TWO ROADS

Dear Reader

When I first met Luke, I realised what a force of nature he was. With the publication of this, his second book of adventures, I admire him (and his energy levels) even more.

Part Dr Dolittle, part young Indiana Jones – and, in its sen[illegible] of camaraderie and friendship, part Richard Curtis roman[illegible] comedy – this is the story of a very 21st century v[illegible] who is a natural successor to James Herriot and Gerald Durre[illegible] love stories about animals that, although warm, aren't afraid to extend into more serious issues. And Luke has both the talent and the experience to tell them.

We hope you enjoy Luke's tales. Do let us know what you think, we'd love to hear from you. Our details are on the last page.

Lisa Highton
PUBLISHER

The Vet

the big wild world

The Vet

the big wild world

LUKE GAMBLE

TWO ROADS

TWO ROADS

www.tworoadsbooks.com

First published in Great Britain in 2012 by
Two Roads
An imprint of Hodder & Stoughton
An Hachette UK company

First published in paperback in 2012

2

A CIP catalogue record for this title is available from the British Library.

ISBN 978 1 444 72182 9

Typeset in Sabon MT by Hewer Text UK Ltd, Edinburgh

Printed and bound in the UK by Clays Ltd, St Ives plc

Hodder & Stoughton policy is to use papers that are natural, renewable and recyclable products and made from wood grown in sustainable forests. The logging and manufacturing processes are expected to conform to the environmental regulations of the country of origin.

Two Roads
Hodder & Stoughton Ltd
338 Euston Road
London NW1 3BH

For Gideon

CONTENTS

1	Something Smells Fishy	1
2	Invincible Scamp	28
3	Making Impressions	39
4	Ticket to Heaven	55
5	Donkeys, Dilemmas and Chimpanzees	81
6	Piggy in the Middle	106
7	Alpha Male	134
8	Born to Fly Pets	153
9	My Precious	164
10	Expect the Unexpected	188
11	Mission Kenya	216
12	Hard to Handle	246
13	Always Be Prepared	275
14	A Really Great Adventure	305

AUTHOR'S NOTE

This is my story. Although this is a work of fact, I have deliberately changed the names of the people and places involved, as well as their physical descriptions, and mixed up different incidents from throughout my career. Accordingly, many of the people described are not based on any real person but are imaginary constructs based on different characters I've encountered in my life so far.

I

Something Smells Fishy

'How am I supposed to do this again?' I said, through gritted teeth.

'Just get the stick in its mouth and wedge it open,' came the ever-helpful reply. 'Be careful, though. Those teeth are razor sharp – it'll take your fingers off!'

I glanced at Sam with an expression of disbelief, not quite sure how or why I had ended up in this situation. We had been best friends for about nine years, even lived together for five of them while at university, and since qualifying we had kept each other updated with the various trials and tribulations of our respective first couple of years as practising vets. I had pursued a career in mixed practice, treating a range of animal species, and Sam had specialised in dogs, cats and exotics.

I had nipped down to visit my friend and catch up on the latest gossip, and Sam, no doubt with a master plan in mind, had somehow managed to rope me into helping him with an in-patient he was looking after over the weekend.

The grey seal, pinned between my legs, looked up at me, twisting its head viciously as I tried in vain to wedge a wooden stick between its teeth.

'You've got to get it to bite the stick, then work it backwards into its mouth,' Sam chipped in, unable to hide the amusement in his voice.

'Why on earth am I doing this when it's your patient? You're the one on call. This is—' I broke off as the seal surged forwards, but I managed to keep hold of it with one hand. When it stopped moving, I realised that, miraculously, the stick was now firmly clamped between its jaws. 'It's in!' I exclaimed.

'*A definite eureka moment!* Think of this as payback for all the times you've dragged me off on some crazy animal-charity mission when we could've been on holiday.' Sam laughed.

'At least we both get involved in the crazy animal-charity missions. Are you going to help me with this seal or just stand there dreaming about your new girlfriend?'

'OK, calm down. Hold it steady and I'll bring the bucket over.' Sam entered the pen and walked towards us. 'Now, tip its head back and feed the fish down its gaping jaws – you need to push the fish right to the back of its throat. They have to go head first so the spines don't stick – it'll swallow them whole.' He paused. 'Mind those teeth, though!'

I looked at him, stony-faced.

'You've got to be kidding me,' I breathed. 'I've got hold of him, *you* slip the fish in there!'

Sam looked at me with an equally stony expression. 'I can't,' he said.

'What do you mean you can't?' I demanded, flashing a hard look at my friend.

'Angle is all wrong from here, Luke. You'll have to do it with your other hand. Hold the seal with your legs and feed the fish from above.'

I tried to imagine this, but only for a fleeting instant. I

wasn't about to start playing a game of Twister with a seal that would rather gnaw on my hands than the fish. 'It's going to get away from me if I let go with my other hand!'

'It won't if you dangle a fish in front of it,' Sam replied, acting as exasperated as if I'd been a naughty schoolboy. 'Besides, I've got a bad finger.'

'I'm not going to have any fingers if you don't help me!' The seal bucked again and I struggled to keep it still. 'Is this why you invited me down here all of a sudden? To help you feed a killer seal?'

I raised my eyebrows, demanding an answer – but Sam was unmoved. 'This seal is eight months old!' He laughed. 'Just a baby! Stop making such a drama about it. Or do you want me to tell Cordelia what her new fiancé's really like? Big, bruiser Luke Gamble – petrified of a little baby seal . . .'

'I'm not petrified.'

'Luke, think of it as a puppy. You're not scared of puppies, are you, Luke?'

It was too late. He'd already snagged me in the conversation.

'No,' I said, 'I'm not scared of puppies.'

'Because, honestly, mate, you look just a *little* like you're afraid of puppies . . .'

'I am *not* scared of—'. I heard how ridiculous I sounded and took a deep breath.

'Look,' Sam went on, 'loads of people would give their right arms to feed a baby seal and you're complaining about a few fingers.'

'Why can't it eat them from a feeding trough?'

'We haven't got a feeding trough.'

'Next time,' I snapped, '*you're* bringing a feeding trough.'

I wrestled the seal's head up a fraction and, looking deep

into its big brown eyes, I sensed a chance and somehow managed to thrust a slimy cold fish down its throat.

'It won't feed unless it thinks the fish is alive,' Sam explained. 'Putting them in a trough would be a giveaway and it would starve. In the sea it would still be learning how to hunt from its mother – you're basically simulating open-water hunting. Or deep-throat fish feeding, however you want to describe it.' Sam paused. 'Dirty mouths, seals,' he added.

'You should know all about that then,' I replied, idly observing the rows of razor sharp teeth as I threaded my hand once again into its mouth.

To my utter annoyance, Sam had been right. Sensing that its last chance of being fed hinged on compliance, the seal had settled and now looked at me expectantly. To my even greater annoyance, it really did look like a big, slippery puppy.

'You know what?' Sam said. 'Jane didn't think we'd be able to do this.'

'*We* haven't done it!' I cried. 'I hope you tell your true love the facts about the situation. I have no idea what wild and exotic thing you've tried to grapple with today but I doubt it required two hands.'

Jane was a local zoo vet who specialised in exotic animals. She was also Sam's new girlfriend.

'There's no way you would have managed it without my guidance,' Sam said, running a hand through his short, spiky brown hair.

'Look, I only nipped over to see you and catch up. I didn't ask to come and feed a dirty great man-eating seal – that's your job!'

'It was washed up on the shore, sick, needy and riddled with lungworm. What would you expect me to do with it? It had lost its mother, had no place to go. No one here was overly keen to help me. You love this sort of stuff – saving lives, remember?' Sam paused. He'd got me, and he knew it. 'By the way, if those teeth scratch the back of your hand, you're going to get a heck of an infection . . .'

I would have sniped back but I felt a tooth scrape my skin and lost my words. 'Your concern's appreciated,' I finally said. 'Especially as I open Pilgrims tomorrow. I'm going to need both my hands if I'm to have a fighting chance of getting the practice off the ground.'

I had spent the last couple of years earning my stripes and learning what being a vet was really all about under the watchful eye of my previous employers, Mr Spotswode and Giles. The time had come, though, for Mr Spotswode to retire, so the practice had been sold to a corporate firm and, being super-commercial, they wanted a town practice to focus on lucrative small-animal work. As the farm work ceased, Giles – the main farm vet – had moved to New Zealand to live with his brother, and the opportunity had presented itself for me to have a go on my own.

It was to be my big chance. I had a huge advantage in beginning with a few farmers who were ready to come with me, but it was still a daunting challenge – especially as it would run alongside a night emergency service I had set up just the year before. It meant I had a fair bit on my plate.

'At least you'll be able to say you can feed a sick baby seal,' Sam remarked as he passed me another fish.

'Useful in the New Forest,' I said. 'I'm sure that the commoners are going to find that skill a real draw. In fact, I was wondering what to include in some posters to advertise the place – now I know – a seal feeding demonstration!'

I rolled my eyes.

'How *is* your saving-the-animals-of-the-universe charity going, anyway?' Sam asked, passing me another small bucket of sprats.

'Great,' I said. 'There are about 200 animal sanctuaries registered with us now, so there'll be plenty more madcap trips for you to come on.'

Over the last couple of years I'd also set up an animal charity called Worldwide Veterinary Service, WVS for short, which aimed to provide free veterinary resources in terms of volunteers, medicines and equipment to non-profit organisations and animal sanctuaries around the world. The more remote, the better. Sam had been with me on my very first trips and, despite regular grumblings, was the one person I could always count on to accompany me on the more extreme and less glamorous adventures.

'Milked any elephants recently?' he gibed. Once, on a trip to India, he had set me up to examine an elephant, knowing full well I had never been within ten feet of one in my life.

'Only you would have done that,' I replied, grinning.

'Only you would have set up a little animal charity to do that sort of stuff for free. I mean, I like animals – but you need your head looked at. Don't you have volunteers going into your house when you're at work, folding leaflets or something? Talk about inviting in the squatters! How does your true love feel about that?'

'Cordelia is totally supportive, unlike some!' I declared, thrusting the last fish down the seal's throat. 'And yes, Tess is still volunteering to help WVS and – for the twentieth time – no, I haven't met her yet. She just goes into the house, folds her leaflets, and then she's off again.'

Tess was a local girl who had found WVS on the Internet. Both she and her boyfriend were into supporting good causes so, on her afternoon off each week, Tess would go round to my house and help run the charity's administration. All this had been arranged by phone and, twelve months later, I still hadn't actually met her in person.

'I'm thinking of asking her to work for the charity full time. We have enough money now and the workload's huge.' I released my grip on the mammal pinned between my legs.

The seal seemed to contemplate the situation, then decided to just lay at my feet, its belly filled with sprats.

'By the way, I've tamed your seal,' I said.

'By the way,' Sam said, a wicked grin forming on his face, 'you stink.'

I looked down at my clothes, which were covered with wet seal smears, and detected the smell of sprats wafting around me. Raising my eyes with a malevolent glare, it dawned on me the real reason that Sam had roped me into feeding the seal.

'Your finger's fine, isn't it?'

'Look,' he pleaded, 'I need to be on fire tonight with Jane. We're going out for dinner and I can't smell of fish! You took this for the team. Just think of all the—'

Sam didn't wait to finish, turning and racing off as I lunged in hot fishy pursuit.

When I eventually arrived back home, having turned heads at the service station, my dog, Leuwen, greeted me with an enthusiasm I had never seen. A 45-kilo Rhodesian Ridgeback, he was clearly a fan of sprats. In fact, he was a fan of most things – except rain – and was my constant companion whenever I was in the UK. Cordelia, my fiancée, had given him to me as a running partner when I was training for the Marathon des Sables, a 152-mile footrace across the Sahara desert to raise money for WVS. Smiling, I gave him a heavy pat before heading inside to answer the ringing phone.

'Hello?'

'That Pilgrims?' came a thick Dorset voice.

I paused. Leuwen was still scrabbling all around me, surely imagining me a single giant sprat. 'Um, yes, how can I help?' I asked, a surge of adrenalin coursing into my veins. It was my first call for the practice I was due to open tomorrow. If it wasn't for Leuwen's slobbering jowls, I might even have forgotten the smell of fish in the excitement.

'Mr David gave me your number – he told me you were starting up. Can you cut?' asked the voice.

Mr David was my biggest farm client. He was the owner and manager of Highmoor Farm, one of the five farms I had confirmed on my books. It was his faith in me that was allowing me to take on the challenge of opening the practice, as the work there, alone, would give me the money to pay my mortgage. Since the practice was to be based out of my house – or, more exactly, my truck – I'd be able to grow things without the gnawing stress of not having enough money to live. Cutting an animal – castrating it – would be part of my bread and butter from now on and this was a great opportunity to get a new client.

'Yes, that will be no problem,' I replied confidently.

'How much do you charge?' the voice asked.

'Well, I charge by the hour,' I said, before quoting my fee. I tried not to gulp as I said it; it sounded a lot, but I knew that the large practices locally charged significantly more. The difference was that they had a lot more facilities, equipment and a back-up team to justify their higher price. Getting my prices right was going to be the key to getting good word spreading about the new practice – especially as it would be the deciding factor in whether new farm clients were willing to try me out. I had to be cheap, but not so cheap as to undervalue my skills. It was a fine line and I'd have to learn how to tread it as I went along.

'It won't take an hour,' was the reply. 'It's just a slice and dice. It won't take half as long. Drugs on top?'

'Yes, drugs on top, but I'm pretty cost-effective,' I said, in as measured tone as I could manage. 'I'll see you straight.'

'You covering the out-of-hours too?' the farmer asked.

The on-call was another essential part of the service I had to offer with Pilgrims. Legally, I was obliged to provide emergency cover to any animal I treated. Since my previous job had been in a super-supportive mixed practice, the on-call had been split between four of us and there was always help if I needed it. Working with my good friend, Rob, we had often traded advice in the early hours for some emergency situation we had to deal with – but there would be none of that now. Rob had gone off to specialise in ophthalmology and would no longer appreciate a three a.m. call to discuss a constipated goat.

There was also the complication that I would be working quite a few nights at the emergency service I had set up about twelve months ago. When my previous employers had decided to outsource the out-of-hours night work, I had decided to have a go at running a dedicated small-animal emergency clinic and take it on. I'd rented out a surgery at night, the business had grown and it now covered nearly all the small-animal vets in the area. While I was lucky enough to have the invaluable help of Sheila, the super capable ex-head nurse from my old job, she couldn't step into the breach when I was short of vets to work nights and weekends. It had meant that while the business was still getting going, I'd have to keep knuckling her down to grow it to a size at which I could afford to pay other vets to come in and take on the bulk of the night work on a full-time basis.

I took a deep breath. There was only one thing to do in times like this: bury my head in the sand and tell myself it was all going to work out fine.

'I'll be on the phone night and day while I get going,' I replied.

The farmer seemed pleased with that. 'Right, then,' he said. 'Mr David told me you're at his tomorrow. I live just up the valley from him – Rainbow Farm. Pines is the name. Can you be with us in the afternoon? Anytime after one o'clock is fine.'

'No problem, Mr Pines,' I said, my voice tinged with excitement – my first new client! 'See you then.'

'Right you are,' said Mr Pines, and hung up.

It was only after the line went dead that I realised I hadn't asked Mr Pines what type of farm animal he wanted me to cut. Whatever it was, I told myself, I would have to handle it. There are some things you need if you're going to be a vet: a love of animals, a love of people and a thorough knowledge of all sorts of species and ailments. But the one thing that you need, above all others, is self-belief.

I told myself it was going to be okay and went looking for my knife.

'Funny smell in here today, Luke,' Phil, the herdsman of Highmoor Farm commented as I stuck my arm in yet another cow to check if she was pregnant.

I grimaced. Despite about half an hour of scrubbing myself in the shower the previous night, the smell of sprats still wafted through my waterproofs, permeating even the thick aroma of the cows. 'Might be fish, Phil,' I admitted. 'Had a bit of a mission with a bucket of sprats yesterday.'

'Ah, is that what it is? I was wondering!' Phil seemed to contemplate whether to take the conversation further but decided against it, squinting to check the cow's number on his clipboard instead. 'This one's about twenty-eight days.'

'Testing me today, Phil?' I replied, with a smile. It was tough to diagnose pregnancy at twenty-eight days – even with a scanner – and Phil knew it.

'Mr David said to make sure you could do the business.' Phil grinned back. 'This is your first routine farm visit as Pilgrims and we'll be seeing you every two weeks so you need to be on top of things if you're going to be our vet. You're on your own now – no Giles to call if you get in trouble.'

I grinned. Phil was right. If I hadn't been sure before, I'd always had Giles as back-up. But there was no chance he'd fly over from New Zealand to help me with a tricky pregnancy scan. It was now my responsibility to work with Phil to ensure all the cows were pregnant when they were supposed to be – and if they weren't, I had to do something about it. I'd have to make decisions that, if they were the wrong ones, could cost a farmer a lot of money.

'What would you do if I told you she was barren and should go on the cull list?' I smiled.

'Fire you.' Phil laughed.

'Well,' I replied, 'I can see it. My luck must be in.'

Phil put a big tick against the cow's freeze brand number on his clipboard. 'That's it, Luke, good job! See you again in two weeks – unless I have an emergency, that is . . .' Phil had a twinkle in his eye. He was obviously relishing roasting the new boy. 'Didn't leave your lights on this time?'

I laughed. Phil had brought this up every time I'd visited

the farm for the last two years, after an epic night when I'd performed a Caesarean on a cow under the illumination of my car headlights. The only slight problem had been that I'd had a flat battery by the time I'd finished the job and had had to get the farm's manager, Mr David, out of bed to rescue me.

'Where are you off to next?' Phil asked. 'Got many farms on your books yet?'

'Funny you should ask. Do you know Mr Pines?'

Phil raised his eyebrows. 'Pretty self-sufficient family – wouldn't think they would often call a vet. They must be desperate!'

'Thanks a lot!'

'No . . . I mean, they really keep to themselves a fair bit. What have you got on?'

I paused, realising he wasn't mocking me. 'Sounds pretty routine – a castration job,' I replied, trying to read Phil's face.

He nodded slowly, with a slight smile twitching at the corners of his mouth that suggested the job might not be so routine after all. 'Down the road then, not far at all. You won't miss it. Rainbow Farm – big old entrance on your right as you drive through the valley. Quite a long track taking you through the forest.' He paused as if he wanted to say more, but evidently decided against it.

I wiped my arms as we ambled back to my car. 'It'll be fine. New business for my first day as Pilgrims!' I said cheerily.

All the same, as I drove away I couldn't help but wonder: what on earth had I got myself into?

Rainbow Farm was indeed easy to spot. The narrow country lane suddenly flared out as it rounded a bend and, beyond that, by about a hundred yards, a break in a thick hedge on the right marked the entrance. A small homemade sign leant casually against one of two heavily battered metal five-bar gates, which swung back against the hedge line on each side of the opening, making it seem like I was driving into the mouth of some cavernous beast.

Thick trees lined the track on each side, which was riddled with potholes and covered with a thick layer of hard-baked mud, jolting the truck as I trundled along. It seemed to go on for about a mile before the forest around me thinned out and I continued on through what could only be described as a huge scrapyard.

Vehicles of every description were stacked on top of each other: old buses, ambulances, a fire engine. A line of ancient Land Rovers flanked each side of the track and a cracked sign reading 'BEWARE – ATTACK DOGS TRAINING' was stuck into the ground just in front of another gate.

'Keep on your toes, Leuwen,' I said quietly to the sleeping form of my dog, sprawled across the back seats of the truck.

Leuwen, my constant companion on my daily rounds and having claimed the back seat of my truck as his own on the day I'd got it, snored softly in response.

Hesitantly, I got out of the truck, looking around for any sign of life. An eerie silence hung in the air. I checked my phone to see if I could call Mr Pines, but there was no reception. I peered over the gate to look down the track, which seemed to be partly grassed over and disappeared into a small clump of woodland.

Realising that the only way lay straight ahead, I unlatched the gate and drove the truck through, jumping out to swing it shut behind me. As I pushed it closed, I heard a bark in the distance. I had gone about two hundred metres when the track swung round to the right and I saw the farmyard directly in front of me, with a crumbling cottage to my left. Paint flaked off the windows and there were holes in the roof. Outbuildings were dotted behind the yard and, pulling up, I turned off the engine, scanning my surroundings for any sign of the owners.

As I readied myself to get out of the truck, there was a huge thud against the passenger door and the head of a monstrous dog suddenly filled the window. I flinched at its fierce barking just as another dog appeared, emitting a low deep-throated growl through the window on my side. Casting a helpless glance through the windscreen, I saw a third huge German Shepherd glowering at me from outside the house. The noise was deafening. Leuwen, normally a horizontal companion on my daily rounds, suddenly leapt up and started roaring back. It was the worst thing that could have happened. Outside, the dogs rose to greater heights of fury. Inside, Leuwen upped the ante. They matched his bet and upped the ante again. All around me was a cacophony of demonic growls.

As claws scrabbled at the doors, I flicked the locks down and wondered what on earth to do. Getting out of the vehicle didn't seem an option and moving the truck would risk injuring one of the dogs. As the farm's new vet, it didn't seem like a good plan to run over the client's pets, whether they were killer attack dogs or not.

Suddenly, a voice shouted and the dogs instantly stopped their baying. A lean figure with unkempt hair came round the corner, a large knife strapped to his belt. Sharp eyes looked at me. 'Are you getting out, then?' the man said.

'Mr Pines?' I asked, cautiously opening the door.

'I'm his son, Tony. Come on, then! You need to go into the

barn – it's over there with the other outbuildings. Don't worry about the dogs. They'll let you alone now.'

With that, he turned on his heel and strode through the yard towards the outbuildings. As he went, he gave a sharp whistle and the dogs raced to his side.

Against all my efforts, I was still shaken. I turned to reassure Leuwen, who still stood upright on the back seat, clearly agitated, then grabbed my box of equipment and drugs. Tentatively, I stepped out of the truck. When I wasn't instantly savaged and mauled to death I breathed a deep sigh of relief. Looking over to see the disappearing form of Tony, I hurried through the yard, past a dilapidated crush, and saw the derelict barn that he was talking about. In the truck, Leuwen watched me go and whimpered. Perhaps he thought I was walking to my death.

The huge barn, lined with heavy cobwebs, was light and airy. At the far end, Tony stood with a man I presumed to be his father. He was older, slightly stooped but with the same rangy physique. They both watched me intently while the dogs, seemingly at ease, trotted around them. All of a sudden they seemed indifferent to my presence and, thankfully, more interested in sniffing out mice or rats than in eating the new arrival.

'Mr Pines,' I said, holding out my hand.

'So you found us OK,' the old man said, firmly shaking it.

'No problem at all.' I turned to his son, with my hand outstretched. 'Hello, Tony, I'm Luke.'

Somewhat bemused, he shook my hand. 'Bit formal, isn't it? We don't normally worry about that sort of thing round here.'

'On my best behaviour,' I said. 'You're a new client.' I smiled as best I could, keen to kick things off on the right foot.

Mr Pines laughed. 'Maybe not for long – all depends on if you can cut Jake for us.'

'Not a problem. We'll get him cut, I'm certain.' I eyed the piles of cow muck on the floor. 'Done plenty of bulls. I've got a good pair of emasculators and, once we dope him up, I'll have them off in no time.'

Tony and his father briefly looked at each other, while a wicked grin formed on Tony's face.

'Jake isn't a bull,' Tony said. 'What gave you that idea?'

'Well, the cow muck, the crush . . .' I began, then stopped, watching Mr Pines slowly shake his head from side to side.

'Oh, no, Jake isn't a bull.' He chuckled. 'Jake's a bit quicker than a bull. He's a bit wilder too! A stallion, Luke!'

'Does your clock start from when you see the animal?' Tony asked, with a smirk.

'How do you mean?' I asked. I had a horrible feeling in the pit of my stomach that things weren't going to go quite to plan.

'He means we have to catch him first,' Mr Pines replied. 'Maybe best if you give us a bit of space while we do that. He's a bit nervy around strangers.'

'He's a bit nervy full stop,' Tony added with relish.

'Once we've got him, it'll be over to you.'

I stepped back as Tony walked past me to grab a long, thin stick that was leaning against one of the walls. It was about eight foot in length with a Y shape at one end. Picking up a neatly coiled rope, he efficiently tied a noose and looped part of it between the stick's two prongs. 'We're going to run him into the pound behind the barn,' he said. 'I'll get this rope round his neck and then we can rope him up in the race. You wait here and keep out of sight as we run him in. Once you hear the gate close, come on through.'

I nodded, my mouth dry. I had never castrated a tame stallion, let alone one that had to be lassoed to be caught.

'You all right there?' Mr Pines asked, peering at me.

'Fine,' I replied, not trusting myself to say any more.

With a curt nod, Mr Pines and Tony disappeared through the other end of the barn while I hung back, waiting in the shadows, listening and wondering what to do.

The principles of stallion castration were fairly straightforward but, although I had the drugs to sedate a horse, knowing what to do and actually doing it were two very different things. I tried desperately to still the butterflies in my stomach. I wasn't a horse vet and felt totally out of my depth. I couldn't walk away from the job, though – it was my first day in practice and I had to stand on my own two feet. There would be other challenging cases I'd have to sort out by myself. The first had just come along sooner than I'd expected.

I thought back to my first night on call several years ago. I'd had to remove a cat's eye with hardly any surgical experience under my belt. With the support of Holly, one of the practice nurses, and a good textbook, it had gone well. I wondered if this would be the same. My gut feeling told me that what lay in store for me outside the barn would make yesterday's seal seem like a lamb.

No doubt Sam would have loved to watch this . . .

Galloping hoofs, wild shouts and the slamming of a heavy gate signalled my cue to enter the arena. Rather unlike a gladiator of old, I picked up my Black & Decker toolbox containing my medicines and equipment, and padded towards the noise with heavy steps.

The pound was about twenty square feet, made of thick six-foot-high wooden planks nailed to cut-off telegraph poles. It looked sturdier than the cottage I had passed on my way into the farm. One end of the pound contained an eight-foot gate, which swung outwards to help herd animals inside, and the other was partitioned off with more thick planks and telegraph poles extending three-quarters across the width. This design effectively created a narrow race about fifteen foot long and four foot wide, with a small gate at the end to allow animals to exit the pound one at a time. It was wide enough to allow a horse a bit of space to walk into but too narrow for it to turn around. I realised that Tony's plan was to rope Jake and goad him into the narrow section, pop a post or two behind him to keep him in place and turn the race into a makeshift stock that would hopefully contain him while I approached with a needle.

Jake was a chestnut stallion that stood about 16.2 hands high. He pranced with high steps, spraying dust around the pound. Tossing his head and snorting in indignation at being confined in the wooden corral, he looked every inch the nightmare horse I had anticipated.

'Right, you stand there.' Tony pointed to a spot near the gate. 'As he comes round, I'm going to loop this rope over his head. Once we've got it on him, he'll go mad for a moment or two – so stay right back out the way. When he settles, let's get him into the race and I'll tie him on. You'll need to get your sedation into him quick, so get it ready.'

He paused, suppressing a smirk. 'We really won't be able to hold him for long,' he said, casting a quick glance in my direction.

Mr Pines held a thick post easily in his wiry grasp and watched as Tony skilfully climbed up one side of the pound, gripping the stick in one hand, the loop dangling neatly between its prongs and the rest of the rope trailing down outside the planks. Leaning over, his face set hard in concentration, he watched as Jake trotted round in circles inside the pen. Reaching forward, he flicked the rope towards the stallion's head. The horse reared and lashed out with his front legs in protest. The rope slid uselessly down his neck and Tony swiftly gathered it up again.

'Not so easy as when we've roped him in the past,' Mr Pines muttered.

I stood, open-mouthed, by the side of the gate. How on earth was I going to do this when the owners couldn't even rope the animal? Fumbling in my medicine box, I pulled out a combination of drugs and started to draw up a super-strong sedation. My only hope was that it would be enough to settle Jake. He was getting more wound up by the minute.

Tony's third attempt was a success and, with a whoop of joy, he jumped down to hold the long end of the rope, the noose tightening around the horse's neck. A large knot, strategically placed, prevented the lasso from strangling the horse – but it was still tight enough not to slip back over his head. Tony flashed me a smile. 'Over to you soon,' he said, with a flamboyant wink.

Leaving Jake a minute or two to settle, I moved round to stand behind Mr Pines. Tony started to pull the horse towards the race, wrapping the loose end of the rope around a thick pole and tugging the animal towards him.

Jake reared and bucked, throwing his weight forwards and back against the rope with frantic energy.

Against the odds, the rope held. With Tony continually winding it around the post, Jake was drawn inexorably into the race. As soon as he was in far enough, Mr Pines rushed forwards with his post and jammed it up behind him to stop him moving back. The only direction Jake could now go was directly up. Rearing wildly, he seemed to challenge me with flared, terrible eyes.

I edged forwards, clutching my syringe.

'You can see why stallions made such good weapons of war,' Tony commented.

'Handy that they can kick with their front legs as well as the back, isn't it?' Mr Pines added.

I had no doubt now: the two men were enjoying this.

'Amazingly handy – almost makes it a bit tricky to inject them into the vein, wouldn't you say?' I replied, with as much good humour as I could muster. My hand darted between the gaps in the planks to touch Jake's neck as he reared.

'Mind your arm, there!' Mr Pines called.

I stabbed blindly into the solid muscle, praying that, once the needle was in, I'd be able to redirect it into the jugular.

Amazingly, the needle hit home and blood was suddenly in the syringe. Quickly depressing the plunger so the drug flowed in, I sprang back, amazed that I had managed to get the sedation into the vein.

'Blimey! You got it in!' Tony exclaimed.

Mr Pines nodded and looked at me. 'The vets normally go for the muscle when they're this wild,' he said.

Feeling a sudden rush of blood to my cheeks, I realised the risk I had taken and it dawned on me what Mr Pines had meant. Although horse sedations were typically given into the vein, the drug would have worked at double strength in the muscle. Had I kept my cool, I would have remembered that and not had to risk breaking my arm. Jabbing Jake in his rump would have been a lot easier.

'It works a lot better in the vein,' I said quietly, hoping Mr Pines and Tony didn't twig that I had no real idea. 'That was enough for a shire horse so hopefully it'll calm him.' I paused, trying to judge whether the drug was taking effect. All I really knew was that the stallion was still filled with fury. 'While it kicks in, I need to get some gear ready. I've left a couple of bits in the truck – be back in a minute.'

I was about to go when Tony called me back. 'Hang on!' I paused and Tony whistled loudly. Jake twitched at the noise, fighting the sedation that coursed through his blood. The three dogs, hearing their master's whistle, appeared from the barn entrance. 'I'll just keep them here, in case they forget who you are,' he said with a wicked grin.

Smiling nervous thanks, I raced back to the truck and climbed in, shutting the door behind me in case the dogs came after me. From the back seat, there appeared a sympathetic muzzle. 'Leuwen,' I said, 'I'm in a world of trouble.' He rested his chin on my shoulder and looked up at me with a cool expression. 'A wag of the tail of encouragement wouldn't go amiss,' I tried.

With a contented grumble, Leuwen lowered his head back down on the seat and closed his eyes.

'Great help as normal, pal.' I slumped in the front seat, kneading the steering wheel. I was even more nervous than I'd known. 'Right, I need to phone someone,' I said. 'I hope he's going to answer.'

I picked up my mobile and frantically scrolled to Rob's number. Pushing it to my ear, I prayed he'd pick up.

'Hello.' Rob's voice echoed down the line.

'Rob, it's me. I need some help.'

'I thought you were opening the practice today? How can you need help on day one?' He sounded amused.

'I've got myself in a right situation. I'm at this farm – something out of *Mad Max* – and I have to castrate a wild stallion.'

'And?' Rob laughed.

'And I've never castrated a stallion before!'

'It's all just a load of balls, isn't it?'

'Rob!' I yelled. 'This is serious!'

'Luke, mate, I just do eyes now – fix them, that is, not cut them out, in case you still aren't familiar with the concept of treating vital organs. I've pushed everything else from my mind.'

'Well, can you imagine this stallion has eyes on its nuts and tell me what to do?' I begged.

Rob sighed down the end of the phone. 'I've only ever done a couple, Luke. Basically, they're like anything else. Just use the emasculators and make sure the sedation is heavy. Remember – when a cow kicks you it hurts, when a horse kicks you it can kill you. You need to ensure the emasculators go on nut to nut. Do the testicles in two parts, the gubernaculum, then the spermatic cord and vessels.' Frantically, I tried to take it all in. 'Don't be tempted to take the testicles off in one bite, as it were. You need to apply the emasculators four times, leave them on for ninety seconds each time. Get some anti-tetanus into the horse, covering antibiotic and anti-inflammatory. Make sure they turn it out into a field after you cut it or the scrotum will swell and don't forget, it'll probably bleed if it has big testicles.'

'What do you mean "bleed"?' I asked, a hint of panic in my voice.

'Well, if you can count the drops of blood when you've finished, don't worry. But if it gushes, well, maybe . . .' Rob paused. 'Luke, I've got to go, my next referral is here – cat with a stromal abscess. Phone me later and let me know how it goes. Good luck!'

The line went dead.

I held the phone to my ear a moment longer, somehow willing Rob to tell me more and trying to digest what he had just said. What was he talking about – do each testicle in two parts? I tried to visualise the anatomy of horse testicles.

There was no more time: Tony was walking towards me.

'Were you thinking of driving away?' Tony laughed as I opened the door.

'No, just a quick call,' I said hurriedly, grabbing my pair of vicious-looking emasculators.

Tony glanced down at the equipment in my hand. 'They mean business, then?' he said.

'No mucking about with these,' I replied with a half-hearted smile.

My emasculators had belonged to Giles and had seen plenty of action. Unfortunately, very little of it had been in my hands. About a foot long, they looked like elongated secateurs with a strange ratchet mechanism on the end. Their job was to enclose the vessels above the testicle and cut through them – but, rather than release, they then clamped on to the severed ends, crushing the vessels and sealing them off so they wouldn't bleed. The hard bit was holding them on for ninety seconds and, if Rob was telling me to do each testicle in two parts – which I hoped would be clear once I got in there – that would mean three minutes of crushing in total for each testicle.

This was not going to be straightforward.

Once the sedation kicked in, I reckoned I'd have about ten minutes to do the job – which, after deducting the three minutes of clamping required for each testicle, meant I had only four minutes to cut down and get the testicles in position for the emasculators to do their work.

'Your sedation's working,' Tony said. 'Thought you'd like to know. You should be able to get in there with him now.'

I nodded, my face set in grim determination. Steeling myself for what I had to do, I headed back to see Jake.

When I approached, Jake was remarkably still. The sedation had indeed worked and I eyed the space between his back end and the pole. 'If I get in there, I won't have the space to move to his side. If he kicks out, I've had it.'

Mr Pines nodded thoughtfully. 'I think it'd be best if we get him out,' he said. 'Your sedation should hold him, but you might need a top-up. He's still quite twitchy.'

As if he was listening to the conversation, Jake pricked his ears and gave a gentle snort.

'Good idea,' I replied. 'I'll give him a bit more and then, if you're okay to get a head collar on him, Tony, we can open the front of the race.'

Being a vet is all about improvising. As Tony dashed back into the barn to grab a head collar and lead rope, I drew up some more sedation – as well as some anti-inflammatory, antibiotic and tetanus antitoxin, as Rob had reminded me – and injected Jake swiftly. He shifted as the needles went in – but, so far so good, the sedation was doing its job.

'Don't give him too much – we don't want him to go down,' Tony said, as he returned, slipping the halter on and opening the gate.

'Don't worry, it's great stuff, he'll be sleepy but won't go off his legs. Much better for me if he's up.'

I was buoyed by how things had gone so far – but no sooner had I spoken than Jake took two steps forwards and his knees buckled.

'He's going down! Quick, Tony, hold his head!' Mr Pines leapt towards the horse as, unable to stand, Jake slumped to the ground. Inadvertently, I gulped. Time was of the essence.

Tony dived onto the stallion's neck, holding his head to

the ground. 'You'd better get this done before he tries to get up!' he cried. 'I don't want to be too close if he starts coming round . . .'

I dashed forward as Mr Pines slipped another rope around one of Jake's back legs, raising it so I could get to the testicles. I moved as quickly as possible, injecting each one with local anaesthetic. Things couldn't get worse. Jake had collapsed under the heavy sedation. The problem was that it wasn't a full anaesthetic, which was too dangerous to give a horse without any oxygen to hand. It meant that he would be in a strange limbo between sedation and general anaesthetic: he wouldn't want to lie down properly but neither could he stand.

Despite Mr Pines's efforts to restrain the raised leg with a rope, Jake began to twitch and pull against it, the hoof flailing dangerously in the air.

'You'd better hurry,' Tony shouted from the head end. 'I won't be able to stay on him if he tries to get up. If you don't get it done, we'll be in a right mess!'

Grabbing the scalpel, I sliced deep into the scrotum, the first testicle popping out. Quickly whacking the emasculators onto the huge ligament, I crushed the handles together and counted to ninety in my head.

Suddenly it dawned on me what Rob had meant: do the ligament separately from the testicle itself.

'You won't have time for the full crush,' Tony grunted, his knee pushed firmly behind Jake's head. 'I can feel him stirring.'

I didn't say a word. The first testicle was now off, and I quickly sliced down for the second.

Mr Pines let out a sudden cry, losing his balance as Jake did a huge bicycle kick with his raised back leg. The hoof whistled towards me, missing my head by a whisker.

'Almost there!' I shouted. 'Hold him!'

Tony almost lifted off the ground as Jake struggled to raise his head. Moving the emasculators to the main part of the second testicle, I prepared for the final crush.

Somehow, Tony forced the horse's head back down and hung on for grim life. Jake's legs thrashed around me.

'. . . eighty-eight . . . eighty-nine . . . ninety!' I snatched back the emasculators and stood back, peering down to inspect my handiwork.

At exactly the same moment, Tony leapt off Jake's neck and flicked the strap on the head collar. The horse hurled himself forwards, lurching into a half-standing position and staggering sideways as he fought the remnants of the sedation.

I peered hard at the blood trickling down the inside of his thighs.

Tony smiled at me and came to stand at my side. Mr Pines, having picked himself up, was busy coiling the ropes back up.

'That blood okay?' Tony asked.

I looked at the drops. 'As long as you can count the drops there's no problem,' I replied, with as much conviction as I could muster.

'Good job,' Mr Pines said, thrusting a bundle of notes in my direction. 'Took you forty minutes, but I reckon you earned a full hour's wage!'

Tony flashed me a smile. For the first time I almost detected a little warmth in his expression. 'Didn't want to tell you before but we've had three vets out to try to geld him and none of them managed it – two of them refused point blank. We didn't know who we'd persuade to do it and then you came along!'

A sudden wave of exhaustion washed over me as the adrenalin ebbed from my system. I nodded my thanks, unable to speak.

'We'll have a couple more next month,' Tony said cheerily, slapping me on the shoulder. 'We'll give you a shout.'

'No problem,' I managed, heading back to the truck, willing my hands to stop shaking. 'Tell your friends I'm open for business.'

I managed a grin. I almost even meant it.

2
Invincible Scamp

'He was wagging his tail and seemed so pleased with himself – we didn't even notice at first.' The woman, her cheeks flushed with the evening's wine and a little unsteady on her feet, giggled.

Her husband, a portly man in his mid-fifties, glanced across at his wife and nodded sagely before placing a hand on the consulting room table and clearing his throat. 'Yes,' he said, 'quite bizarre, really. Never expected it, of course. But one wouldn't, would one? There we were, having dinner with our next-door neighbours, and Josephine, here, looked out of the window and said she could see Scamp in the garden. How he got over the fence, I've no idea. It's seven foot high for a start. Incredible he would even attempt it.' He reached out with his other hand to pat Scamp, who was still wagging his tail as he perched on the rubber mat between us.

I shook my head, utterly amazed at the little terrier's composure. He seemed totally oblivious to what could only be described as a horrendous injury. Viewing him from the left-hand side, he appeared a picture of perfect health; it was only when you examined him from the right that it became apparent he was nothing of the sort – his right hind leg was hanging by a thread. Or a ligament, to be precise.

'What time did you first notice him in the garden, Mr Bixby-Smithe?' I enquired, studying the leg and trying to work out why the poor little dog hadn't bled to death through a severed femoral artery.

'Well, what's the time now?' he asked, with a smile. He glanced at his wife, clearly a little unsure about the timeline of the evening's entertainment.

'It's ten past midnight,' I replied, trying not to let a hint of weariness creep into my voice.

'Oh, well, he was there about eight o'clock I think.' Mrs Bixby-Smithe laughed nervously, and leant forward to talk to Scamp. 'That's four hours ago, you poor little mite. To think we left you out there with that horrible leg! You poor, poor naughty little Scamp!' She planted kisses all over the dog's head.

'You see, we thought nothing of it at first, had a chuckle about it, and decided to let him sniff about the garden, all quite comical, really. Then we went through for drinks and . . .' Mr Bixby-Smithe tailed off sheepishly, watching his wife, who was still kissing the dog.

'We forgot all about him!' Mrs Bixby-Smithe exclaimed, pausing for air and wrapping her arms around the hapless animal. Poor Scamp was now having to fully support half her bodyweight on his three remaining legs.

To Scamp's credit, he was taking it all in his stride – even enjoying the avid attention from his owner. One leg missing or not, he wasn't about to miss out on this affection.

'Yes, oh dear, it does sound rather awful, but we had our drinks and it was only when we got back home that we remembered Scamp was still in next door's garden . . .' Mr Bixby-Smithe hesitated. 'Beautiful garden, mind,' he added, as if that somehow made up for Scamp being stranded there.

Poor Scamp had already been through enough, I decided. I eased him from under Mrs Bixby-Smithe and scooped the bemused dog up from the table, gently passing him to Sheila, my super-experienced head nurse. Briefly fixing the Bixby-Smithes with a disapproving frown, she smiled down at Scamp before swiftly leaving the room, Scamp protectively wrapped in her arms.

'Oh, where are you taking him?' Mrs Bixby-Smithe wailed dramatically. 'My poor little pooch!'

'Well,' I replied, 'I need to sort out his injury and then I can get him back to you – but it will be the morning before he's ready to go home, so the best thing you can do is head back and get some sleep.'

I presented Mr Bixby-Smithe with a consent form and wondered if he was in any state to sign his own name.

'I shan't sleep until he is safely back at home,' Mrs Bixby-Smithe replied.

'I'm sorry,' I said, more firmly this time. 'This is going to be a complicated business, I'm afraid. We'll do our best for Scamp, but it's going to take some time – and I won't be able to save that leg.'

Both Mr and Mrs Bixby-Smithe looked at me open mouthed.

'You don't mean . . . you'll cut his leg off?' Mr Bixby-Smithe cried, momentarily sobered by the news.

'I'll be honest,' I said. 'It's incredible that he's lasted four hours. It sounds as if he scaled the fence and got hooked up on it on his way over. He's literally ripped his leg off. I just can't believe that he hasn't lost more blood. It looks as if he's torn through his femoral artery. The leg must have twisted round, dislocating the joint – but, somehow, the rotation must have clamped off the vessel as it tore through . . .'

Mrs Bixby-Smithe suddenly swayed. Thinking she was about to faint, I dashed round to offer my arm as support. Frantically, she latched on to it and hauled herself back upright.

'Enough!' Mr Bixby-Smithe declared, with the air of a haughty colonel. 'We're quite traumatised by the whole ordeal! This is preposterous! First you want to cut our dog's leg off and now you manhandle my wife!' He fixed me with a piercing look, as if I were a recruit he was drilling. He extended a finger and jabbed it in my direction. 'You are absolutely certain you can't just, well, you know, stick it back on?'

I looked at him as I eased myself out of his wife's grasp. 'Sadly not, Mr Bixby-Smithe. The best thing I can do is get that wound closed up and prevent infection getting into the stump. The leg is literally hanging off and—'

Mrs Bixby-Smithe swooned again, her whole body lurching into me. Mindful of her husband's accusing finger, I let her prop herself up against me but tried not to get too close. Every time I edged even an inch away, she staggered a little bit more.

'My poor little Scamp!' she wailed, burying her head in my shoulder. 'Oh, will he survive this terrible injury?'

I was beginning to think I was trapped in a Merchant Ivory production. I even took a quick peek around to make sure a secret camera wasn't filming me. 'He's made it this far, hasn't he?' I said, trying to sound reassuring. 'Look at what he went through to try to join your dinner party. He'll definitely come through a little anaesthetic if he can still wag his tail after doing that to himself!'

'I'm not so sure about a three-legged dog,' Mr Bixby-Smithe muttered, reluctantly opening his arms to accept his wife.

'He'll be able to run like the wind,' I said. 'I promise. Look, why don't you take a seat in the waiting room and we'll call a taxi for you?'

Mr Bixby-Smithe turned on his heel, still holding up his wife, and took a great stride towards the door. As he went, he too began to crumple. He stopped and steadied himself on the door-jamb. There was clearly enough wine still flowing in his veins that, if he had suffered the same injury as poor Scamp, I doubted he would have felt a thing.

Finally regaining his balance, he disappeared through the door. 'Oh, that won't be necessary!' he called. 'We'll drive home.'

My stomach lurched. This nightmarish situation was getting worse by the second. There was no way I could let the couple drive home three sheets to the wind. And I couldn't let poor Scamp be orphaned as well as cut off one of his legs.

'Not a worry,' I said, hurrying after them and putting my arms on each of their shoulders. We bustled down the corridor and into the waiting room. 'Sheila!' I called.

Sheila appeared in front of us. Over the tops of the Bixby-Smithes' heads, she opened her eyes fractionally – a message to me that she could handle this. 'I've already called you a taxi,' she said to them. 'Just take a seat. It'll be here in five minutes. How about I take your card details so you don't need to worry about settling things later on?'

Realising that Sheila's no nonsense attitude implied she was not the sort of woman to broker an argument with, Mr

Bixby-Smithe mutely reached into his pocket and held out a gold card.

Bidding them goodbye, I hastily made an exit, thanking my lucky stars for Sheila, and went to have a proper look at Scamp.

The dog gazed at me from his cage, still seemingly relaxed and indifferent to his predicament. His head, half cocked to one side, had an expression that almost seemed to imply that he wanted me to throw a ball for him rather than attend to his terrible injury.

'You're a character, aren't you?' I said, opening the cage door and giving him a gentle stroke.

Scamp's bright eyes gleamed up at me as he digested the question. Clearly deciding to agree, he wagged his tail fiercely.

'We'll get you sorted out, pal, don't you worry,' I murmured, as the surgery door swung open behind me.

'Are you talking to yourself again, Luke?' Sheila laughed, evidently having managed to send the Bixby-Smithes safely on their way.

'Just having a chat with our stoical friend here,' I replied, gently closing the cage door. I shook my head in disbelief at Scamp's fortitude. 'That little dog is a hero. He was so desperate to join his owners for dinner, he tore his leg off in the process.'

Sheila had a way about her when she laughed. It seemed, for a moment, that I was the most sombre creature in the room. Even poor Scamp, maimed as he was, was in a more cheerful mood.

We began to get everything ready for the operation.

'Well,' I replied, finally summoning a grin, 'I hate to throw a curveball but he could have been just trying to escape them.

Sort of understandable,' I added, 'considering the way Mrs Bixby-Smithe was smothering him.'

Sheila gave me one of her withering looks. Then her eyes opened wide and she stared dreamily into the middle distance. 'Let's assume, just for the sake of a romantic notion, that he was so bereft at his owners going for dinner that he sacrificed a limb to be reunited with them . . .'

'Ah!' I said. 'You're in one of *those* moods. I was going to say that there was also the possibility Scamp was more interested in the neighbours' cat than in watching Mr and Mrs Bixby-Smithe through the french windows – but I'm sure you're right.'

'All this work is turning you into a hardened cynic,' Sheila sighed.

'It's turning me into a hardened vet. Basically, I'm a Spartan in disguise.'

Sheila fixed me with a reproachful look. 'Well, would the Spartan vet like to help get things organised for this operation rather than just stand there watching his Spartan nurse do all the work?'

'See what I mean?' I exclaimed. 'The battles never cease!'

Twenty minutes later, Scamp was anaesthetised, and the operation under way. Removing the leg didn't take long as Scamp had managed to do most of the job himself. The tricky bit was tidying everything up so the wound would heal nicely and he wouldn't be bothered by the stump.

The blood vessels had all contracted and almost sealed themselves off during the trauma. Not for the first time, I marvelled that the little dog had survived – and, to all intents and purposes, appear bright and happy afterwards.

With one eye on the pulse oximeter, which monitored Scamp's vital signs during the anaesthetic, Sheila appraised my handiwork. 'Do you think Spartans would be bothering with intradermal sutures? Isn't that a bit too delicate for a fearsome warrior?'

'OK.' I chuckled. 'I'm a delicate Spartan – I can live with that.'

'One thing I did mean to ask you, since you're the ultra-capable Spartan vet, is what we do tonight if you get called out on a calving? You're on-call here at the emergency service, but I'm presuming you're on-call for Pilgrims as well?' Sheila raised an eyebrow.

She had hit the nail on the head – and it was a nail I had desperately been trying to avoid. Pilgrims, my fledgling practice, didn't quite have its own surgery yet – I was working on it – and to finance myself in those early days I was still fully committed to the emergency service. Tonight I was doing two jobs at the same time. A tricky business – and one that only a Spartan vet could hope to accomplish.

'Well, there is the possibility,' I said, 'that I might be just winging it a touch. But we can do it, can't we, us two old comrades? I can nip out, do a calving and you can man the fort here until I'm back.'

I ventured a laugh, to test her mood. There was no doubt that what I was doing wasn't strictly the *best*. I was trying to pull a double duty on-call and get away with it.

'And if you're out on an emergency calving and a fitting dog turns up?' Sheila asked, the humour gone from her voice.

'Look,' I admitted, 'I know this is bad, but it's incredibly short term – I spoke to Bob last week and he's keen for a few extra bucks on a regular basis. If he joins me full time then it'll take a load off and I'll start to have a regular pool of vets to help us out.'

A fantastic small-animal vet, Bob was the senior assistant

at a busy local practice in the neighbouring town. His practice had recently subscribed to my emergency service, and before Bob had got too used to the easy life with no nights on-call, I'd somehow managed to twist his arm into helping me out.

'Just bear with me a few weeks . . .' I paused. 'Please?'

Sheila sighed. 'Bob will be fantastic if you can get him to join the team, but seriously, you can't provide two on-call services – you know how busy we're getting down here. If the worst-case scenario does happen, we're going to be in trouble.'

Sheila was right. The emergency service had taken off; I now covered the out-of-hours duties for twenty-eight practices in the surrounding towns, centralising the work by running it out of one hospital. I also knew that, without Sheila I'd be floundering hopelessly, trying to keep things afloat. The two of us had pretty much built the service up between us, covering all the nights ourselves, but now, with between five and ten emergencies each night, it was non-stop. There was no chance of sleep, so we needed to expand the team and give ourselves nights off. While the veterinary work was one aspect, the administration was another.

Sheila managed it effortlessly, but, to compound matters, as the practice had grown, her duties on the night-to-night running of things had increased. She now had her own nursing team to organise and needed to know that, if she wasn't on duty herself, the nurse on-call would have a competent and reliable vet who would be able to work unsupported.

'If it really goes mad, we can phone Bob and I'll beg, but Pilgrims is quiet and the odds are so small that I'd get a double emergency, I mean—'

'Don't tempt Fate!' Sheila cut in. 'Let's just focus on getting Scamp sorted out and hope there isn't a calving or a fitting dog rung in.' She gently stroked Scamp's snout. 'How did you persuade Bob to commit anyway?'

'I took him a bottle of whisky and upped my financial offer,' I joked.

'I suppose he must be saving up for something,' Sheila said, with a smile in her voice.

'How about he just loves healing?' I protested.

'Bob is no one's fool – he must be trying to put some aside for his forthcoming nuptials. Which reminds me – how are things progressing with Cordelia?'

It was a loaded question. Along with the rest of the team in my first job, Sheila had watched my developing relationship with Cordelia, a vet who worked in another local practice.

'Going just great, thanks,' I replied evasively, feigning intense concentration as I started to place the final skin sutures over Scamp's freshly modelled stump.

'Is that "Going great, mind your own business", or "Going great"'

'Look how neat that wound is. Scamp's going to be streamlined!' I exclaimed, pointing at the finished leg and looking innocently at Sheila.

Sheila remained silent, a thin smile on her lips.

'It's a sensitive subject,' I said. 'I'm meeting her family for Sunday lunch this weekend. It'll be the first time I'll join the whole clan for a meal, big day and . . .' I paused. How best to phrase it?

'The pressure to impress is acute!' Sheila finished, almost clapping with joy at the gossip she'd be able to spread.

I shook my head in despair, knowing that the first thing

Sheila would do in her break would be to text all my old work colleagues with this news. Scamp, groggy from his anaesthetic but apparently sensing that the situation required his input, did what only a tough three-legged dog would do – he wagged his tail.

3
Making Impressions

'Right you are, Luke, she's over there. How are you keeping, then? Nice to see you again, been a while. Sorry it's a Sunday but can't plan these things – you know how it is.'

That was how Mr Hootle spoke. He had barely time to take a breath between sentences. He continued to chatter away as I pulled up at the yard and turned off the engine.

Sunday morning had come around in the blink of an eye. Keen to impress at the big lunch with Cordelia's family, I'd smartened up and just slipped on a clean pair of shoes when the call had come in. Attending an emergency at Mr Hootle's farm was never a disappointment: there was always a drama and this call promised to be no exception – I just didn't want to be late for lunch. It would be the first time I'd met the whole family since I'd popped the question and was intent on making a good impression.

The drama was a cow that had calved and subsequently prolapsed her uterus straight afterwards. It was a serious emergency and time was of the essence. To make matters worse she had gone down in the crush in which she was being held. Mr Hootle had phoned about twenty minutes ago and, thankfully, I had three clear hours before I was due at Cordelia's. Reckoning it would be okay as long as I didn't delay, I'd jumped straight into the truck and headed over.

'Been great, thanks. Things are getting busy, which is a good sign, even started taking on some equine work, which I never expected,' I replied, a broad smile on my face as I moved swiftly round the back of the vehicle to get my equipment ready.

Mr Hootle nodded enthusiastically. 'Oh, that's good news, you've done well there, haven't you? Very good! Careful with horses, though, temperamental creatures – can't trust them. Thanks for coming so quick for this one. She's in a bit of a state, reckon we'll have a job on.'

'How long has she been prolapsed for?' I asked, pulling up my waterproofs.

'Oh, well, I phoned you right away, Luke, no messing about. Haven't had any bother with them calving up until now, but she's wild as the hills, this one, and once I pulled the calf out – dead one at that – she pushed her womb out about ten minutes later. It's got to go back in but it'll be hard this one, Luke, she's down in the crush and stuck fast. I couldn't move her. Must be an hour, all said and done, since I calved her.'

As I got ready, Mr Hootle wrung his hands and paced anxiously up and down.

Time was important; the cow had pushed her uterus out after the calving – mainly because she was exhausted. The problem was that, the longer the uterus was outside the cow, the more it would swell and become harder to push back in. To compound matters, it sounded as if the cow had collapsed in the crush and, depending on her position, getting the bulging tissue back inside her could be difficult. After all, we wouldn't have gravity to lend a hand.

'Is it a full prolapse?' I asked, following Mr Hootle as we wove between a couple of barns.

'Oh, yes, everything's out, right mess, Luke. You'll manage, I'm sure, but it'll be a job.' Mr Hootle gestured ahead to where the beast lay.

I looked at the cow and inwardly groaned. She was a huge Charolais-cross and was lying wedged at the bottom of a large metal crush, unable to stand, move forwards or backwards, with an ever-spreading sheet of thick tissue spilling out of her back end as the womb continued to pull itself out. Effectively it had turned itself inside out and was lying on the concrete around her feet. Her back legs were tucked forwards under her and she was lowing sadly, her great eyes rolling.

I glanced at the still form of a huge dead calf lying to one side, and Mr Hootle, noticing my observation, pointed at it. 'Look at the size of that one, Luke,' he said, shaking his head sadly. 'Real brute. Stuck fast he was. I got the thing out but it was too much for her. She went down as I got him and the rest followed.' He paused. 'You don't mind if I sit down, do you? It's my knees, you know. Not much room for two of us up there anyway.'

I eyed the race running up towards the back of the crush. It was about three feet wide – and with the cow wedged and collapsed at the end of the crush, it was going to be tight space for me to get behind her and work. Mr Hootle, anticipating a difficult calving, had herded her into the race and shut her in the crush so he could work safely on her with her head restrained. Only it hadn't gone to plan. She'd collapsed and now getting any manoeuvrability around her was nigh on impossible.

'No problem, Mr Hootle,' I said, with as much confidence as I could muster. 'I'll just get some jabs ready and then I'll get up there and have a go.' I drew up some injections to give to the cow.

'It's just my damn knees, Luke.' Mr Hootle chortled and sat on a bale at the end of the race. He was out of my eyeline now but I could still hear him chuntering away as I prepared the syringes. 'Going just fine, except my knees. Knees are useful things, Luke, and mine are starting to ache a bit. Not like yours, I expect. You're looking fit – just as well. You'll need to be to sort this one out.'

I tried to suppress a smile but couldn't. The farmer's ceaseless cheer and quick-fire talking were infectious.

'What have you got there then, Luke? Couple of horse drugs? Don't mind if they are, as long as they get the job done.'

It was an old joke. Not so very long ago, he'd summoned me when I'd been a new, fresh-faced vet. I'd had to resort to a horse drug to remove a potato stuck in one of his cow's throat. 'These are pretty universal drugs, Mr Hootle, don't worry. The first one is a local anaesthetic, so I can give her an epidural and relax the back end. The second one will go into her vein and stop her pushing the uterus back out as I try to push it back in.'

I edged my way up the race to get behind the cow. Carefully pinpointing the spot between the vertebrae at her tail base, I inserted my needle. 'We're also going to need some sugar and a couple of buckets of water,' I said, depressing the plunger on the syringe. 'And a plastic feed bag, if you've got one.'

'Right you are, Luke. I'll get some sugar from the house.' Mr Hootle climbed to his feet, awkwardly with his rusty knees. 'Why do you need sugar? What's all that about?'

'It's an old trick that Giles used. We'll cut the plastic feed bag in half and get it under her uterus. Then we can wash it off, pour on the sugar and it should shrink. Leaves me with less tissue to push back inside her and makes it all less swollen . . .'

The senior farm vet in my old practice, Giles was one of the most practically minded vets I had ever met. While I wasn't convinced that pouring sugar on a prolapsed uterus would have been favourably looked upon by my old university professors as 'best practice technique', if it was good enough for Giles, it was certainly good enough for me.

'Just before you go,' I said, climbing over the metal rails to move around the front of the crush, 'could you quickly give me a hand to get this other jab into her neck?'

'Right you are Luke. We'll need a rope to hold her head, I expect.'

Mr Hootle disappeared for a moment as he walked round the outside to the front of the crush. As he went, I thought I could even hear his knees creaking – but it was probably my imagination.

The cow, wide-eyed with pain, tossed her head angrily as I opened the side panel of the crush. Her neck, restrained between two thick bars of metal, which prevented her from going forwards or backwards, tensed as I approached and she flung her head sideways towards me. The danger wasn't from her short horns, more that she could trap and break my fingers between her head and the bars of the crush. Then nobody would be pouring sugar on her uterus today.

As Mr Hootle distracted her and slipped a rope over her horns from the front, the cow bellowed. I used the opportunity to jab my needle into her neck with the hope of finding the jugular. It was a deep neck, with no visible vein, but in a cow of her size, providing I gauged the right anatomical spot, it would have been hard to miss something the size of a small hosepipe. With some relief, I saw blood gush back into the syringe. I quickly injected the smooth-muscle relaxant and nodded my thanks to Mr Hootle.

As Mr Hootle disappeared to get the supplies I had requested, I climbed back into the race and knelt down to examine the cow. She was badly torn around the vulva and gave a desperate moan as I examined the mass of swollen uterus on the concrete.

I faced a notoriously difficult challenge. Fully prolapsed uteruses require huge amounts of patience and strength. The plan was to clean the tissue off, then slowly work it back into the cow, starting at the edges. Weighing about 30 kilos, with more tissue than a man could easily fit into his arms, it was a mission of logistics trying to feed everything back through a relatively small hole. Resigning myself to getting a bit mucky and figuring I still had a good couple of hours before I was due at Cordelia's, I began the procedure.

Mr Hootle returned, clutching his bag of cane sugar in one hand, a feed bag and a bucket of water in the other. I sliced the feed bag up the sides, slipped it under the uterus as best I could, then poured the water over the tissue to clean it. The cow, in marked distress, had passed faeces all over it. The combination of cow muck, water and uterine tissue meant I was swimming in filth within about ten minutes. I looked up at Mr Hootle, who watched me carefully. Cordelia might just have to wait . . .

Once the uterus was clean, on went the sugar. Unable to get the cow's legs behind her, I had to lift the tissue onto my lap and try to push it uphill, back into her pelvis.

About half an hour later, with the uterus no further in, I paused to catch my breath.

'How are you doing there, Luke?' Mr Hootle asked anxiously. He was watching me from the end of the race as I sweated, strained and cursed, every inch a battle.

'Just fine, Mr Hootle, bit of a tricky one this – she's really working against me and the space is . . . difficult . . .'

I grunted. Having moved to a horizontal position with my face pushed up against the back end of the cow, I was desperately trying to get purchase to push the tissue.

'Have you got an empty wine bottle by any chance?' I asked, through clenched teeth.

'A wine bottle, Luke?'

'A wine bottle . . .' I wheezed. Gravity was against me. Every time I thought I'd gained ground and relaxed for even a second, the uterus came spilling back out.

'Wine bottle – bit of extra reach, is that the plan?' Mr Hootle chirped. 'Right you are, Luke! Need to get that in, don't we?'

'We do.' I strained, trying again for one big push. I hadn't been keeping track of time, but I reckoned I still had an hour before I needed to be with Cordelia. If the wine bottle did the trick, I'd even have time for a shower. There was no way I wanted to meet the in-laws covered with cow muck and uterine discharge.

'Here we go, Luke,' said Mr Hootle, re-emerging with the wine bottle. 'Hope this does the trick! You see, I think we might have another problem . . .'

I paused to catch my breath, the wet mess of blood, muck and uterine fluid cold against the side of my face. 'What's that, Mr Hootle? I didn't quite hear . . .'

I took the wine bottle and began to judge how I would do this. Mr Hootle kept on chattering. I only caught the odd word, but that was enough.

'Just been watching that one in the yard, Luke. She's been trying to calve down for a few hours, reckon we'll have a job with her as well. We'd best look at her once you've sorted this one out, don't you think?' I blinked up at him, his shining, hopeful face, completely clean of uterine muck. 'You'll get them sorted, though, Luke. No problem on that score!'

This was going to be tight. Another calving, and this present job still not finished. Cordelia would kill me if I was late – but I couldn't let the cows down.

I closed my eyes for a moment to count to ten and rally my strength. Then, focusing hard, I heaved in one gigantic effort to reduce the uterus and hold it inside.

The bulging tissue gradually reduced, but wouldn't stay in until I managed to push it completely inside and over the brim of the pelvis. My face was on the concrete in an appalling pool of blood and faeces, my arm engulfed up to the shoulder inside the cow, as I tried desperately to get the uterus to stay where it was supposed to be. It was time for the wine bottle. I reversed it so I was holding it by the neck, then swiftly pushed it into the cow to give my arm the necessary extra foot of reach. Then I pressed the womb completely inside.

'Are you getting it reduced, Luke? Is it working? What a job this one is!'

I couldn't reply. I was using all my strength to keep the tissue inside her. Although it was back in place, I still couldn't get it to drop down into her abdomen due to her position and size. 'What a job indeed, Mr Hootle.'

I had to come up with a unique solution.

'I need four mls of oxytocin,' I panted.

'Haven't got my glasses, Luke. Where will I find that one?' Mr Hootle said. I heard my drug bottles rattling around as he delved into my medicine box.

'Small bottle, green label,' I wheezed, straining to keep the uterus from spilling back out.

Mr Hootle chatted away as he drew up the drug. I closed my eyes, my arm numb with fatigue.

'Stick it in the muscle, Luke?' Mr Hootle chirped. I nodded and watched through one squinted eye as he injected the cow.

The plan was that the uterus would now rapidly contract inside the cow and around my arm. It was the only way I could think of keeping it inside her and reducing the huge volume of tissue straining to spill out. As I felt it start to shrink, I decided how to place thick nylon sutures around her back end and effectively seal her up so nothing could come back out. The wine bottle had been amazing but, until the cow stood up or I could get her legs behind her, I just couldn't reach far enough inside to properly position the uterus. This was my only hope of sorting the problem – either that or I would be lying there for several days to come. I doubted whether either the cow or I would survive that long.

Tentatively, I started to withdraw my arm. As it came out, I held my breath, watching for any sign of the uterus coming straight back out. A minute passed before I turned and scrabbled for a needle and thread, swiftly looping sutures to seal her back end.

'Right you are, Mr Hootle.' I managed to smile through my mask of blood and muck. 'Let's get some calcium into her and sort this calving out!'

An hour and a half later, I leapt into the truck. Behind me, Leuwen raised his head to consider the apparition that had appeared in the front seat. Having determined that I was just about recognisable, despite being covered head to foot in dried blood and muck, he gazed at me with an expression that could only have been interpreted as pity before closing his eyes and resuming his sleep.

'Thanks for the support,' I murmured to his slumbering form.

My only chance of being even semi-presentable for lunch lay in racing home, washing and grabbing some clean clothes. I hadn't wasted time cleaning myself at the farm, and since most of what covered me was now dry, the truck would be able to suffer me for half an hour without too much contamination.

With a cheerful wave to Mr Hootle, who stood in the yard, holding the heifer calf we'd successfully pulled out of the second cow, I slipped the truck into reverse and glanced at the time.

I felt sick. I was going to be at least an hour late. As if it had read my mind, the mobile began to ring. Pulling over, I reached to answer it. 'Hello?'

'Hi, it's me.' Cordelia sounded cheerful. 'Just wondered how you're getting on?'

'Bit of a nightmare – been at Mr Hootle's. He had a prolapse and a calving so a bit of a double whammy,' I blurted. 'I'm just leaving now. I'll race home to wash and change.'

'Well, Abe, Eddy and my dad have just gone for a walk and we're just waiting for Isabella, who'll be coming from the station.' Cordelia paused, as if she were divining a plan. She always had a plan. 'Why don't you come straight here? You can wash off before lunch and anyway, no one will mind if you're a bit grubby – let's face it, they may as well get to know you in your normal state.'

I glanced at my face in the rear-view mirror and was appalled by my own reflection. I was one of the living dead. 'I'm really horrible, I mean absolutely covered, and I haven't got any decent clothes.'

'It'll be fine. We don't stand on ceremony here.' Cordelia had already made up her mind. That meant my mind had been made up as well. This was going to be trickier than the prolapse. 'Better you're grubby than make everyone wait and spoil the lunch. I'll explain to the family what you've been doing so, don't worry, you can make an entrance.'

I could hear her grinning as she disconnected.

Looking back at Leuwen, I sighed. 'Would this impress you?' I asked.

He didn't even open his eyes.

The sunlight dappled through the trees as I rumbled over the cattle grid and entered the forest. Slowing to navigate around a small group of donkeys clustered on the side of the road, I noticed two of the young ones were lounging on the narrow lane, heavy heads swaying slightly as they stood motionless on the tarmac, indifferent to the big truck trying to edge past them. Sounding the horn had no effect and, only when I was about to hop out of the truck and move them manually, did they playfully skip out the way.

Looking at the time, I breathed a slight sigh of relief. I was not, after all, as late as I might have expected. As long as I could find the house, get showered and Cordelia had tracked down a clean shirt for me to borrow, all would be well.

Rounding a gentle bend, I began to drive up a steep incline, slowing to peer out of the window. According to my map, an unmade track off to my left would take me to the house.

While the sheer size of the truck usually guaranteed I had

right of way through any oncoming traffic, it was an absolute swine to turn. As I spotted the track, I didn't swing out far enough and completely misjudged the manoeuvre. A tree one side and the corner post to a large fence on the other were fairly unforgiving – so, angled across the road, I started to reverse to begin what effectively would be a five-point turn. Grinding the gears, I cursed and Leuwen sat up in the back seat to see what all the fuss was about.

'OK,' I muttered. '*Now* you're interested. You want to witness my advanced driving skills, do you?'

Leuwen's eyes were fixed on the hill ahead. Realising that something else had snagged his attention, I turned my head to follow his gaze.

Three figures stood silhouetted at the brow of the hill. Each carried a large stick and seemed to be dressed in thick ragged shirts. Stocky in build, they had halted their descent down the hill and were now keenly observing me make an absolute mess of turning into the drive.

Perhaps they were potential clients. I tried to keep my cool and smashed my fist into the steering wheel. Driving like this in a huge truck with PILGRIMS painted on the side was not the best way to win over new business. I kicked the truck into reverse again, but again made a meal of the turn. Now it would have to be a seven-point turn.

I felt my cheeks flush. The three men were getting bigger as they approached, looming like the front rank of an advancing army. I willed them to just walk on by and let me get on with it.

It was only when they were close enough for me to see their expressions that it dawned on me – the three men weren't planning to walk by at all. In fact, they were waiting to follow me into the drive.

I could see a grin form on the face of the youngest man. The older one, in the middle, was observing me with mild curiosity while the third, clearly the slightly older brother of the youngest, just looked perplexed as to how I could possibly have passed my driving test in the first place.

Winding down the window, I tried a cheerful wave. The three men looked stoically back. 'Do you think I'm scoring points for a great first impression?' I murmured to Leuwen.

After what seemed an eternity, I managed to get the truck onto the drive and rattled along it to the house. As I parked, Leuwen regarded me flatly. Then, catching sight of Cordelia – who was coming out of the house to meet us – he began to wag his tail frantically.

'You don't do that when you see me approach the truck,' I complained, giving him a stroke.

Cordelia, looking radiant in a summer dress, walked towards the car and opened the back door. Leuwen's whole body was wiggling with excitement. This was fairly impressive for a huge Ridgeback and the truck shook vigorously from side to side.

'Oh!' Cordelia gasped, looking at me properly for the first time. 'I don't know what to say . . .'

'Well, it's been eventful. I think I may also have just impressed your dad and brothers with some masterful driving skills. Making a great first impression here.'

'The plan was for you to get in the shower before you met everyone,' she said, her nose wrinkling at the sight and smell of me.

Before I could reply we heard heavy footsteps on the gravel.

'Might be a bit late for that,' I said, looking over her shoulder.

The three men, having followed the truck up the track, walked towards us.

'Luke,' Cordelia said cheerfully, 'it's time for the introductions. Meet Abe, Eddy and Daddy . . .'

My face caked in blood, late and unable to drive my vehicle, I did the only thing I could. I stepped forward and held out my hand.

'Bit of a tight turn there,' Eddy said, with a warm smile as I shook his hand.

'I'd probably have made a better job of it blindfolded.' I laughed, turning slightly to shake Abe's hand.

Both brothers were unflinching about the fact that I resembled a creature from the depths of a black lagoon. They gave firm, strong handshakes before stepping back to allow Graham, Cordelia's dad, to meet me.

I cleared my throat apologetically. 'Mr Sharp,' I began, 'it's nice to meet you. I'm sorry to be in such a state . . .'

'Luke,' he said, a smile cracking a weathered and capable face, 'Graham will do . . . Looks like you've been hard at work. Best grab a shower and then Abe or Eddy will show you where to get a drink. I've got some local ale in the garage – make yourself at home. I'll be keen to hear about your eventful morning over lunch.'

Graham's hand felt like oak and I remembered that, aside from a successful career in NATO, he was an accomplished carpenter. In his retirement, he spent most of his days outside in the forest, rearing livestock and felling trees.

A smaller, slighter character appeared behind the three men and regarded me with cool appraisal. In contrast to Abe and Eddy, who were both blond, six foot and stockily built, this man was whip thin with mousy brown hair, a slightly hooked nose and a penetrating stare. 'This is

Gwyn,' Cordelia said. 'He's a friend of the family who has come to visit.'

I nodded hello and stepped forward to shake Gwyn's hand. 'I'll wait until you've had a wash!' he said, with a nasty laugh. 'That's the problem with vets – all the horrible places you spend your days sticking your arms.'

'Well, it pays the bills,' I replied, smiling politely.

'Dirty money, my father used to call it – and for a good reason!' he sneered, looking at Abe and Eddy smugly.

'Gwyn's father was a vet,' Cordelia said, filling the silence as I wondered what to say. 'They lived down the road from us when we were growing up.'

'That's nice,' I managed.

'Well, it was at the time,' Gwyn said, giving Cordelia a sly smile. 'Never something I would consider – not lucrative enough for my ambitions – but it was nice when I was younger.'

'Well, each to their own,' I said, somewhat confused. 'What did you do instead?'

'I'm an investment banker. We tend not to get too much blood on our suits in my line of work.'

I smiled back at him, meeting his stare with one of my own. Before I could reply, Cordelia took my arm to steer me away. 'Time for you to shower and have a good scrub,' she said, with a twinkle in her eye. 'My sister's in the house, so you can meet her on the way through and then, once you're presentable, you can have a beer with the boys and tell us all about your adventures.'

Cordelia began to lead me away. Naturally, my stench followed us.

'What about Leuwen?' I asked, kicking off my boots by the back door. 'Does he need to be shut in the truck?'

'Oh, no, he'll be fine,' Cordelia replied, nodding in the direction of the garage where Graham was tossing Leuwen some sort of treat. 'He's already proving a hit.'

Leuwen looked immensely proud of himself. Without giving me a second glance, he trotted into the building on the heels of Cordelia's father.

'So what's the deal with Gwyn?' I said, as we stepped into the kitchen.

'Gwyn?' a voice piped up from the depths of the kitchen.

'This is Isabella,' Cordelia said quickly as I turned to meet the figure approaching me.

'Gwyn,' Isabella said cheerfully, taking my hand with a smile, 'is Cordelia's childhood sweetheart . . .'

My mouth must have dropped a fraction, because Isabella – a slightly shorter, brunette version of Cordelia – gave a knowing laugh. I looked at Cordelia, who returned my gaze innocently. 'Time for a shower,' was all she said.

I nodded and hurried towards the bathroom, remembering the ale I had been promised once I was clean. I had a sneaking suspicion I was going to need it.

4
Ticket to Heaven

'You want us to go to the Gambia?' Sam's plaintive tone echoed down the line.

'It'll be nice and sunny for you,' I replied. 'I've got all the documents ready – copies of our vet certificates and deposit cheques for the flight. I'm about to post them off now.'

The silence buzzing down the line told me more than Sam's words ever could.

After what seemed like for ever, he glibly retorted, 'It'll be full of tsetse flies and slave traders.'

'That was a century or two ago,' I said. 'Well, the slave traders anyway.'

'And I'm guessing that, once again, you'll be dragging me to some luxury resort by the sea for a bit of R and R?'

I wished he could have seen me grin. Now he was getting the idea. 'Absolutely! Though I thought we might head up-river a bit and see some donkeys as well.'

'Well, how could you go to the Gambia and not spend time with donkeys?' Sam sighed. 'That would borderline insane.'

'Look, I've spoken to the lady who runs The Gambia

Horse and Donkey Trust. They're desperate for veterinary help to get them off the ground. It's exactly what we do.'

'Correction,' Sam stated. 'It's what *you* do. I just muddle along making us look good.' He paused. 'More to the point, we're both going to have to swing time off work. You've got the emergency service *and* Pilgrims *and* . . .' Here, he launched in for his *coup de grâce*. 'Aren't you supposed to be gearing up for *the* wedding of the year next month?'

He had a point. But I had another.

'I know Jane's away with her mum on holiday because you've told me a million times,' I replied. 'See, Sam? I've used my initiative. You also told me you wanted a week away – so this is perfect. In fact, it's more than perfect, it's all set – I'm heading into the post office right now. Cords is having her hen weekend, Rob is going to cover at Pilgrims for some extra cash. I have Bob-a-dob-dob covering me at the emergency service. It's a perfect window of opportunity.'

I had him on the hook. Now I just had to reel him in.

'Who the heck is Bob-a-dob-dob? One of your imaginary constructs from university?' Sam gibed.

'He's a vet—'

'Well, I figured.'

'—who works locally. He's great. I'm massively twisting his arm into working with me on the emergency service front.'

'He won't go for it,' Sam said. 'He sounds too sensible. But I guess you've always got your trusty Sheila to run the show.'

'I'll be seeing her in a minute. I'm on my way to the hospital now via the post office. I'll pass on your regards.'

'Absolutely! And to the other one . . . What's her name?

Holly? How's she? Still laughing at you all the time? Have you got her slaving away during the nights for you as well?'

Holly was one of the senior nurses from my first practice. She spent 90 per cent of her working day in hysterics and was best friends with Sheila. They both knew Sam well from various Christmas parties and social events that he'd attended and, needless to say, they'd all hit it off immediately. Laughing at me and my various adventures was a great way for disparate strangers to bond.

'Holly's great – still at the old practice, but if things progress with Pilgrims, I hope to win her over.'

'One step at a time, Mr Empire Builder,' Sam said. 'You keep getting these sandcastles set up and the tide could be only moments away.'

'Which is why a week away will be just the thing to recharge the batteries and get us both in the zone,' I responded, pondering the truth of Sam's joke.

'Remind me why I should take annual leave to work in the Gambia?'

'Because,' I said, 'you don't have a huge number of other options. Your girlfriend is away, you need to use up your holiday allowance, you don't have any other friends and, most importantly . . .' Here was my own *coup de grâce*. ' . . . it's cheap beer.'

For the longest time, Sam did not say a word. Then a little cough announced his decision. 'Next week, did you say?'

I'd noticed the advert in a weekly publication called the *Vet Times*. It simply stated 'Vet wanted to help support a new charity in the Gambia'. Without thinking about it much, and knowing I'd be able to trick, coerce or blackmail Sam into being my buddy, I'd phoned the number and spoken to a very positive and focused woman called Heather.

She and her sister, Stella, had spent their childhood in the Gambia and had vowed to help the animals and people there when they grew up. Stella had set up a chimpanzee sanctuary, and Heather the Gambia Horse and Donkey Trust (GHDT). As a fledgling charity ourselves, I thought WVS could only benefit from being involved, and Heather's warmth and passion for her project had fired me up. It sounded as if WVS would have a good mission on its hands and, before I headed into work and before Sam could change his mind, I resolved to post copies of our veterinary certificates to Heather, who needed to get permission from the Gambian vet council for us to go.

As I drove the truck into town to visit the post office, Leuwen tagging along for the ride, I made sure my mobile was powered down. If it was on, there was always a chance Sam would call up with some plaintive excuse – perhaps he had an ingrowing toenail, perhaps it was his mother's friend's sister's birthday – and I didn't want to give him the slightest sniff of backing out.

As I jumped out of the truck, I saw a small crowd clustered around the post office entrance. I approached, wondering what all the commotion was about. Glancing at my watch, slightly concerned that a long queue would make me late for the night shift, I joined the crowd.

'He's a vet!' a voice sounded. 'Says so on his truck. He'll know what to do.'

I almost looked over my shoulder to see if another vet was behind me. As the eyes of the small crowd swivelled to fix on me, I brokered a smile. 'What's the problem?' I asked, looking around for an injured dog or half squashed cat.

A rather stout woman stood in the middle of the group and gestured towards a postman. He was peering at something that seemed to be balanced on top of a gatepost to the left of the post-office entrance. 'Baby bird,' she said brusquely. 'It needs help.'

'Oh, I do hope you can help it!' another voice cried. 'So lucky a vet's turned up!' I found the voice in the crowd. It came from a tall lady holding a small, bespectacled boy firmly by the hand.

'A baby bird?' I said, surprised.

'Well, it looks like one to me,' the postman said, turning to fix me with one eye; the other staring off somewhere to my right.

Momentarily distracted by the gaze of the cross-eyed postman, I peered at the gatepost.

'He's not sure,' the stout woman said quickly.

'It's a baby pigeon,' I replied, craning my head upwards towards the roof of the building.

'A baby pigeon!' the tall lady echoed, as awestricken as if we'd uncovered a chest of buried treasure.

'Yes,' the stout woman said simply, nodding in agreement.

'So,' the postman gruffly surmised, 'it's a baby pigeon which has fallen out of the nest in the gutter. What do you want to do with it?' He looked at me, demanding an answer.

I looked closely at the bird. 'Has anyone touched it?' I asked, in an attempt to get a handle on the situation. Thoughts of what Sheila would say to me if I pitched up for my night shift clutching a baby pigeon hurtled into my mind.

'No,' the postman said. 'I noticed it by chance when I came for the collection, so no one's been near it. Come to think of it, I need to get on. Hope you do well with it.' Clearly deciding enough was enough, he gave a curt nod and promptly marched away. The baby bird was, apparently, my responsibility now. It wasn't quite the same thing as finding an abandoned human baby on the doorstep, but it felt close.

Almost as if to signal the postman's abrupt departure, it started to rain.

'Oh, Toby, we have to get home. The nice vet will look after the pigeon now,' said the tall lady and, throwing me a smile, she too headed off.

'Yes,' the stout woman said, departing with a hearty slap on my back.

I stood there alone, the other bystanders and well-wishers shuffling off to find shelter from the downpour. In the space of a few minutes, it was only me, the rain, the gatepost and the baby pigeon. What few feathers it had fluffed out and it seemed to cringe into itself, unsure what to make of the rain.

'Did it fly down?' a small voice said behind me.

Startled – I had thought I was alone – I turned. A girl of eleven or twelve was standing there, quietly watching from the shelter of a purple umbrella.

'No, I don't think so,' I said. 'It's far too small. I guess it fell. But it doesn't seem to be hurt. Its wings must have helped a bit. As long as it hasn't been touched we might have a chance.'

'We shoot them at home,' the girl ventured.

'Right,' I said, turning to look at her. All I needed, I thought – I was late for work, stuck in the rain with a baby pigeon, and a twelve-year-old girl was mocking me.

She smiled sweetly and nodded gravely. It was the most curious look. 'I live on a farm,' she explained. 'My dad calls them flying rats. Then he goes to get his gun.'

'They carry psittacosis,' I replied, as much to myself as to her. Craning upwards again, I considered the guttering.

'Nasty disease if you catch it. If you go to Trafalgar Square – don't feed them.' I looked back again, quickly checking that the girl didn't actually have a shotgun hidden on her person. 'This one's a baby,' I said, 'and we're in the country. So, if no one has touched it, we should be able to get it back in the nest.'

'I thought you said we shouldn't touch them,' she said.

'Human smell means the mother will reject it – if I wear gloves, it should be fine.'

The girl nodded indulgently. 'I could always call my dad.'

'No!'

'Don't you like my dad?'

The rain was getting heavier, and so was my head. 'I'm sure he's a very good farmer.'

'He'd have shot that bird already.' She smiled.

I decided to ignore the sweet little murderer for a moment and, distractedly, tried to fathom out where exactly in the guttering the nest was.

'I think the nest is at the end there,' she said, pointing upwards.

Sure enough, she was right. I could just about make out some sticks and a tail sticking over the corner of the building.

'How are you going to get it up there?' she asked.

Slightly annoyed, I bit my tongue.

'My dad has a ladder.'

I shot her a look.

'He uses it to climb up things.'

I nodded. It wasn't very helpful.

'Those builders over there might have a ladder too,' the girl said. 'All you'd have to do is ask, but you'd have to be polite.'

Underneath her purple umbrella she was the very picture of politeness. I wondered if this was what she did, wander all over the country dispensing helpful advice.

But, yet again, she was right. She gestured towards a row of terraced houses on the opposite side of the road. One of them had some scaffolding on the outside with a big sign pinned on the front of it: 'RICHARDS AND RICHARDS – BUILDERS AND GENERAL REPAIRS.'

I peered towards the scaffolding. Some figures were milling around, their silhouettes visible as they sheltered from the rain under a tarpaulin. 'Not a bad idea,' I said, smiling at her for the first time. 'If you could keep an eye on the bird, I'll be right back.' I took a few strides, then looked back. 'No shooting it, though. We can sort this.'

The girl looked disgruntled, but nodded all the same.

Soaked to the skin, I hurried to the scaffold, the envelope I was planning to post still clutched in my hand. As I passed the truck, I cast a look at Leuwen, who watched me through the back window, an almost bemused expression on his face.

'You're better off in there, mate,' I called. 'This little girl would have you shot in a second . . .'

Keenly watched by both Leuwen and the girl, I approached the scaffolding and pushed my way through the gap in the tarpaulin hanging down from the first platform. Three men, who had been engaged in eager conversation, went suddenly silent and shot me a piercing look. I felt as if I'd walked into a Wild West saloon.

'Hi,' I said tentatively. 'I'm sorry to bother you, but I don't suppose you have a ladder I could borrow for five minutes?'

They considered me archly, each dragging on a self-rolled cigarette.

'You want a ladder?' one repeated, his hands like calloused

plates, a faint sprinkling of plaster dust over his torn shirt and boots.

'Baby bird – fallen out of a nest just over the road. I just need to pop it back and job done.' I forced the words out quickly, trying not to sound too much like a crazy woodland eccentric.

'You're that new vet who's set up, aren't you?' another man asked.

'Yep, I was just posting a letter,' I said. 'I don't normally treat baby birds, to be honest . . .'

'Is it one of those pigeons that roost up there every year?' the third builder said, oblivious to my weak joke.

'It's a pigeon.'

'Hate bloody pigeons,' the man cut in. 'Flying rats!' His two friends laughed at that one. 'Maybe you should shoot it.'

I looked over my shoulder. The opening in the tarpaulin fluttered apart and, through the sheets of rain, I could see the girl standing demurely under her umbrella, thinking exactly the same thing.

'Look,' I said, pretending I agreed, as if I were drawing him into some ridiculous conspiracy, 'there's a little girl over there and she's really upset. It'll take two seconds. I reckon I could just pop it back and that will be a ticket to heaven right there.'

There was a moment of pause as the builders clearly thought about the situation. Then the one in the middle spoke up: 'Can you do that then?' he said with a twinkle in his eye.

'What?' I replied.

'Get us a ticket to heaven,' he said, his friends beaming broadly.

'I'll try to put in a good word,' I said confidently, smiling back.

'You've got a contact, have you?' the builder said.

'I've got a contact – her number's in the phone box,' one of the others chipped in helpfully. In response, the three of them roared with laughter.

When the joke was finally over, I tried again. 'What do you reckon?'

'Don't think we've got one here. It's not long enough . . . Simon, have we got one over the other side?'

One of the men rolled his eyes and, with a nod for me to follow, trudged out of the shelter, into the rain, heading back over towards the post office. 'All this for a flipping pigeon,' he muttered, throwing me an evil sidelong glance.

At last, we drew close to the post office. The little girl swivelled to meet us. 'All right, Simon,' the girl nodded.

'All right, Stacey,' the builder replied. 'That your bird, is it?'

'Flying rats,' she said.

The builder stopped dead and gave me a withering glare. 'I thought you said she was upset?' he demanded, rain streaming down his face, plastering his shirt to his chest.

I threw looks all around me, desperate to find another little girl to pin the blame on. All I could see was Leuwen, staring at me from the back of the truck. Behind the rain-drenched glass, he looked disappointed.

'Okay, I admit it!' I said, exasperated. 'It was me! I'm the one who was upset! I just can't stand the idea of this baby bird drowning out here. Okay?'

Simon and Stacey shared a conspiratorial look. She lifted the umbrella as high as she could so that Simon could duck underneath it. It was more than she'd done for me.

'All right, Mr Vet,' Simon said. 'Let's get you this ladder. We wouldn't want you crying yourself to sleep at night.'

I followed him to a garage just behind the post office, where the drains were rapidly starting to overflow.

'This is all we've got,' he said, pointing at a long rickety ladder propped on its side horizontally down the edge of the garage.

'Will it reach?' I asked, trying to eye up the distance.

'Oh, it'll reach,' the builder replied casually, dragging the ladder out with one hand. 'If you stretch . . .'

I nodded mutely. Grasping the ladder, I headed over towards the bird.

'You going to climb up, then?' Stacey piped up as I returned.

'Yes,' I said, tight-lipped. 'That's what you want, isn't it?'

She shrugged.

'I just need to grab a glove from the truck . . .'

Leaving the ladder by the post office, I raced back to the truck, opened the door, threw the envelope onto the seat and rummaged around for some rectal gloves. Leuwen, fed up with watching his master make a fool of himself, lifted his head lazily to greet me.

'Yeah, just keep on laughing,' I said. 'I suppose you'd shoot it too, wouldn't you?'

He whimpered miserably. I had forgotten how much Leuwen hated rain.

'It's letting up,' I said. Over my shoulder, I heard the builders laughing. 'Which is more than I can say for this lot.'

By the time I returned, Simon had been joined by his workmates. Underneath her umbrella, surrounded by builders, Stacey was apoplectic. Her face had turned purple with rage. 'You said I was really upset?' she thundered.

'Look,' I said, 'I've already explained that. I was embarrassed. It's me. Me who's upset.'

'I told you we shoot them!' Stacey protested.

'I thought you were joking,' I replied, leaning the ladder against the wall and taking a deep breath.

Stacey glowered at me as I gently picked up the bird with a gloved hand.

'Bloody ugly things, pigeons,' Simon said.

I looked at the helpless bird. There was no denying it was exceptionally ugly, tufts of feathers sprouting out from a fat little body with a bulbous head.

'The mother's up there – she might attack you,' one of the builders chirped.

Ignoring the running commentary, I picked up the ladder and positioned it against the wall, testing its stability with a gentle shake. The guttering suddenly seemed a long way up.

The baby pigeon, seemingly unconcerned by the whole chain of events, sat motionless in the palm of my hand.

'Simon, any chance you could just steady the ladder for me?' I asked, trying not to sound feeble, even though my heart was pounding with every rung I ascended.

Simon looked at his friends as if irritated to be singled out by name, but slowly walked over to casually place a hand on the ladder.

'Thanks,' I said quietly.

'What are you going to do if the mother does try to peck your eyes out?' Stacey shouted, encouraged by the builders who seemed to be discussing what they would do when I fell.

'Blink!' I replied.

Deciding there and then that I needed to just get this done, I fixed my eyes on the nest and pushed myself further up, my arm outstretched.

Near the top of the ladder, I paused to contemplate what to do next. The nest was about three feet above me. To try to put the bird back where it belonged, I would have to climb near the top of the ladder and reach out over the side. I could only imagine what the builders would say if I dropped the bird.

Glancing down, I could see that a small crowd had gathered. The builders and Stacey had been joined by a late flurry of customers for the post office. Now the rain had stopped, I had clearly become an attraction for every passer-by who happened along. I took a deep breath as I perched precariously on the brink of disaster.

I inched up another step, willing myself to keep going. The prospect of what would happen if I fell thundered through my mind. It wasn't the broken legs or the mocking of the builders that bothered me most: it was the amount of abuse I would get for the rest of my days from Sam, Rob and everyone else who knew me.

I cursed myself. I should have phoned the RSPCA – what was I thinking, risking my life for a pigeon?

As I leant outwards and upwards, angling the baby bird to the side of the nest, there was a collective intake of breath. The mother pigeon, seeing me approach, immediately flew off and I noticed that there was one other chick in the nest. Gently tipping the bird into the mass of twigs, I gulped and quickly grabbed the ladder with both hands.

There came a small round of ironic applause from the builders. As I climbed down, my heart was beating like a machine gun.

'Quite brave that,' Stacey said.

I looked at her, trying to gauge if she was mocking me again. To my shock, it seemed that she wasn't.

'But you still should have shot it.'

'Just earning a ticket to heaven, Stacey, that's all.'

With that, I made a hasty retreat to the truck.

Posting the envelope, I decided, could wait until the morning.

It seemed like an aeon before we were on the plane, winging our way to the Gambia – but, in truth, the whole trip had been organised in less than a week.

'Pleased to escape?' I asked Sam, whose compact frame nestled comfortably in the economy seat.

'This is my favourite bit of our trips,' he said, with a smile.

'What – the flying?' I replied incredulously, never having been a fan of it myself.

'No – the bit where I sit here with plenty of space and you squeeze, sweat and curse for however long we're trapped here for.'

He gave a cruel laugh. In response, I only grunted, my legs already jammed up against the seat in front.

'It's a quick one – just five hours or so and we're there. I can handle it,' I said, popping my hand on the armrest between us. 'Besides, I can always spread sideways – you know you love it.'

'You're the one who hates to be touched,' Sam said, placing his hand on mine as he spoke. 'It's never bothered me.'

Instantly, I ripped my hand away. Sam gave a victorious laugh.

'You'd better make the most of this,' he went on. 'You won't be able to have these adventures when you're married, you know, can't neglect your wife by constantly being away. How do you two have a relationship, anyway, if you're working all your nights at the emergency service and spend your holidays abusing my good nature?'

It was something that had been on my mind. 'I'm grafting

to set up our future life and Cords is behind the charity. She believes in it. I'll get the businesses settled, find the work–life balance and it'll all turn out just fine.'

'Oh no, don't tell me there is never going to be an end to these adventures. I'm clinging to the prospect of you settling down and leaving me alone,' Sam moaned.

'How about you and Jane?' I said, changing the subject.

'Truth be told, I'm keen to have a break. Jane isn't best pleased with me at the moment.'

'Oh no?' I asked. 'She saw you in daylight?'

'No,' Sam said gravely. 'I got a letter from Susan.'

'You mean *the* Susan?' I said, surprised. Susan had been Sam's first girlfriend – the one he had dated at school and who had left him for the captain of the rugby team. Once that relationship had petered out – all two weeks of it – she had stalked him throughout our time at university, with a plethora of phone calls and letters. Sam had been broken-hearted at the time but had remained steadfast in his resolution not to take Susan back – which had only escalated her desire to win him over.

'Yes,' he said, pulling a letter from his top pocket and handing it to me. 'I haven't heard from her for a couple of years, and then, out of the blue, *this* arrived.'

I unfolded the crumpled sheet of paper and scanned it:

Hi, Sam,

Long time no hear . . . Thought I'd drop you a line and see how things are there.

I have something to say to you but I'm not quite sure how to put it. Well, let me start by saying you're stalking me in my dreams, chasing me, hunting me. I want you to catch me but you just can't for some reason. Trust me, it really turns my world upside down. But the strange thing is, we're still in school, still in school uniform, but at a location unknown to me.

I suppose it's my subconscious that's getting to me as things weren't said and done when we split up. Peter was never serious about me. I was confused, I didn't know what I wanted and I let you go. I'm so sorry I'm bringing that up all these years later – but I just keep feeling things were never settled between us, that chapter was never finished or closed properly on our lives . . .

I'll understand if you want to break contact with me and remove me from your Facebook and email contacts after I say what I'm about to say but I need to get it out. I don't want to cause problems with you or Jane, but I just can't seem to find closure. I feel, deep down, that you are my soul mate, but circumstances led us in different directions and our paths were never to meet again. I think that's why you're haunting me in my dreams. If I'm wrong then so be it, but at least it's out in the open.

I'm going to remove you from my Facebook but if you still feel that we can be friends, please feel free to request me as a friend again.

Sorry to drop this on you like this but it has been bothering me for a while and it's starting to affect me physically too.

Kindest regards,
Susan

'Going from hunting to haunting is a bit of a jump.' I laughed.

We marvelled at the letter. It seemed to be a missive from another world. Sometimes it was easier to talk to animals than to women.

'Tell me about it,' Sam replied. 'It's not funny – I thought she'd stopped all this stuff five years ago.'

'I can't believe you actually showed it to me. I mean, no surprise you can't catch her in the dream – you were never any good at that – but how are you going to take the Facebook rejection? Please tell me you didn't show this to Jane.'

'She was there when I opened it,' Sam said miserably. 'I didn't have much choice.'

'I can't believe I'm saying this,' I began, 'but it genuinely looks like you're in demand . . .' I paused. 'Wait a minute – have you written back?'

Sam's eyes almost popped out of his head. 'No! Of course I haven't. What I've done is get on a plane with you on some godforsaken charity mission. The solution will come to me during the week ahead. I was hoping you'd be able to offer some sensible advice. Fat chance.'

Sam put his headphones on to stop me wading in – but I hadn't finished. 'You want to know my honest opinion?'

Sam paused, one headphone in, one out.

'I think you should send her some flowers,' I said, 'with a card apologising for hunting her in your school uniform . . .'

With a flourish, Sam slammed his other headphone into his ear and reclined in his seat. Reaching over, I tucked the letter back into his top pocket. 'Try to think about the donkeys you're going to help,' I said. 'Mind you, when she hears about this trip, she'll dream about you chasing her down on a donkey.' I considered this. 'How are your riding talents these days? You might even catch her if you were on a donkey . . .'

Sam's mouth twitched as he clamped his eyes shut and turned away.

Martha brooked no nonsense. Tall, wiry, tough and with flaming auburn hair, she stood out from the crowd as we inched our way through Customs in Banjul. Smiling faces offered us a hundred taxi rides as we pushed out into the bright sunshine and she strode confidently ahead of us, talking to us over her shoulder in clipped sentences. Her English was heavily accented with the strong Germanic influence of her homeland.

'I manage for the moment on behalf of Heather and Stella,' she said, her green eyes piercing and direct. 'You spoke to them, *ja*?'

'Yes, I've spoken to Heather at length,' I replied. 'She placed an advert for veterinary help, so that's why we're here.'

'You are going to run clinics?' Martha enquired.

'We're going to do whatever we can, but the plan is to set up some follow-up vet teams and see how best we can implement some sustainable help,' I said, quickening my pace to keep up.

'Why don't we run?' Sam murmured from the back, trailing a bit behind me, laden with two heavy packs.

'What?' Martha stopped mid-stride, turning suddenly to look at Sam.

Almost bumping into her, I turned to look at my friend.

Embarrassment was etched on Sam's face. He tried a smile. 'Keen to build up a sweat, you know. Got these heavy bags, great to power on, be super-efficient and all.'

'You want to run, or are you being sarcastic?' Martha asking, her eyebrow arched.

'Just joking,' he said quietly. 'Sorry.'

'He's got a lot on his mind,' I interjected. 'He's fine.'

'Woman trouble?' Martha mused, nodding as if to confirm her own assessment of what might be on Sam's mind.

'Very intuitive. Nothing gets past you.' I laughed, twisting my head towards Sam, who shook his head and mouthed silent abuse in my direction as we started to move forward again.

Reaching a dilapidated white minibus, Martha nodded a greeting to two Gambians in the front seat, who leapt out and rapidly snatched up our bags to begin loading them neatly into the boot.

'We are driving straight to camp,' Martha said. 'It is a little while so you can sleep on the way.'

Sam tried to smile politely back but managed more of a grimace.

'How far?' I asked, folding myself into a well-worn seat.

'At least eight hours to Sambel Kunda – many of the roads up-river are quite bad,' Martha replied.

'Eight hours!' Sam protested. Then, realising that Martha would probably unload him from the vehicle for grumbling, he quickly added, 'That's fantastic! I mean, I'll really be able to catch up on some rest.'

'*Ja*, that's good. You need to get some strength and will have time to clear your mind.'

Slamming the side door shut, Martha climbed into the front with the Gambians.

'I think my mind is beyond help,' Sam mumbled. 'Which is why I'm accompanying my friend on yet another insane adventure.'

Ignoring his comment, Martha turned over her shoulder and handed us each a printed pamphlet. 'You can read about the project here – you'll be staying in the camp at Stella's

Chimpanzee Rehabilitation Project. We don't have anywhere for you to live in the village and, besides, most people who come like it in the jungle.'

'Chimpanzee Rehabilitation Project?' Sam asked. 'You mean you'll be returning him to the wild?'

Martha looked at him. 'That's funny,' she said, without any humour. 'Stella set up the programme in 1969 and it's the oldest chimpanzee rehabilitation project in Africa. They are orphans who have been saved from the illegal pet trade and relocated to live on the sanctuary of three islands in the river.'

She broke off to talk to the driver, seemingly discussing the best way to get out of the airport.

'Where do you find these animal-charity people?' Sam gently moaned. 'Do I have some sort of sign on my head that says, "Victimise me"? Why don't you get any of this sort of attitude when we go places?'

'I also don't get hounded by girlfriends from my school days,' I replied. 'I guess we're just different.'

'You didn't have girlfriends at school,' Sam retorted. He must have spoken a little too loudly, because Martha suddenly turned her attention back to us.

'Your girlfriend is still at school?' she asked, aghast.

Sam rolled his eyes. 'No, it's just a letter.'

'You are too old to go out with school girls, I would have thought? Is this what is troubling you?'

'I . . . I mean, it's an old girlfriend. Long story, honestly, I—'

'He's getting over someone called Susan,' I cut in.

Distracted by the driver, Martha turned back to the front of the van.

Sam's eyes were daggers. 'What is all this, Luke? Chimpanzees? I thought you said we were going to be working with donkeys.'

'Stella is Heather's sister. She helps chimps, Heather helps the donkeys, and together they help the community. The projects are linked. Don't worry about it – we're staying with chimps! How great is that? You're going to feel right at home!'

The countryside flashed by as we drove inland, heading east along the River Gambia. As we left the city, the landscape seemed more savannah than jungle and, reading the background information in the pamphlet, I noted that the country was the smallest in Africa, only 4,300 square miles in size – about half the area of Wales, with a population of only about 1.5 million. Historically, between the seventeenth and nineteenth centuries, one in every six people taken as slaves was from the Senegambia region in West Africa. The British were responsible for the majority of the trafficking although they were quicker to outlaw it than the local Gambian chiefs, who took more than half a century longer to decide it violated basic human rights.

The journey took slightly under the eight hours Martha had estimated and, finally, we arrived at our destination. The village was comprised of about thirty buildings of varying sizes, all with thatched roofs and mud-brick walls.

We spilt out of the vehicle to stretch our legs, and gulped fresh air. Sam let out a groan. 'Those last four hours – what happened to the tarmac?' he gasped.

'It is a work in progress,' Martha replied, with a grin. Like me, she was beginning to enjoy Sam's plaintive tone. 'It has already been like that for the last five years, apparently. Chrissy, one of the previous managers here, told me there are fifteen hundred miles of road in the Gambia and a thousand of them are uncovered. Now you know why everyone likes to live in Banjul.'

'Fantastic way to keep the population local,' Sam commented drily, rubbing his back.

Taking up our packs, we started the dusty walk through the village.

'We walk through the village and then down to the jungle by the river. Your accommodation is there, near the chimps,' Martha explained.

'Can't wait for a refreshing shower and a cold beer,' Sam chirped.

Martha laughed. 'Beer – maybe I can get you tomorrow, but not now. Also,' she added, 'it is a bucket shower and we have no electricity. Welcome to the Gambian bush.'

Sam looked at me – I got the sense that if he could have turned me to stone, he would have done so. In the end, he made do with a string of curses so unutterably disgusting that even I was shocked.

It had been a busy few days and the donkey regarded us wearily.

'Oh, boy,' Sam said quietly. 'I have no idea how we're going to sort this one.'

I didn't reply. My own thoughts echoed his words. This one was going to be a challenge.

It had been hectic at the clinics. The Gambian villagers had been incredibly friendly and, as word had spread that we were there to help the local charity with veterinary supplies and expertise, donkeys and horses had come from far and wide.

An essential means of transportation in a region where a motorised vehicle was far too expensive for a family earning only two hundred pounds a year, horses and donkeys were everywhere we turned. Often being driven by very young children, the donkeys pulled homemade carts loaded with everything from groups of people, balanced precariously on top of each other, to other animals tied to boards, on their way to a local market.

We had travelled to several villages and set up outreach clinics, treating mainly wounds and skin problems. The wounds were typically from the crudely constructed rope harnesses, which invariably bit deeply into the animals' skin. Bathing and spraying these wounds, and trying to explain how to manage infected lesions, were the mainstays of our work. Many of the pack animals suffered a range of infected wounds over their withers and along their backs where their harness had failed to distribute the pressure of the heavy loads evenly.

'They need to rest these animals,' Sam said. 'All well and good us treating them for now, but if they don't let the sores heal over they'll just open up again.'

Martha had allocated each of us two assistants and we had worked back to back, a line of animals stretching away from us in opposite directions, our medicines and supplies piled high on a low wooden table between us.

The assistants, all of whom spoke English, smiled and chatted as we worked. Every animal was wormed and given a cursory health check. Our most important role was to teach the owners how to correctly tie the straps around their animals.

Towards the end of a long morning, we had been asked to see a donkey that was too sick to be brought to us. In a rare respite from the queue of patients, we had seized the opportunity to go and take a look and now, together with the four assistants and Martha, we gathered around the poor animal to work out how we could help it.

'How long has he been like this?' I asked softly.

'About two weeks,' came the reply.

I nodded and bent down to take a closer look at the injury. The unfortunate donkey was only young and had been run over by a cart coming in the opposite direction to the one in which it was heading. Unable to move out of the way in time, probably due to its own heavy burden, it had twisted to get out the way, but slipped at a crucial moment and its left hind leg had been run over. Somehow, it had managed to hobble around for the last two weeks, despite the fact that its hoof had been ripped clean off. Now in front of us, unable to stand, it sported one of the most horrible injuries either of us had ever seen. The ulcerated and infected stump at the end of its leg was swollen, with flies nibbling away at it.

'So what will happen?' I said, bewildered as to why no one had taken the trouble to finish the poor animal off.

The donkey's owner said nothing. He only shrugged.

'It won't get better,' I continued, looking him hard in the eye. 'It can't regrow the hoof.'

'They normally just abandon them,' Martha interjected.

'You mean, literally just take the rope off and let them go?' Sam said, amazed.

'They know they're no good any more. Gambians don't eat horse or donkey meat, so they let them go. We knew this one was here, which is why we brought you, so you can see the problems.'

'Great,' Sam said, a touch testily. 'We can see the problem. The key thing is what we can do about it.'

Sensing Sam's change of tone, Martha looked at him as she answered. 'The key thing is what any of us can do about it,' she said. 'That is why you are here.'

'Will they object to us putting it to sleep?' I asked, trying to put aside the anger I felt at the sheer apathy of those who were supposed to care for the donkey.

'We always have a lot of trouble with this. Is there anything you can do to help it?' Martha replied. Even though she had been hardened by the familiarity of the situation there was a note of desperation in her voice.

I looked back at the donkey. It stood there stoically, helpless, hopeless and resigned to its fate. 'Well, we can't leave it,' I said simply.

'If you're thinking of buying it off them, you will be swamped by hundreds of mutilated and crippled animals,' Martha said.

Sam swore under his breath. 'They don't care about it,' he said. 'Why can't we just take it away?'

'Because as soon as you take it away,' Martha replied, 'that's when they will care about it.'

'Well, it's hopeless, then!' Sam snapped. Promptly, he sat down on the dirt, cross-legged. It was more than the donkey could do. 'Luke won't leave it, they won't let it go. I need shade and a drink. It's going to be a long wait.'

It was the first time Martha's face cracked into a smile. I turned to look at my friend, who simply shrugged and flashed me a grin.

'Martha, who do we need to speak to in order to resolve this situation?' I asked.

'The village chief,' Martha said.

'Right!' Sam exclaimed. 'Let's go and make an appointment!' With surprising sprightliness, he was on his feet and walking off towards the cluster of mud-brick buildings.

'Sam, wait!' Martha yelled.

Dramatically, Sam paused. 'We need action here, or Wonder Boy over there is never going to let us go back to the chimps and our bucket of cold water. We need to do this,' he declared. 'We can't just sit here doing nothing. And if we have to speak to the chief to get it sorted, then speak to the chief we shall!'

Martha looked at him for a moment. '*Ja*,' she said. 'This is good. This is great! But, Sam . . .'

'Yes?'

'Sam, the chief's hut is in the opposite direction.'

5
Donkeys, Dilemmas and Chimpanzees

The morning light burst through the treetops and pierced the seams of our tent. It was still early, about six a.m., but the Gambian sun was already hard at work. It wasn't only the intense heat that was making me feel uncomfortable. Sam, still snoring, turned over and pressed himself against me.

'Wake up!' I said, shaking him fiercely until he opened his eyes with a sudden snort.

'What?' Sam spluttered. 'What d'you do that for?'

'You're contaminating my personal space and we can't be lying around lazing all day. Or have you forgotten?' I climbed out of the tent flap and dragged Sam with me. 'We've got someone to see.'

Sam's efforts to see the chief the previous evening had been in vain, but we had managed to secure an appointment to visit him today. Frustrated, we had dosed the donkey with painkiller, treated the infected stump with purple spray in an effort to keep the flies away, and headed back to base for a bucket shower and a deep sleep.

Our camp was right on the edge of the River Gambia and the thick brown water drifted peacefully past as I stood on the bank and gazed out towards the rising sun. Three islands, located serenely in the middle of the river, were home to the chimps of the rehabilitation project and I scanned the shoreline of the closest island for a glimpse of the remarkable creatures. They were talkative at dawn and I could hear them chattering away, but seeing them in the canopy of the trees was difficult.

'How many live on those islands?' Sam's groggy voice sounded behind me as he emerged, pulling a T-shirt over his head.

'The project is home to seventy-eight,' I replied, recalling the pamphlet Martha had given us.

'I suppose we need to get over there to check them out.'

There was a sudden splash and both Sam and I looked to our left. About a hundred metres away, the second half of a large scaly body was sliding into the water.

'OK,' Sam quickly added. 'Maybe we shouldn't swim – not unless this whole donkey business gets too desperate.'

Footsteps sounded along the trail behind the tent and Martha's figure soon became apparent. 'Morning,' she began, striding purposefully towards us. 'You hear the chimps?'

'Hard not to,' I replied, smiling.

'Would you like to take the boat over there and see them?' she asked. 'Now's the best time of day. They'll be right on the shoreline waiting for their food.'

I exchanged a hopeful look with Sam and we nodded eagerly.

'*Ja*, that will be no problem.' Martha smiled. 'You can go with one of the boys while I prepare things here. The boat's only two hundred yards up the river.'

When we just stood there, she flapped her arms like a mad

buzzard. 'Well, go on!' she exclaimed. 'They won't wait all day! And we've got too much to do when you get back.'

Five minutes later, Sam and I clambered down the bank into a wooden boat. One of the Gambian lads, Joseph, who was employed in the project, threw us a cheery smile and fired up a little outboard motor rigged up on the stern to push us into the river. We had only gone ten yards or so when he suddenly cut the engine and pointed frantically to our right.

'Hippo!' he cried, anxiously swerving away as momentum carried us forward.

'Where?' Sam asked.

'Now under,' Joseph replied, clearly agitated.

Sam looked at me, confused. 'What does he mean "under"?' he asked.

'Basically,' I replied, 'imagine Susan, bulked out on pies, underneath this boat – the biggest man killer in Africa . . .' I saw Sam's face drop. 'Not cool.'

Nobody said another word. Sam and I sat stock still. Our eyes darted at the water. The hippo had come from nowhere, and despite Joseph's efforts to avoid it, there was now a risk that it would come up under the boat, irritated by our intrusion onto its river, and promptly destroy it.

'So we might get a swim, after all . . .' Sam muttered, his voice tailing off as he scanned the surface of the river.

We drifted for a couple of minutes, until we were certain the hippo hadn't taken too much offence. Then Joseph kicked the outboard back into life and we sped away.

Once clear, we looked back. Where we had been hovering, the hippo had surfaced, its nostrils just visible above the water line. 'Is that a common problem?' I asked Joseph.

He nodded and grinned. 'They can crush the boat – big problem. We always check everywhere before we go in the water but that one was a surprise. Very rarely we can get caught out, I would be in trouble.'

'I think we'd all get in a lot of trouble if that hippo is as tenacious as Susan,' Sam said.

As we approached the main island, Joseph killed the engine again and we drifted close to the shore. Picking up some buckets laden with fruit, he began to throw them onto the land.

'Do we get out?' Sam asked, standing up.

'No, no, no!' Joseph replied, eager to make Sam stay still. 'Too dangerous. We throw the food, the chimps will come. If we got out they would attack you and tear you apart.'

'The chimps?' Sam cried.

Joseph paused, one bucket still in his hand. 'You don't think chimps can tear you apart?'

'Well, I—'

'Chimps *can* tear you apart.'

Glumly, Sam retreated to the end of the boat.

'This whole little adventure is just danger, danger, danger,' he said. 'Luke, you realise we can see these animals really well on TV without any of this, don't you?'

'You can't get a TV this big, though, can you?' I replied, watching the effect of breakfast being served.

Almost as the food landed, the chimps began to appear. There were about thirty animals, ranging in size and age from small youngsters to a couple of huge adult males. Together, they bounded about with squawks of delight, hungrily scooping up the food and eyeing us with as much enjoyment and curiosity as we watched them.

'That one there is Africa,' Joseph said, pointing out an adult female who, picking up an orange, sat down and coolly regarded us from her vantage-point on a rock.

'Her mother had been caught and killed, her parts harvested for witchcraft. Africa was rescued as a baby and Stella brought her here. She now has a daughter of her own.' As he went on, Joseph pointed out different chimps, telling us their backgrounds. 'That one heading over to climb that tree is Mischief – he's a terrible chimp. You need to watch out for him, he will not know you.'

'What do you mean, "watch out for him"?' Sam asked. Instead of tucking in like all of the others, Mischief was eyeing us strangely and climbing a tree. 'He's not going to try to jump on the boat, is he?'

Joseph opened his eyes wide. 'If you can see, he is missing a finger on his right hand. He was found caught in a snare for the illegal pet trade by park rangers. The authorities were going to confiscate him but Stella heard about him, intervened and he was brought here. He is very naughty.'

Sam kept his eyes fixed on the cheeky chimp, certain he was about to pounce. I saw him risk a look back at the river, just in case the hippo was coming back at us from behind.

'How do you integrate them?' I asked.

'It is complex,' Joseph said. 'It depends on the age of the chimp. We are now at capacity but there are three groups – juveniles that are five to eight years old, sub adults, aged eight to twelve, and then the adults of twelve and older. The youngsters must be adopted by one of the adult females before they meet an alpha male or he will kill them.' Joseph paused to consider his point. 'They have ninety-eight point seven per cent the same DNA as us. The alpha males – you see Gabriel over there – they're as strong as five men.' He gestured to a huge chimp sitting at the back of the troop, towering above a smaller male who was busy grooming him.

Sam and I looked at Gabriel. Briefly, he glanced back, aloof to our intrusion onto the edge of his island.

Suddenly something splattered into the boat. Joseph swung around and instantly kicked up the engine.

'What the . . .!'

Another projectile landed on the side of the boat, showering us with juice and pulp. Sam scrambled one way, then the other. I grappled with him to try to make him stay still. He was rocking the boat.

A manic sound filled my ears, as yet more projectiles rained down on us. What I had thought were pieces of fruit and peel, chewed up and spat out, was something altogether darker. It was brown and fetid and it was everywhere . . .

Joseph's eyes were wet with tears he was laughing so much.

'Can't we move out the way?' Sam protested, sniffing his shirt and wrinkling his nose. 'What the heck is this?'

Joseph tried to steer us away from the shore but his convulsions of laughter stopped him from making any headway. Somehow, none of the projectiles seemed to have touched him. He drew a big hand across his eyes to wipe away the tears.

Following the trajectory of the missiles, I could see the shape of Mischief high up in a tree, raising his arm, ready to bombard us yet again.

'What is he throwing?' I asked, wondering where he was getting all this muck from so high in a tree.

Time seemed to stop – and suddenly I knew the answer to my own question.

'Joseph!' I said. 'You need to reverse the boat now! This isn't funny.' I realised, suddenly, that this was a joke Joseph shared with the chimps. Raucously shrieking, Mischief hurled yet more of his own faeces in our direction.

'You have got to be kidding me!' Sam yelled, his face going red. 'I mean this is beyond abuse!'

Sam looked at me furiously and, suddenly, seeing him splattered with chimp poo, his face red and his spiky brown hair standing on end as if in outrage on its own accord, I also couldn't help myself. It was probably the highlight of the chimps' day and my own explosive laughter joined their chorus.

As if sensing we had passed an initiation rite, Mischief let out a shriek of delight and scampered down the tree to bound across the shoreline and stand in front of the boat, whooping with glee.

'They like you now,' Joseph managed, catching his breath.

'I'm not sure anyone else will today,' I replied, looking at the brown smears all over my shirt.

With a farewell wave, we headed back to shore.

After a quick wash and a change of clothes, we left Joseph behind and headed for the waiting minibus. Martha was waiting there, wearing a knowing grin. I wondered if she knew exactly what she was sending us to when she'd urged us to visit the chimps.

'First,' she began, with a glint in her eye, 'now you are clean, we are driving to the village for your appointment with the chief. One of the children is very sick there so we may not get much time.'

'What's wrong?' I asked, concerned.

'Malaria,' Martha stated, clearly hardened to the news of a child being fatally ill. 'It is a big problem here. The child will probably die. The parasite seems to be resistant to the normal medication they use to help.'

A thought popped into my head. Because our trip had

been so last-minute, we had only had time to get a new malaria product from the doctors. It was by far the most expensive tablet on the market but you only needed to start the course the day before you arrived in a malaria area. It had been our only option. 'Martha, can you wait two minutes?' I said. 'I need to race back to the tent.'

Sam looked at me quizzically. 'Your makeup?' he asked.

'Our tablets!' I shouted, running off towards our packs. 'Malarone – a new wonder drug – it treats malaria as well as prevents it!'

Racing back to the tent I scrabbled together our Malarone tablets and returned.

'We can give these to the child to take,' I said breathlessly. 'They may help – I don't know, but it's worth a try.'

'What about your own protection?' Martha said steadily.

'We'll be home in just a couple of days. We can pick up more tablets when we get back. I'm sure we'll have enough in our bloodstream to protect us for the next few days – and, anyway, we *cover* ourselves with anti-malarial spray.'

Sam rolled his eyes before, finally, nodding. 'He might speak the noble truth.'

Without further ado, Martha took the pills and told the Gambian driver to get going.

The village huts were of mud brick with thatched straw roofs and, as we ducked into the gloom of the largest, it was immediately clear who the village chief was.

Facing us were five figures, but the middle one was an impressively built man with a hugely swollen leg. He looked at us calmly as we sat respectfully on a rug on the hard dirt floor.

'Elephantiasis,' Sam whispered, as Martha made the introductions and explained the work we had been doing.

I had heard of the disease but never seen it in the flesh. I tried not to stare at the huge leg. Caused by a thread-like parasite transmitted by mosquitoes, it infects the lymphatic system and can be very difficult to treat. A major cause of disability in sub-Saharan Africa, I was nevertheless surprised to see the village chief stricken by it.

'I have some dogs that need treatment,' the chief said, breaking my train of thought with his sudden direct statement.

'May I ask what is wrong with them?' I said, momentarily pushing the thought of his swollen leg from my mind.

Before the chief could reply, Martha interjected, 'That is no problem,' she said flatly, flashing me a look of mild annoyance. 'We can look at them without any trouble.'

'I want them fixed,' the chief said, casting a friendly look in my direction.

'We were wondering about the donkey with the missing hoof. May we have permission to take it?' Martha asked, with her usual directness.

'What do you want it for?' the chief replied, with a chuckle. His associates laughed with him. 'It is useless!'

'We wish to stop its suffering.'

No sooner had Sam spoken than Martha and I looked at him in surprise. 'It's never going to heal,' he continued. 'It's simply dying horribly out there. We can make it feel at peace, end its pain.' He hesitated, unsure whether to go on. 'We'd be delighted to treat your other donkeys as well as look at your dogs,' he concluded.

There was a momentary silence as the chief considered the outspoken visitor in his midst.

'What about the ones with the fly sickness?' he said. 'I have one horse with this.'

Sam nudged me.

'Yes, I know what you mean,' I piped up. 'We have some treatment for that.'

'The treatment is very expensive,' Martha added.

I assumed the chief was referring to the horse equivalent of sleeping sickness, which is fatal to both animals and people, and carried by the dreaded tsetse fly. It infects a host with a protozoan parasite that invades the lymphatic and circulatory system. Trypanosomiasis, as it is known by its proper term, is a horrible disease.

The chief paused to consider our request and looked directly at Martha. 'You are helping with the mouthpieces?' he asked.

Martha nodded.

'I have some with bad mouths I would like you to see. I am grateful to Heather and to you for all your work. The project is much needed and a big help to us.'

The Chief looked left and right at his associates. 'You may have the donkey,' he began. 'I will see there is no problem. But perhaps you will see my animals now?'

The chief began to move, gesturing us on our way, but before we had gathered ourselves, Martha spoke up: 'There is one more thing . . .'

The chief looked up, surprised.

'There is a boy,' Martha began. 'He is the nephew of one of our workers at the chimp project.' She paused. 'He has malaria. Luke and Sam have some new medicine that may help him.'

I cleared my throat to interject. 'The dose is just one a day I think,' I said, producing the tablets. 'I hope they work – it's a new medicine and might just treat it . . .' I tailed off, uncertain if I had done the right thing to even raise hopes.

The chief fixed us with a stern look. Finally, slowly, silently, he smiled his thanks and we took our leave.

'Phew!' Sam exclaimed, once we were outside. 'Well, that wasn't too bad. He drives a hard bargain, but at least we have the donkey. Bit of a result that, Martha.'

'*Ja*,' Martha said flatly. 'It is good.'

'What's up, Martha?' I asked, concerned at her despondency. 'Surely that's the best result we could have hoped for. The village chief is right behind us, despite Heather not being here. Doesn't that prove the project's valued?'

'It is just that . . . perhaps the medicine was not such a good idea.'

Sam and I stopped in our tracks and looked blankly at her.

'*Ja*,' she explained, her expression, normally so neutral, suddenly pained. 'If the boy dies, then it is possible your medicine may be blamed.'

'I hadn't thought of that,' Sam said.

'But you said he was dying anyway,' I began.

'It is not so simple,' Martha went on. 'We shouldn't interfere with the village people. I think we have done badly with this. Heather is not here to advise us.'

I could hardly believe what I was hearing. 'The medicine can't do any harm!' I protested. 'Surely it's better we tried to help than not.'

I was complaining too bitterly, and even I knew it. In my heart, I could see Martha's point, and a gnawing doubt that we had been a bit reckless crept into my mind.

'Nothing we can do,' Sam chipped in, seemingly oblivious to the potential implications Martha was trying to explain. 'Put it from your mind. Let's just hope it helps the kid. Whose nephew is he anyway? If they're in the project, surely they'll know we're only trying to help.'

Martha's face was blank. 'Actually,' she replied, glassy eyes on Sam, 'you have already met the boy's uncle. He took you out to see the chimps this morning.'

I was silent.

'Joseph?' Sam mouthed. 'Well, surely that's a good thing!'

For the longest time, not one of us spoke. Finally Martha broke the deadlock.

'No,' she said. 'You do not see. You *will* not see. This is a very bad thing. It gets worse. If there is any implication our medicine could have harmed the boy, we may even be accused of witchcraft.' Martha was silent. 'Our staff will then leave,' she whispered. 'Every last one of them . . .'

Sam opened his mouth to speak, but thought better of it, and promptly clamped his lips shut.

'Martha,' I said, 'the tablets really might help. It's better we try than not. I mean, imagine how we would feel if the poor kid dies and we hadn't even tried.'

Martha could do nothing but nod. Slowly, we started walking again.

'The best we can do,' she said, 'is continue with our work. The chief will have put the word out immediately, so there will be a queue.' She sighed heavily. 'There will be a long day now.'

Sam stopped, momentarily, dragging his heels to lag a few paces behind. 'You're so full of cheerful news . . .'

As he spoke, we rounded a corner and, taking a deep breath, saw exactly how much mayhem awaited us.

'Just a couple of horses and dogs the chief's lined up for us to treat, then!' Sam concluded.

Despite us having already run a treatment clinic in the village the previous day, the line of animals seemed to stretch back at least a hundred yards. Dogs, horses, donkeys and people milled about everywhere. We had come from a virtually deserted street to what seemed like a beast bazaar.

'Where are my trusty assistants?' Sam shouted, over the noise. 'I am ready to heal!'

'What's come over you?' I laughed. I was still unable to take in the scope of what lay before us. 'Suddenly you're the Donkey Man?'

'Buddy, I've always been the Donkey Man,' Sam replied, with a smirk. 'Why do you think Susan still wants me?'

I looked apologetically at Martha, who rolled her eyes. 'I think some of the chimp poo has affected him,' I said.

'I think the chief liked him,' she said.

'He certainly liked him enough to get all these animals together for us to look at,' I replied. 'Well, in for a penny and all that . . . Let's get on with it.'

Quickly setting up a table and getting out our meds, we once again started to work through the animals.

The usual wounds presented themselves and we treated them rapidly, settling comfortably into a routine. Heather had told me on the phone before we came out that the most important and useful thing we could do was educate the owners on how to treat their livestock. I endlessly demonstrated how padding should be applied under abrasive ropes and showed owners how to tie knots, bathe wounds and keep flies away. I explained that oil and battery acid wouldn't help, that wounds needed to be kept clean and rested. I had no idea how much fell on deaf ears but everyone seemed to nod gratefully as Sam and I diligently washed, sprayed and injected horse after horse and donkey after donkey.

It wasn't long before a large grey horse approached me, so skeletally thin that I was amazed it could walk. Instinctively, I examined its withers for the typical injuries we were seeing.

As I was doing so, the owner, an elderly Gambian farmer, stopped me and gestured to the mouth.

I nodded and moved back to the horse's head. As I gently opened its mouth, both the horse and I flinched, the animal in pain and me in shock. Instead of a smooth pink tongue, an ulcerated infected mass flashed before me. The poor animal's tongue had almost been amputated, and the most horrific deep cut ran horizontally across the thickest part of the muscle.

'How did this happen?' I asked, a hint of anger creeping into my voice.

The Gambian shrugged.

I tried to rein back a tide of frustration. This wound was no accident: it was the result of neglect and cruelty.

'At least he brought him to see you,' Martha said, her voice sounding from behind my shoulder.

Stepping forward, she peered into the mouth. 'This is one of the worst I have seen. No wonder the horse is so thin.' She sighed. 'They have no idea . . .'

'This horse is as good as dead,' I said, trying my best to remain calm. 'It can't eat like this. It probably goes through agony every time it drinks . . .' I risked a look at the farmer. 'And the odds are that he's still working it. How on earth did this happen? I can't see any sign of cancer or growth – this is an inflicted injury.'

'Senegalese bits,' Martha explained, as I looked at her blankly. 'It's what the chief was referring to when he asked me about the mouthpieces.'

I looked into the horse's eyes. They rolled about in their orbits, but I thought that, for the briefest of moments, they fixed on me and froze, as if the animal was begging me to understand.

'They're crude pieces of metal that go round the lower part of the mouth with a sharp piece of metal wedged on top of the tongue,' Martha explained. 'The reins are attached so that the slightest pressure will be very painful and the animal will yield. It allows the children to work the strong animals. It's how they break them – the Gambians are not natural horsemen.'

'And too much yanking does this?' I said in disbelief. 'It simply cuts the tongue off?'

'Yes,' Martha said simply. 'This one was too wilful . . . or the children too cruel.'

'What can we do?' I asked, a momentary feeling of despair washing over me.

'Heather was donated five thousand snaffle bits by a charity called SPANA. They're kind on the mouth and don't damage the animals. The people know these other bits are bad but they have no alternative. This man also knows his horse can't be fixed. The only reason he's brought it here is to get one of the new bits. They have these Senegalese mouthpieces because they are cheap and readily available – and they know no different. They even make them out of rope for the donkeys to do the same thing.'

I moved forward and patted the horse, making the farmer wait while I injected it with painkiller. Meanwhile, Martha went to get him a snaffle bit – a smooth bar of vulcanised rubber that would be infinitely softer on the poor animal's mouth. The painkiller would last a day but it was all the good I could do. He grinned appreciatively and led the horse away.

I stood there, helpless and angry.

As I pondered the predicament, and my heart went out to the poor horse, Sam walked over with a swagger. 'Right,' he said, brushing his hands off on his shorts, 'I'm going to start on the dogs while you stand there daydreaming. Time for a bit of home territory now – I'll leave the unenviable task of dealing with our poor donkey amputee to you two and get going with some neutering.'

I nodded, my eyes still watching the grey horse disappear in a trail of dust. At least I could put the donkey out of its pain, I thought and, leaving Sam, I quickly got together the drugs I would need for the next horrible job.

Together, Martha and I went back to see the donkey from the previous day. It was tied to the very same tree where we had seen it yesterday. I wondered if it had been given water, and felt immediately bad as I tripped over a bucket that had been placed under its nose. There were bad things here but good as well.

'*Ja*,' Martha began. 'We must now put it down. But we can't do it here. We must do it away from the village. The chief has given us the donkey, which means we must lead it away out of sight or we will cause trouble.'

'It can hardly walk,' I protested.

'It has to,' Martha said, stepping forward and untying the rope from the tree.

It took an age to lead the donkey about half a mile down the dirt track to the edge of the jungle, which dropped away towards the river. We walked at a very slow pace so as not rush the poor animal, and kept going until we were completely out of sight of the village.

'Now you can do it,' Martha said.

I nodded miserably. The donkey, resigned to its life of suffering, stood there looking at me. I bent down to draw up the lethal injections.

Martha's hand suddenly clamped over my own. 'What are you doing?' she demanded.

'Drawing up the juice to put it to sleep,' I replied curtly.

'You cannot inject it,' she said, her hand still fast around mine. 'Hyenas come this close to the village. Vultures will scavenge the carcass. There is the risk of animals taking chunks of meat from a freshly dead donkey. Even the village dogs will come here.' She paused. 'No – you cannot risk it.'

'Martha!' I gasped, exasperated. 'How do you propose I kill it if I can't inject it? Can't we just bury it?'

Martha kicked her heel against the ground. She was right – the ground was like concrete, and we had no spade.

'Don't you have a bolt or something?' she asked.

'A bolt gun? No!' I cried. 'I don't have any sort of gun! I've come from England – how could I have brought a gun with me?' I was aware my voice was rising, and struggled to rein myself in. 'Can we burn its body?' I asked, flailing for another solution.

'It will attract too much attention. Firewood is also a precious resource – we would use too much wood.' Her brow furrowed in concentration. 'And the risk of the fire spreading here is also too great. If we do this, we must do it quietly and without fuss – or the chief will never give us permission again.'

'I think a dead donkey by the side of the road will attract attention no matter what we do,' I replied.

We stood in silence. I didn't want to get frustrated or angry with Martha – none of this was her fault – but I could feel myself teetering.

'We'll roll it towards the jungle, down this slope into the vegetation,' Martha finally said. 'A dead donkey in the ditch will not attract attention – it will quickly disappear. Are you thinking of slicing its throat? I am not sure I can be comfortable with that.'

I looked up.

'Martha,' I said, 'don't worry, I am not considering trying to cut its throat. That doesn't bear thinking about!' I paused. 'We'll need to get a gun from someone and do this thing humanely.' The poor donkey had already gone through enough, I thought. 'The least we can do is make this as pain-free as possible. I mean, we *have* already dragged it a kilometre on three legs.' I looked almost angrily at Martha, the super-efficient organiser who, for once, was stumped as to what to do.

'Tobaski was just before you arrived . . .'

'Tobaski?' I asked.

'*Ja*, it is a public holiday. The families all slaughter a sheep or a goat as a sacrifice. Everyone dresses nicely.'

I looked at Martha blankly, wondering what she was talking about and how it would help us euthanase the donkey.

'It is in commemoration of Abraham's willingness to sacrifice his own son Ismail, in the name of Allah – it coincides with the end of the annual pilgrimage to Mecca. They kill many sheep and goats by cutting the neck . . . I just do not think I could let you do it to a donkey.'

'No, Martha,' I insisted. 'It would be horrific. That method of slaughter is not good.'

Martha stood transfixed, her eyes on the donkey, her brow furrowed in concentration. The struggle of knowing what was best to do was impossible for both of us. I realised she was just saying things that came into her mind because we were running out of options. The idea to slash its throat was one of absolute desperation – and not something either of us could contemplate actually seeing through.

'I do know that, but there are no guns here,' she said quietly. 'They are illegal.'

We stood in silence, both of us wondering how we could humanely put to sleep the poor donkey without drugs, bullets or any easy means at our disposal. Suddenly a plan began to formulate in my mind. 'Martha, I've never done this,' I said, 'but I have heard of it once. A friend of mine once told me a story of how he was driving at night in South Africa and hit a cow. He had to kill it because it was in terrible pain and he only had a penknife. He cut its aorta.' I paused. 'Well, we're in a similar boat – I mean, we're in a better situation because if I sedate this donkey heavily, it shouldn't even feel the cut . . .'

Martha looked at me oddly. 'In the neck?' she asked.

'No,' I said, 'not the jugular. I told you – I promise we're not cutting its throat. I'll cut the aorta – the main artery. I'll cut it inside.' I was not sure she understood.

'How will you cut it inside?' she asked anxiously. 'You don't mean . . . stab it in its heart?'

'Nothing like that. I'll rectal it and sweep a scalpel blade upwards, through the intestinal wall. I'll sever the main blood vessel. It's the artery that feeds the whole body. The donkey should bleed out in minutes . . .'

'There will be blood gushing?'

I could see that she still didn't understand.

'It won't bleed outside at all,' I replied carefully, still weighing up if there were any other alternatives. 'The blood will fill its abdomen inside . . .'

'Will it be painful?'

'The key thing is we'll make sure it isn't.'

I rummaged through the drugs I had brought and drew up a very strong sedation. I imagined the donkey to be the wildest colt I had met and planned to make sure the poor animal didn't suffer during its final moments.

Knowing any further delay would get us nowhere, I stepped forward. Before Martha had time to debate any further or start talking about cutting its throat again, I injected the donkey into the vein. There was no going back now, I thought, steeling myself for what had to be done.

'We'll give it a few minutes to take full effect,' I said, as much to myself as to Martha, who stood silently, holding the halter with one hand and resting her other hand on the soft brown nose. 'Then I'll make the cut.'

The time passed quickly and, as the donkey's head swayed with the effects of the drugs I had administered, I clasped the scalpel blade between my index and middle finger, and gently eased my hand into position.

Not quite knowing the technique, and only having heard about it as rumour at vet school, I gently felt upwards through the rectal wall until I could detect the strong vibration of the huge artery. Planting my feet a little wider, I took a deep breath and then cut up quickly, through the wall of the intestine. I sliced in an arc through the thick, pulsing vessel, about the size of my finger, in a bold, definite slash.

Instantly, I could feel the blood gushing out. The donkey didn't flinch. Instead, he swayed, not knowing what was going on. As I removed my arm, he regained his balance and stood there, so heavily sedated he seemed oblivious to the fatal injury I had just inflicted. It was strange: I had euthanased so many animals in so many ways, but this felt so much more brutal, more personal somehow. Guilt and sadness washed over me.

From cut to final breath, it was four minutes before the donkey collapsed and then died. It was probably the longest four minutes of my life.

Scooping up my stethoscope, I bent down to listen to the heart one final time. Then, heaving the donkey over, I rolled it down the bank as Martha had directed, the scrub and vegetation camouflaging the carcass. By tomorrow, I doubted it would be there – the hyenas would make short work of it.

Martha stood by the road watching me as I walked back towards my equipment. As I picked up my things, neither of us spoke a word.

'I've neutered six dogs in the time you've taken to put down a donkey,' Sam declared, as we returned to the buildings. 'I mean, what were you doing? Talking it to death?'

'Bit more complicated than that,' I said. 'I'll tell you about it later. How many dogs left to do?' I was keen to change the subject, the rawness of the euthanasia still at the forefront of my mind.

'Four,' Sam replied, as he waved his anaesthetised patient away from the table. 'We can get them done in the next hour if you stop mucking about. Joseph has joined us from camp . . . He's itching to be your trusty assistant.'

Joseph appeared from behind the table and flashed me a big smile.

'I have the set-up of power here,' Sam said. 'It's as slick as you can get – prep, op, recovery areas all organised. I have the assistants all in the zone and the force is strong in me, Luke.'

Sam paused, glancing from me to Martha and back again. 'What on earth has got into you two?' he asked. 'Don't get all sensitive on me. You were doing that donkey a favour. And, besides . . .' he leant in conspiratorially, and I was distinctly aware that he still wore the faintest whiff of chimp faeces '. . . we have the perfect opportunity to throw something truly horrible at Joseph while he helps monitor an anaesthetic.'

Joseph looked up from the dog he was stroking.

'How is your nephew, Joseph?' Martha suddenly asked.

Joseph nodded. 'God will decide,' he said calmly and, picking up the dog, he brought it over to me. Across the poor dumb animal, he looked me in the eyes. 'Thank you for the tablets,' he added softly.

Then it was on with the day's hard work.

'This has been a mission of power, as you would say,' Sam said, tipping a bucket of cold river water over his head.

'Our last morning scrub,' I replied, distracted by a bird flapping in the trees above us. 'Can't you hurry up? Martha's waiting for us in the minibus and you aren't even dressed.'

'You know, I quite like donkeys,' Sam said, quickly towelling himself down and grabbing a T-shirt.

'That's not unexpected. I always had you down as an animal lover,' I replied, with a half-smile.

'It kind of puts things into perspective, doesn't it?' Sam continued. 'These sort of trips . . .'

'Well, that's a bit of a role reversal.' I laughed. 'Don't get all deep and meaningful on me. We've got an eight-hour road journey before the flight. If you're going to witter on, I might just take my chances with the crocs and swim back to Banjul.'

'I mean, the chief has elephantiasis, the animals are in a right pickle and the boy is dying of malaria. Sure does put the whole Susan issue into perspective.'

I'd wondered how long it would be before we were back to Susan. 'What are you going to do about her?' I asked.

'I'm going to invite her to your wedding,' Sam said, straight-faced.

I looked at him in shock, having forgotten whatever was moving around in the tree, as I digested the information. 'You're *what*?'

Sam laughed. 'That got your attention!'

I looked at my friend and shook my head. 'She'd be so disappointed if you weren't in school uniform.'

'Guess what?' Sam said.

I looked at him blankly.

'I'm in the clear!' He beamed. 'I had a text from Jane, in one of the rare moments I managed to get some mobile reception out here. Susan has sent another card to the house.'

'Another declaration of undying love?' I asked, all ears at this groundbreaking news.

'I told Jane to open it and read it to me,' Sam went on. 'Turns out Susan is now getting married, herself. She just wanted to inform me that she's realised we really aren't meant to be after all.'

'Wow, that was quick!' I chuckled. 'She found a husband fairly sharpish. Mind you, with her taste in men, maybe it wasn't too hard.'

'Well,' said Sam, suddenly coming across as wizened and wise, 'there might be a downside to all of this. Between you and me, I reckon Jane's going to be keener than ever now.'

'Come again?'

'Well, now she knows her man is in constant demand, women chasing me from my past, it can only fire her up!' Sam pronounced.

'Or make her realise you dated some very "special" people when you were younger?' I replied.

Sam sighed.

'Come on, Don Juan. Martha will be getting impatient – we'll be behind schedule.'

'Perish the thought,' Sam said.

We grabbed our bags, gave our tent a final check and headed up to the minibus to find Martha surrounded by local Gambians.

'Oh, boy. This doesn't look great,' Sam murmured.

Looking at the group, I saw that Joseph was deep in conversation with one of the men I had seen with the chief the other day. 'I think this is about the boy,' I said quietly, as we got nearer. 'They're in such deep discussion . . .'

'Martha doesn't look happy,' Sam said.

As I wondered how the next few moments would turn out, Joseph saw us, his face splitting into a broad grin. The rest of the group, realising we were approaching, all fanned out, smiling as well. Joseph clasped each of our arms in turn.

'I gather your nephew's a bit better, then?' I asked happily.

'Yes, he is much better today,' Joseph replied. 'Your magic medicine has helped him. We are all so grateful, thank you.'

I looked at the other people and saw suddenly that they were Joseph's family. I realised that he must live with his extended family and their children as well; they had all come to say goodbye.

'The chief has given a blessing to you and Sam this morning in the village,' Martha said.

'Well, well, well!' Sam beamed. 'I am feeling truly blessed today, good news all round.'

'His woman troubles are sorted,' I said to Martha, by way of explanation.

'I think he finds women awkward,' Martha replied, stony-faced.

As the villagers waved us goodbye, I sat back in the minibus and contemplated the trip: the plight of the animals we had seen; the hard environment and the lack of education that contributed to it; the donkey with the hoof missing; the horses with their partially amputated tongues and all those wounds covered with battery acid. It was just like Sam had said: it put everything else in my life into perspective. As I dozed off, my mind flashed to the image of the baby pigeon outside the post office. All in all, I decided, it really was a big wild world.

6

Piggy in the Middle

'You can't do that, can you?' Fred said earnestly.

'There are maggots in the joint,' I replied, studying the farmer. 'It won't get better with antibiotics, it's too far gone. We've got no choice . . .'

Fred looked at me as he considered my point. About five feet ten inches, in his late fifties, he had milked on the farm for the best part of forty years. With his flat cap slightly tilted at an angle, he looked every inch the country farmer. 'Are you sure you can take the claw off?' he asked. 'What happens if something goes wrong with the other one?'

'Well, most people calve them down,' I answered, 'get the lactation off them and send them on their way. If something nasty does happen to the remaining claw, then, I'm afraid they're done for. On the other hand, I've amputated a claw before, and the cow has carried on in a farm for years – it's up to the farmer and how lucky they feel.'

Fred didn't move. He looked, instead, at the cow's foot, which was roped up and suspended in the air. Locked in the crush, she let out a low moo in mild protest at her predicament.

'Right,' he said uncertainly. 'Best get on with it then, if you think it's the only thing to do.'

I nodded and started to rummage around in my footbox, pulling out a flutter valve, normally used for giving a bottle of calcium into a vein. It was a long, flexible rubber tube, usually connected with a needle at one end and a bottle at the other.

'What have you got that for?' Fred asked, a smile flickering across his face. 'She doesn't need calcium, does she?'

'No,' I replied, moving towards the cow as she shifted her position in the metal confines of the crush. 'The plan is to use the flutter valve as a tourniquet – it's elastic and I'm going to strap it around the leg, just below the hock, then inject local into the vein below that.'

The cow was an Ayrshire, and her misfortune had been to accidentally stand on a sharp piece of flint that had worked its way up between the two claws of her right hind foot. The blood and muck that had wedged in there as a result had been a magnet for flies and, in the space of probably only two days, they had invaded a wound on the inside of the outside claw to the extent that I could insert my index finger beyond the knuckle, deep into the cow's flesh.

Fred watched me with keen interest as I felt gently below the improvised tourniquet for the vessels I needed to inject. 'So you're going to cut the whole outside claw off then?' he asked, breaking the moment of silence.

'It's a tough call – but she's a young cow. When this heals nicely she'll be back in the yard.'

Fred lifted his cap to scratch his head through a tangled mop of brown hair.

'Most problems occur in the outside claw of a hind foot because that's where they put seventy per cent of their weight, so it's no surprise it's that one that's injured – but her inside claw, the medial one, looks great. I promise you, she'll be able to walk just fine after this. Haven't you had a claw amputated in the past?'

Uncomfortably, Fred replaced his cap. 'Can't say we have,' he said. 'I mean, it's not the sort of thing you think of, cutting off a claw. Seems a bit drastic, but she isn't getting better. I thought you'd tell me to shoot her.'

I nodded, concentrating on injecting the local. 'This is the best way. I'm injecting regional anaesthesia – the idea with the tourniquet is that the local numbs the whole foot and stays around in the leg while we do the business.'

'Not sure I can watch this,' Fred replied, wincing as he watched me pull out some wire and a scalpel blade from my box.

'It won't bleed much,' I reassured him, checking the ropes and making sure the cow was steady. 'The idea is I slice up between the claws, then saw through one of the little bones at the top of the hoof – that way, it'll heal over, no problem. Basically, you have to imagine this claw like one of our fingers – there are three bones in each of our fingers, just like there are three bones in each of the cow's claws. The joints bend different ways from ours, but the principle is that I need to amputate the finger – or claw – just below the knuckle.'

'And you don't stitch it over, just leave it open?' Fred exclaimed, surprised.

'No messing about. We'll bandage it, change it after three days, then keep the next bandage on until it falls off. It'll heal over, I promise. There's no way I could stitch it even if I wanted to – there's just not enough skin. Anyway, it'll heal naturally, by granulation.'

'The wound will be huge!' Fred protested.

In fairness to Fred, it *was* a gory operation. Amputation of a toe doesn't sound so bad for people but for a cow, when she only has two and puts all her weight on them, it really is a big deal. It was also a last resort – but, as horrendous as it was, Fred and the cow's choices were limited. Infection and maggots in the joint meant that it was either amputation or death.

Threading my wire into the deep cut I had made, I positioned myself to the side of the cow and, taking a sharp breath, began to saw rhythmically. Cutting through the flesh was no problem, but I needed to go through the bone, just above where the top of the claw joined the foot. If I accidentally went through the joint, the skin wouldn't heal over it because any cartilage left on the joint surface would stop granulation.

I moved my arms fast and the wire bit quickly. Part of the plan of sawing it off as swiftly as possible was also to generate heat and hopefully cauterise some of the vessels. I heard the satisfying grinding as the wire found its mark, chancing a quick glance to Fred to reassure him. I grinned to see that the farmer was watching me through a gap in his fingers.

The claw dropped onto the concrete floor with a dull thud. 'There you go!' I declared breathlessly. 'It's off.'

'Is that it, then?' Fred asked, coming closer to peer at the severed stump.

'It's not delicate surgery,' I replied with a grin.

'It's like how they chopped off soldiers' legs in the Napoleonic wars.'

'It sure is.' I laughed. 'Except they gave them whisky.'

'She can get an extra ration of biscuit tonight,' Fred declared, patting his cow, unable to take his eyes off the wound. 'You can see all the tendons and everything there. It isn't bleeding at all,' he added, amazed.

'I'll wash the exposed tissue, spray and bandage it – but we're almost done. When I take the tourniquet off, it may bleed a bit, but the thing to do is just wrap another bandage over the top of it.'

Fred picked up the claw from the yard floor and studied it intently.

'You reckon she'll be all right now?' he said sceptically, flicking off some of the seething mass of maggots that were now wriggling out of the severed digit.

'I do,' I said confidently, washing the stump with antiseptic solution and getting my bandage material ready. 'We mustn't take this bandage off, though, not for a few days – no matter what. It needs to clot up and we'll only disturb it. I promise you, this will heal fine.'

This farm call was a big deal in more ways than one. I had met Fred only once before, when I had been in my previous job, with Mr Spotswode and Giles. After the sale and split-up of the large and small animal work, he and his brother, not having any bond with me, had elected to go with the big farm practice on the outskirts of town – but out of courtesy to Giles, who had been their farm vet for the best part of twenty years, they had promised to try me out once I was up and running. This was my try-out and, if I won the contract, it would mean fortnightly routines and all their drug orders – which would increase my turnover by a quarter.

I wondered if I had been too bold. The wound looked as gory as that of the donkey I had seen in the Gambia the other week and, while I was putting on an ultra-confident show, a sudden fear went through me. I hoped this wouldn't end the same way.

'Brother!' a loud male voice shouted behind me.

Startled, I jumped up, dropping the end of the bandage I was winding around the cow's foot.

'Brother!' the voice shouted again, a sense of urgency in his tone. 'Quick, we've got a sinker!'

Fred looked around, frantically. 'Coming!' he yelled. 'Luke, when you've finished, let her down – we'll be by the bottom field. Got to dash.' With that, he raced past me in the direction of the voice.

'Well, girl,' I said, stepping back to look at the luminous green bandage I had thickly wrapped around the cow's foot, 'this bandage is looking sharp – we'll be able to see you in the dark with that on there . . .'

Somewhere behind me, I heard a tractor revving up and driving off.

'There's trouble on the farm,' I said, patting the cow's hind leg.

Removing the tourniquet and lowering the foot, I waited with bated breath to see if the green bandage would suddenly start to turn red as the pressure was released. To my great relief, it was looking good. Soon the painkiller would kick in and the cow would begin to feel a lot better.

'Better to have only half a foot than be turned into burgers and steak,' I said.

The cow lowed mournfully. Then, seemingly taking my point, promptly raised its tail and passed a large cow pat, missing the bandage by millimetres.

'Job well done,' I said, and turned to leave.

I scooped up my equipment and headed back to the truck to catch up with Fred and see what drama was unfolding. Guessing the bottom field lay at the end of the main farm track, I bumped along for a good mile before passing through a large open wooden gate into a gently sloping grass field. In the far distance, I could just about make out a beaten-up red tractor and two figures dancing about in front of it.

Driving up to the tractor, I killed the engine and climbed out.

'This way, Brother!' said the voice I had heard in the yard. 'Throw it further!'

'I'm trying to!' came the reply. 'What do you think I'm doing?'

'Whatever it is, you're not doing it well enough. She'll go if you're not quick!'

Fred grunted. As I watched, he flung out a rope into what appeared to be a ditch at the edge of the field. 'Fred, what's going on?' I asked, walking up to him. It was only as I got within five feet of the ditch that I saw the almost vertical ten-foot drop into a river. Totally unfenced, the bank plunged towards the water's edge. Although the water wasn't fast-flowing, the river was about twelve feet wide and clearly very deep.

At the bottom, directly below where Fred was prancing about, a large black and white cow was paddling frantically, just about keeping her head above the water line.

'Fancy a swim?' shouted the voice of Fred's brother.

'Luke, this is Louie. Louie, Luke,' Fred said, his face screwed up with concentration as he swung the rope again.

I looked at Louie, and did a double take. Whereas Fred was typical of a local farmer, with his flat cap and country ways, Louie looked totally out of place. His hair was swept back in a thick black ponytail, a screw protruded through his left ear and his torn T-shirt depicted a half-naked lady strumming a guitar.

Shorter than Fred, Louie had a stocky, powerful build and he grinned at me manically in return.

The rope missed and Fred cursed under his breath as he pulled it back in.

'Throw it higher, Brother!' Louie shouted, prancing around beside him.

'You do it, if you think you can do better!' Fred replied, flinging the rope again.

I looked down at the cow, which was clearly reaching the point of exhaustion. 'How about the fire brigade?' I ventured.

'No phone reception,' Louie replied, with a grudging laugh. 'They'll take ages and make a right song or dance about it. We do this every year.'

'We tried them once,' Fred said, by way of explanation. 'We lost the cow, took all afternoon.'

'They have a specialist animal-rescue team now,' I commented.

'Do they rescue baby pigeons as well?' Louie shouted, and gave me a wink.

I groaned inwardly.

Fred missed the cow again.

'It's not going to make it, Brother.'

'Hang on,' I heard myself say, as I peered down the bank. 'If I scramble down there a bit, I'll be a lot closer.'

A thick root protruded halfway down and the cow was drifting directly below it.

'You'll be a lot wetter,' Louie replied, laughing.

'Maybe I can get some purchase on that root,' I said, lying on my front and pushing myself half down the bank. 'I might be able to drop the loop over the cow if she comes within reach.'

'Then pass the rope to Fred and we can pull her in,' Louie said.

Fred looked at me and wordlessly handed me the rope.

I had never thrown a lasso in my life but, with a longer reach than the farmers, and hanging over the drop, I flung it towards the cow's bobbing head.

The rope hit her and slid off.

'You throw like a girl,' Louie blurted.

'Helpful, Louie, thanks for that,' I replied, pulling the rope back in.

'Any time!' he roared.

'We could use a long stick – lower it over her head,' I said, racking my brains as to any better means of getting it on to the cow. I didn't even want to think about how we might drag her back up the bank.

'Not a bad plan, Tarzan,' Louie said. 'I'll get one and you keep trying.' Promptly, he disappeared.

'Tarzan?' I repeated.

Fred shrugged with a big smile, made a mad sign with his hand by the side of his head and indicated I should have another go.

'If we don't get her before long she'll go under the bridge and that'll be that,' he said.

I looked further down the river and could just about make out a large concrete bridge in the distance. 'We've got a while,' I said. 'The current doesn't seem too bad.'

'Only because she's fighting it,' Fred observed. 'The middle of the river is stronger than it looks. If she gives up, she'll be down there before you know it and we can't get to the river beyond the bridge.'

Focusing hard, I swung the rope again. Miraculously, it dropped over the cow's head. 'Quick!' I shrieked. 'I've got her!'

Fred reached down and grabbed the end of the rope, bellowing for Louie to return from his foray in the woods.

I turned to scramble back up the bank and lost my

footing as the root snapped, leaving me sprawled on the mud. Unable to clamber up, I clung there, my only other option to drop into the river. 'Could do with a hand,' I said, through gritted teeth.

In reply, there was only silence, the gushing of the river suddenly louder in my ears. Above me, I could just about make out Fred tying the rope around his tractor.

'Fred!' I shouted.

'Hang on,' Louie's voice replied. 'We're just going to lift the cow.'

Idly, I wondered what would happen if I fell into the river and drifted beyond the bridge. At least, I thought, it would be the end of these crazy animal rescues.

The cow was now hanging by its neck as it floundered in the water. I twisted my head to watch the proceedings, my fingers digging into the soft turf above me, the tips of my toes pushed as far into the edge of the bank as possible.

Using the tractor and the head rope to anchor the cow, I saw Louie climb into the cab and lower the forks attached to its front, level with the top of the bank.

'Careful!' Fred exclaimed. 'Don't want to strangle her!'

'It's your turn,' Louie said.

'No it's not, it's your turn,' Fred replied.

'I did it last time!'

'You're younger than me, you do it!'

'I always do it. What if I fall in?'

The cow splashed around suddenly, flailing forwards with its front legs to bounce against the bank. The movement seemed to tighten the rope under her head, increasing the pressure. She let out a sudden, strangled moo. I wasn't doing so good myself.

'It's your turn,' Louie went on. Then, hooking one end of

a very long thick strap to one of the two forks on the front of tractor, he hoisted himself up and leant out over the river, a long hooked pole in his hand.

'That would have been fine for the head rope,' I managed.

'What?' Louie shouted. Hanging over the river, he dropped the free end of the strap into the water upstream of the cow and fished with the long hook under her chest from the other side.

I watched, amazed, as he leant right down over the water's edge, his legs gripping the tractor fork.

'Bit more to the left!' Fred shouted.

'You mean right,' Louie said, his voice choking.

'No,' Fred replied. 'Left!'

'Your left or my left?'

'Just *left*!' Fred cried. 'Go on, grab it!'

'Your left facing the same way as me or facing the other way to me?' Louie uttered, his face purpling from hanging upside down.

'If it was my left facing the other way to you then it would be the same as your left,' Fred thundered.

Louie considered it. 'No, it wouldn't!'

'Yes, it would!'

'No, it wouldn't!'

This pantomime was going on too long. I pictured the cow being dragged along, disappearing under the bridge – with yours truly coming quickly after.

'Wait!' Louie cried. 'I've got it! I see what you mean.' He paused. 'It *would*, wouldn't it?'

'Yes, it *would*!' I summoned all my strength and screamed, 'Hurry up! Go left and you'll get it!'

Somehow Louie managed to hook the free end of the strap underneath the cow. Hoisting it up, he attached it to the other fork of the tractor. Then he dragged himself back along the fork from which he hung, swung down onto the top of the bank and leapt up into the cab. Beside him, Fred tugged on the ropes, clearly adjusting the strap so that it tucked snugly and supportively behind the cow's front legs, flush against her chest.

'Raise her up!' Fred shouted.

The tractor arms steadily heaved upwards and, as the pressure of the head rope eased off from around the cow's throat, she let out a low bellow, her legs paddling wildly in the air. Slowly, by degrees, she ascended the bank.

'OK!' Fred shouted. 'Go back!'

As the cow came level with the top of the bank, Louie reversed the tractor, pulling her half over the lip of the drop. As she struggled forwards, Fred rushed forward to loosen the strap and head rope.

'Quick, Brother! Get that strap off her! If she gets up and away she'll be all caught up in the tractor.'

'I'm going as quickly as I can,' Fred replied, dodging the cow's lethal kicks as she heaved herself into a standing position.

'OK, she's all set!' Louie whooped.

The cow trotted forwards, seemingly none the worse for wear after her watery ordeal.

'Fred!' I shouted.

There was a moment of silence.

'Who was that?' Louie began.

'I don't know,' Fred replied, with humour in his voice. 'Can you hear someone?'

On the bank below them I began to fume. The cow's ordeal might have been over, but I was still in the thick of mine.

'I swear I heard something,' Louie said, 'but I'm not sure what . . .'

Fred laughed.

'Hang on – is it a baby vet in distress? Has it fallen from its nest?'

If I'd been close enough, I might have thumped them. 'Side-splittingly funny,' I replied.

The two faces appeared above me. Plaintively, I looked up. 'Guys? Please?'

They shared an ominous look.

'Stacey is our niece,' Fred said, by way of explanation.

'Helping out a pigeon one month and a drowning cow the next,' Louie declared, peering down at me. 'What a hero!' The screw in his ear gleamed brightly.

'Guys, it was only a pigeon . . .'

'Pigeons have feelings too, is that it?'

I was seriously losing my purchase, and was beginning to suspect the joke had finished a long time ago. Above me, the two farmers threw sidelong looks at each other. Each one of them broke into a smile.

'He chopped the claw off 192 this morning,' Fred said.

'Which one?' Louie replied.

'The back one,' Fred explained.

'Left or right?'

'Left,' Fred replied, thinking.

'The outside claw?'

'Yes.'

'Your left or my left?'

I exploded. 'The lame one!' I cried. 'The injured one! Which one do you think? Did they put another screw through your head when they put one through your ear?'

Above me, Fred's explosive laughter ricocheted through the undergrowth.

'I take as many screws as I can get!' Louie joined in as Fred doubled over, wiping a tear from his eye.

That was it. I felt the earth shift underneath me. I heard their laughter billow out and take over the bank. It seemed, then, that even the cow was joining in, a low, sonorous mooing joining in the chorus.

The picture of those two brothers guffawing was the very last thing I saw as I plunged away from the bank, grappled in vain for something to hold on to, and crashed into the icy water.

After that, the laughter only got louder.

Time was racing as I drove to my call. Sodden from the waist down, I had managed to find a spare shirt but my bottom half would have to remain soaked until I'd finished for the afternoon. I looked at the clock. I was late but it had been a good day. Thanks to my dashing heroics with the cow I potentially had two new clients – and, if I secured the farm, the financial pressures of opening Pilgrims would be significantly eased. The timing couldn't have been better: Cordelia and I were due to be married in a week and were in the closing stages of completing on the house we planned to move into once we got back from honeymoon.

I looked out of the window; thick grey clouds loomed on the horizon. There would be none of this in South Africa, I thought, picturing our forthcoming safari and ten days of blissful relaxation and enjoyment.

The emergency service had been really busy as well but Bob had finally committed to coming in with me and the sense of relief was huge. Having given up his day job, he was focusing on the lucrative night work. He and Sheila were more than capable of getting it sorted while I concentrated on building Pilgrims. I was still working a couple of nights a week, but the difference it made to my life, not having to be on permanent standby and down there every other night, was amazing.

In the first year of running the emergency service I had worked two and a half nights out of three for an entire year, even with the trips abroad for the charity. I was good at small-animal emergency surgery but absolutely frazzled by spending more time in the hospital than at home. My house felt like a holiday home in its own right. It had all been worth it, though, with the nest egg I had built up. I had a business and was in a good place to get married.

Leuwen yawned from the back of the truck as I indicated left and pulled into the driveway for my next call. I was deep in the forest and the call was from an elderly lady who I didn't know; her dog had been treated at the emergency service a few nights ago, and she had asked Sheila about her sick pig. Sheila had mentioned Pilgrims to her and suggested that I could help.

Checking the windows were open enough to give Leuwen some air while I was away, I parked in the shade and, grabbing my treatment box, got out to admire the timber-framed house in front of me. Winding clematis traced up the walls and a large wooden veranda jutted out at the side. It seemed a little crooked and the place oozed a sense of disorganised rustic charm.

'Hello?' I called, my feet crunching on the gravel drive.

A sudden squawking made me jump and I sidestepped a couple of chickens that bolted out of a shed to my left.

'Hello?' I called again.

'Come in!' shouted a voice.

I walked up to the door and gave it a gentle push. Inside, the walls were lined with rosettes of every colour, a lifetime of competing and showing displayed proudly. As I turned into the kitchen, a heavy scent of saddle soap and oiled leather hung in the air. 'Hello?' I called, hesitating by the kitchen door.

'Come on through,' shouted the voice again. 'Get in here!'

Slightly unsure where I was supposed to go, I walked through the kitchen, a pile of china plates and glasses stacked on worktops, and pushed open a thin wooden door into a study. A broad table heaved under a mountain of magazines and a handsome tabby cat gave a cool miaow as it appraised me from a shelf to my right.

'Go on,' sounded the voice again. 'You can do it, power through.'

I walked forward, a strange popping noise emanating from the room beyond. I gave a steady knock on the side of a glass door before walking into the lounge to the sound of heavy applause.

Ms Conelson reclined in a large armchair, swinging her arm at the television. She looked to be in her mid-sixties, of medium build, with grey hair pulled back in a tight ponytail. She wore a pair of glasses that she seemed to constantly push back as they slid down her nose. Without even looking at me, she gestured to an empty seat.

'Last set, five–four. If he breaks him here then he's won!' she exclaimed, delighted.

I looked at the tennis on the TV and took a seat. I'd forgotten just how soaked I was, and promptly jumped back up again.

'Oh, that *was* a good shot, wasn't it?' Ms Conelson cheered, clearly thinking I was jumping for joy. 'I used to leap around like that,' she said, her eyes still transfixed by the ensuing volley. 'But gone are the days. Now I just cheer wildly sitting down!'

She was so excited by the tennis that she had barely looked at me.

'Game, set and match!' she declared, as the volley finished and the applause once more sounded around the room. Grabbing the remote control, she flicked off the TV with a flourish and finally turned to me.

'Quite a gripping one,' I said, returning her warm smile.

'Oh, yes, can't beat a good tennis match,' Ms Conelson said, looking me up and down. 'Do you play?'

'No,' I said. 'Hopeless, I'm afraid, but my fiancée is pretty good.'

'Keep an eye out for those tennis coaches,' she replied, with a twinkle in her eye. 'They're a randy lot. I should know – I married one!'

For the first time, she seemed to notice my bedraggled state. A peculiar look came over her face and she twitched with amusement. 'Been raining this morning where you've been?'

'No, just went for a quick swim with a cow – as you do,' I replied. 'Sorry I'm a mess.'

'Not a problem, young man. Would you like a slice of cake and some lemonade?' Ms Conelson heaved herself out of the chair and grabbed a homemade walking stick that was leaning against a bookcase.

'I'm all set, thanks, very kind of you.'

'Right, well, how can I help you?' Ms Conelson said calmly.

'Oh, sorry, I'm the vet – Luke.' She considered me with a blank expression. 'You took your dog, Peanut I think, to the emergency service last night and mentioned you had a sick pig. I phoned this morning. How is Peanut doing?'

'Ah, yes, how forgetful of me, you're due here at three and three it is!' she declared. 'Peanut is right as rain, I'm proud to say. She had a cracked tooth, split it on a stone and was in terrible pain, but they pulled it out quick as a flash and she's back to her usual mischief. Out down a rabbit hole, I expect – she'll turn up and I'll introduce you at some point.' She paused, clearly ready for business. 'Come on, then! Let me take you to see Bertha. She lives just past the orchard. She'll probably still be flat out.'

I followed Ms Conelson out of the back of the house into a large leafy garden. Crossing a neat lawn, bordered by evergreens, we followed the winding garden path through a small patch of woodland to a block of buildings beyond. Wooden stables, shaped in a large L, gave off the aroma of freshly applied creosote and I saw brown and grey muzzles poking out over the stable doors as we navigated a large muck pile, scattering another group of chickens clustered around it.

'You've got quite a menagerie here,' I said.

'Oh, yes – horses, donkeys, sheep, alpacas, ducks, chickens, dogs, pigs and cats, not to mention some giant French lop rabbits. Do you do much with rabbits?'

'I used to, but nowadays not many farmers ask me to treat their rabbits.' I laughed.

'They have their own remedies for them, I suppose. I often feel the same way about my chickens – I have a seemingly endless supply of them. No idea where they all come from but they're everywhere.' Ms Conelson waved her stick as the chickens clucked around us.

Just beyond, I saw a little playhouse, with an open blue door and thatched roof. 'This is Bertha's house,' Ms Conelson cheerfully said as we approached. 'Now, then. It seems quite quiet . . . Where is she?'

I looked for the fence line but couldn't see it. 'It's quite a big garden, Ms Conelson,' I commented.

'Call me Judy.' She paused. 'It's even bigger when I leave the back gate open,' she muttered, 'and everyone can wander off into the forest.' For a moment she looked perturbed. 'It just isn't the time of year for Bertha to go out for the acorns,' she said, 'and she won't at the moment anyway. They let them into the forest to sweep the acorns up – but you probably knew that already.'

I nodded. Pigs are very tolerant of acorns, which poison cows and horses. 'I saw a nasty case of acorn poisoning in a New Forest pony not so long ago,' I said.

'That's rare. Normally the ones bred on the forest know what isn't good for them, clever little things. Did you save it?'

'It needed a drip,' I replied, 'but it pulled through, thankfully.'

'Oh that's good,' said Ms Conelson, cocking her head to listen as we approached the playhouse.

A sudden squeal erupted from within.

'Aha!' Ms Conelson exclaimed. 'She *is* in there!' She stood and shook her head. 'She mustn't feel up to coming out and saying hello.' Ms Conelson ventured forward and poked her head inside the house. 'Oh dear, you poor old girl . . .'

I moved closer and, as Ms Conelson cleared the doorway, I too peered inside.

The playhouse was two storeys high, with a ladder at the back leading to the upper level. Tucked behind it on a thick layer of clean straw, there sprawled a giant saddleback, with eight piglets huddled against her.

Bertha gave a low snort, realising an unfamiliar visitor was in her midst.

'She's just so flat,' Ms Conelson explained. 'Really hasn't picked up after farrowing and I'm getting quite worried about her.'

She was huge, bigger than almost any other pig I had seen. I judged that she must have weighed more than two hundred kilos.

'How old are the piglets?' I asked.

'Two days now,' Ms Conelson replied. 'There were nine piglets, but she squashed one. Then, yesterday, she simply went off her food – and this is the sickest she's ever been.'

'I think she has something called MMA,' I said, squeezing into the playhouse and squatting down. Bertha, anxious about my intrusion, snorted repeatedly and twisted her head to get a better look at me. Around her, the piglets began to squeal and scrabble for better positioning at her teats.

'What's MMA?' Ms Conelson asked.

'Mastitis, metritis and agalactia syndrome – occurs in pigs about two days after farrowing. No one quite knows what triggers it but sows go off their feed very suddenly and the odds are she has a hot and swollen mammary gland.'

'Oh dear,' Ms Conelson said, worried. 'That sounds rather serious.'

'Is she quite a steady pig?' I asked, tentatively reaching out to rub Bertha's neck.

'By steady, do you mean will she let you stroke her?'

'I have to check underneath her and I don't want to stir her up.'

'She has attacked strangers in the past,' Ms Conelson admitted, 'but she seems quite tolerant of you. Frankly, I'm amazed she let you into her house. Do you want me to come in?'

I looked around. With me and Bertha in the playhouse, not to mention a litter of piglets, there was little room for another adult.

'I think it would be a tight squeeze,' I replied, gently

placing my hand on Bertha's side and sliding it backwards to feel her wiry coarse hair. 'I don't want to crowd her.'

Bertha shuffled and snorted.

'Steady, girl,' I began. 'I just need to feel under your tummy. Ideally, I'll take your temperature as well.' I teased my hand into the group of piglets that wriggled against it, pushing me out of the way to get back to their feed.

Gently probing along Bertha's underbelly, I quickly identified one large swollen mammary gland.

'It's this one,' I said, as much to myself as Ms Conelson, keeping my eye firmly fixed on Bertha in case she leapt up.

'It's going to be hard to escape if she gets upset,' Ms Conelson said, watching intently from the doorway.

Checking the other glands, I removed my hand and the piglets all pushed forwards again. 'I think she's too sick to worry much about me,' I replied. 'It's often just one gland that's mastitic. We'll need to get the milk flowing or these little ones will starve. I also need to check her temperature.'

I turned to open my box and get out my thermometer – but, as I did so, Bertha decided that enough was enough and with a sudden movement, she leapt up behind me.

'Watch out!' Ms Conelson cried.

I flattened myself against the wall of the playhouse, twisting to push myself out of the doorway, but I was too slow. In an instant, Bertha was pressed against me. In another instant, she had knocked me to the floor. As I scrabbled to my knees, I was face to face with the huge sow. She snorted derisively, and I saw with sudden fear that she was blocking the only exit.

'Bertha, Bertha, it's all right!' Ms Conelson cried, from outside the playhouse.

Bertha stood motionless, the piglets scurrying around between us. I froze, pinned in the corner.

'Hello, Bertha,' I said, as calmly as possible. I tried to fix my eyes on her but all I could see were pictures of how my being savaged by an adult pig might result in the postponement of my forthcoming wedding. Or, at least, the wedding night . . .

Bertha snorted in response.

'Are you okay in there, Luke?'

'Good news that she's up,' I replied, watching the pig.

'You need to scratch her nose,' Ms Conelson said. 'She likes that. You do that, no sudden movements, and I'll just grab something from the house to distract her.'

'Right,' I replied, listening to her footsteps retreat into the distance. 'Well, Bertha, let's see if you fancy a scratch, shall we?'

I took a deep breath and slowly extended my hand towards Bertha's snout. She moved forwards, closing the gap between us, her huge snout only inches in front of me. Raising my hand slowly above her wet nose, I placed it palm down between her eyes and began to gently rub up and down. 'Need to give you some antibiotics,' I chatted. 'A jab to reduce your fever and something to get your milk going and you'll be back on track . . .'

Slowly Bertha's eyes half closed and, within a couple of minutes, she lay down. She was still completely blocking the door – but, on the plus side, she didn't want to savage me any more.

I breathed a sigh of relief and kept rubbing her, wondering where on earth Ms Conelson had got to.

After a few moments, Bertha began to snore.

Taking my opportunity, I reached over with my spare hand and rummaged around in my medicine box. Deciding that taking Bertha's temperature might not be strictly necessary, I quickly drew up the injections I needed to administer.

Bertha seemed totally relaxed and I resumed rubbing her nose and neck. Pushing down hard with one hand, I eased the needles into her thick muscle with the other. Amazingly, aside from a slight snort at the last one, I managed to get the jabs in and Bertha was out for the count.

What felt like ten minutes later, I heard footsteps outside.

'Luke? Are you still in there?'

'Yes, still here,' I replied. 'Bit tricky to leave, to be honest.'

'Sorry,' Ms Conelson said. 'Peanut had come back and made a right mess of the kitchen. I had to clear it up – she'd got into the bin. She really is back to her old self.' She paused. 'Look, I'm going to push this wellie through the window. It'll distract her and you can get out.'

'A wellie?' I asked, amazed.

'She goes mad for them, chews them up,' Ms Conelson replied. 'I have a whole supply of them in the house for her. Fantastic for emergencies.'

'Well, she's fast asleep at the moment, but the good news is that I managed to inject her,' I said.

'That's great,' Ms Conelson said. 'Are you comfortable?'

I considered the madness of the question. 'It's a lovely playhouse,' I replied, 'but I was planning on going home tonight.'

'I've brought some cake and lemonade. Thought you might like it while we wait.'

Bertha snorted in her sleep.

'Wait?' I asked.

'Why, wait for Bertha to wake up, of course! I think it's the best way. She's a very deep sleeper, but I worry that if you do wake her, she'll be startled and go for you. She was so very protective of her babies when she had a litter last year.'

I considered my predicament. I was only four feet away from the exit – so near, yet so far. 'How long will she sleep for?' I enquired pensively.

'She power naps,' Ms Conelson said, 'so I don't think she'll be out for too long. If you reach up, I can get this through the window.'

I looked round and saw her tapping at one of the Perspex windows. Stretching up, I opened it to receive a small green wellie and a plastic carrier bag, which contained a flashlight, a small bottle of lemonade and a slice of cake in a Tupperware box. 'You've thought of everything, thank you. Does this happen to all the vets you have round?'

'Oh, yes,' Ms Conelson said. 'Almost every time.'

Rummaging around in the bag, I pulled out the cake and, shrugging to myself, took a bite. 'This is delicious!' I exclaimed.

At that exact moment, my phone started to ring. The sharp noise blasted out and, as I reached into my pocket, Bertha's eyes shot open. With a huge snort, she leapt to her feet and spun round.

Pinned by her back end this time, I froze as the piglets, once again disturbed by their mother's unpredictable movement, scrabbled around in panic.

'The wellie!' Ms Conelson yelled. 'Show her the wellie!'

'I can't get to it,' I replied, as Bertha turned her attention to me, a dangerous glint in her eyes.

Instinctively, I threw out my hand to cover my face, but as I did so, the piece of cake I had been clutching spun into the opposite corner of the playhouse.

Bertha stopped and sniffed the air. Turning, she waddled over to the discarded piece of cake.

Seizing my opportunity, I grabbed my box and dragged

myself outside. In the whole history of mankind, never has a man run away from a pig with as much desperation.

Once outside, I slumped onto the grass.

'Well, I'd say that was successful,' Ms Conelson exclaimed. In the playhouse, Bertha, having munched up the cake, had discovered the wellie and was now tearing it apart. 'She hasn't eaten for two days! Your injections must have done the trick.'

'Either that or your homemade cake, Ms Conelson . . .'

'Got to be on your way, Luke?'

I looked at the phone. I'd missed a call from Sam. 'No, just a friend,' I said.

'Well, lucky he phoned! I didn't want to say anything but Bertha's power naps often last a couple of hours . . .'

We walked together, back through the house, where the gap-toothed Peanut watched me curiously. Near my truck, I paused to make my goodbyes.

'You'll come again, of course?'

'Any time Bertha needs me.'

I was about to slide into the truck, Ms Conelson on her way back inside, when a sudden thought occurred to me. Turning around, I called out to her. 'Judy,' I began. In the truck, Leuwen had woken up and was eager to say hello. 'After all that, there is one thing I need to ask you.'

Ms Conelson turned back to me. 'Anything, Luke. What is it?'

I reached through the window and gave Leuwen a friendly rub on the head. 'Do you have any more of that cake?'

'So how far did you go down the river?' Rob asked, clasping his pint glass.

'Not far,' I replied, shaking my head at the memory. 'I sort of clung onto the bank at the bottom and they dragged me up.' There was going to be no way Fred and Louie would let me forget it.

'Did you get the contract?' Sam asked.

'I did,' I said, casting a sideways look at Rob, anticipating his forthcoming outburst.

'So that's another one for me to do while you gallivant away! Your new-found pal – Bob-a-dob or whatever you call him – is working your nights and I'm running your increasingly busy practice! Some study break this is turning out to be! I get two weeks to revise for my certificate exam and I'm going to spend most if it propping up your practice. If I fail, honest to God, you'll be in for it.' Rob took a deep pull on his beer.

'And you accused me of spending my holidays suckered into doing his work overseas!' Sam guffawed. 'At least I get a bit of sun when I help him.'

'It's not holiday,' Rob said defensively, 'it's study leave.'

'You do get quite a bit of "study leave", though, don't you?' I mused.

'Look,' Rob said, raising his eyebrows, 'do you want me to cover your honeymoon or not?'

'I'm eternally in your debt,' I said, raising my glass in salute. 'If ever the time comes when you need a return favour, just let me know.'

'No chance – you'll enucleate all my patients. Remember, I know your approach to eyes . . .'

'You should see his approach to lame donkeys,' Sam said.

'I heard about that – horrendous! And the chief had elephantiasis?'

'Massive leg,' I said. 'Nasty business.'

The three of us took a drink together.

'Are we doing a good job keeping your mind off the big day tomorrow?' Sam said, nudging me in the ribs. 'I mean, Cordelia will be at home with her nearest and dearest, getting ready . . .'

'And here you are with us!' Rob replied with a smile.

I nodded.

'Gwyn's there, isn't he?' Sam asked.

'Who's Gwyn?' Rob said.

'Gwyn is a close and personal friend of the family – and, I hasten to add, Cordelia's childhood sweetheart,' Sam said, with relish.

'You have got to be kidding! What a brilliant twist to the evening – you know what'll be going through his mind?'

'It gets worse,' I said. 'Do you know what he said to Cordelia this morning?'

The two of them looked at me expectantly.

'He apparently told her he thought he may have made a very grave mistake in letting her go.'

There was silence as Rob and Sam digested the news.

'What does he do?' Rob asked soberly.

'Successful investment banker,' I muttered.

'Is he good-looking?'

'Well,' I said, 'he has a slightly hooked nose.'

'So basically, Blondie, he's tall, dark and handsome,' Rob quipped.

'We're both tall,' I replied. 'And my nose is perfect . . . and you're blond as well so don't knock it.'

'How did you uncover the comforting gem about his unrequited love for your betrothed?' Sam chipped in.

'I asked Cords if he'd said anything about our wedding tomorrow and she just told me. In fairness, she was laughing.'

'He'll be trying his luck tonight,' Sam said.

Rob and Sam looked at each other and then burst out laughing as my mouth dropped a fraction.

'Best get another round, then!' Rob said, grinning, and slapping me on the back, he headed off to the bar.

7
Alpha Male

'Stop! Hold on, there's a fish eagle over there!' I said, immensely proud of myself, perched next to Cordelia on the raised back seat of a modified long-wheelbase Defender.

The thick Afrikaans accent of the guide drifted up to us from the front of the vehicle. 'Whereabouts?'

The other four paying occupants of the vehicle all strained to peer at the treetops that surrounded the lake.

'About ten o'clock to the direction the jeep is facing, perched up there, right in the distance. You can see him with binoculars!' I declared.

'Good spot there, Luke,' the guide said, glancing briefly at the trees, not bothering to use his binoculars. Stocky, rugged and every inch the bush safari guide, he exchanged a half-smile with the local ranger sitting next to him.

'Big birds, aren't they?' a crisp English voice commented from the row directly in front of us. Its owner turned to give Cordelia and me an encouraging smile, just as eager as us to soak up as much game as possible on these drives.

I nodded, feeling very pleased with myself.

'They are big birds. It's good to keep your eyes open,' the

guide continued. 'If everyone looks to our right there are about four elephants in the tree line, there is also a giraffe moving away from us on the track – and, about two hundred yards up here, you're in for a treat. Ladies and gentlemen, there are two leopard cubs in that tree . . . Now, if you could keep quite still and quiet, we'll get close to them.'

As we edged forwards, Cordelia nudged me in the ribs and I sat there, my chest deflating at a million miles an hour, before a big grin spread over my face. Slowly, the leopards came into view.

'Do you think there are any fish eagles in the trees around here you want us to look at?' she whispered.

The wedding had gone perfectly – well, perfectly for most of the people attending. Sam and Rob had made it their personal mission to sideline Gwyn from the proceedings. True to form, he had parked his top-of-the-range BMW coupé convertible right outside the church. One of the first guests to arrive, he had swaggered in with a sideways sneer in my direction.

Rob and Sam immediately clocked him, conferred and then waited until the church was half full before Sam informed him that the space he was parked in was reserved. Outraged, Gwyn had moved his car a few spaces away, only to be told by Rob, five minutes before the service was about to start, that his car was now blocking an emergency exit.

'There's a hedge by the side of it! How can that be an emergency exit?' Gwyn had groaned.

Rob pretended to look abashed and apologetic. 'Don't shoot the messenger, pal,' he said, shrugging his big frame. 'Take it up with the father if you like – but that will only delay the service.'

Gwyn ended up parking about half a mile away down the narrow forest lane and returned too late for the ceremony.

Unsurprisingly, he left the reception early. I think he had to wash his hair.

We had flown off on our honeymoon the following day and were enjoying a four-night stay at a high-end safari camp on the edge of Kruger National Park.

Deciding to leave the game spotting to the experts, I settled back in my seat, the wind whistling through my hair, and felt the thrill of a magical honeymoon. The game drives were fantastic and it was a chance to see wildlife in a way neither of us had ever had the opportunity to see it before: healthy, fit, magnificent animals in their natural habitats.

The lodge itself was tented luxury. Deep in the bush, the camp was staffed to the teeth, with every whim catered for. Each meal was a three-course affair with wine and champagne, and the tents were more like mobile palaces, with wooden floors and en-suite facilities. The game drives started at five a.m. each day and lasted three hours and were repeated in the afternoons, leaving at four p.m. Walking safaris to look at the local flora and fauna were available in the middle of the day, and every trip out was in a maximum group size of six, with one experienced guide accompanied by a local ranger.

'So, what do you two do when you aren't on honeymoon?' a man, who was in our vehicle for most of the game drives and who had supported my ludicrous discovery of a fish eagle, ventured as we sat down for a communal dinner later that evening.

In his late forties, his black hair flecked with distinguished grey at the sides, he looked comfortably middle-aged and regarded us with a friendly expression. An attractive lady sitting to his left, at least ten years his junior and layered with makeup, looked at Cordelia and me expectantly.

'We're vets,' I replied, as our wine glasses were promptly filled by the super-attentive staff. 'How about you?'

'Well, I honeymoon a fair bit – this is my third in actual fact.' He laughed, putting an arm around his companion. She gave us a smile that almost extended beyond the corners of her lips, flashing a set of artificially whitened teeth.

Dropping his arm, he continued, 'Name's Gary. I'm an airline pilot – fly the 747s long haul. Don't have much to do with animals, but you'd be surprised how many come on the planes!'

'You mean normal passenger jets take pets?' I replied, tucking into the mountain of food that had just been placed in front of me.

'Depends on the route you fly,' he replied. 'But on virtually every plane bound for Australia from the UK there will be three or four dogs and a couple of cats stashed in the hold. It's not great, to be honest. I really don't like it myself. Bit of a dog lover and most of the companies that fly them do it with no frills.'

'Really?' I asked, still getting my head around the fact that dogs and cats flew with the bags on normal passenger jets. 'They're just in the hold?'

'Wooden or plastic boxes. Wood is better, I think, but plastic's easy. They fly as cargo. They don't sedate them, which always concerns me – not that we can get to them down there if anything happens, anyway. It's against IATA regs so they have to chance it.' He put a large piece of steak into his mouth and chewed.

'IATA regs?' I said.

'International Air Transport Association regulations,' he answered, mid-chew.

'Sedation would lower blood pressure and so does high

altitude,' Cordelia explained. 'The two may not be a good combination.'

'OK,' Gary said, nodding as he thought it through. 'So, if they have a bad heart or something, it would make it worse if they were sedated and then flown.'

'I work with Gary on some of the flights,' his new wife joined in. 'I'm in charge of cabin crew. We flew a Boxer once. It was just put in this horrible plastic container. It was so unhappy. Many of them are fine, don't get me wrong. It's just we also have a Boxer and I looked at this one when it came off at the other end – poor thing, it was in such a mess . . .'

'Just in time for quarantine! Thirty days in Australia,' Gary added.

'Oh, you were so worried about it, weren't you, my sweet?'

Gary nodded, slightly embarrassed.

'If you moved out there, would you fly your dog?' I asked, thinking about what Gary was saying.

'We'd have to,' he replied. 'But we'd make sure he travelled in comfort, wouldn't we, Lorraine? None of this bare plastic-crate business for Rocky! He'd make it through, of course, but it sure is rough . . .'

Lorraine nodded enthusiastically. 'He'd make it, and he'd have no choice. We'd never leave dear Rocky.'

'Tell you what, you should get into that as vets – someone needs to.' Gary laughed and drained his glass of wine.

I was about to reply when, suddenly, a loud trumpeting noise blasted through the air. A sudden scrape of chairs and scurry of feet signified something serious was happening and we all looked at each other uncertainly.

Our guide, a big South African, confidently appeared in our midst, clutching a rifle and striding purposefully through the banqueting tent to one of the jeeps parked outside. He signalled to several of the men who were doubling as general help for the camp, before turning to our group.

'There is a male elephant in musth,' he said. 'He's a handful – but me and the boys will take care of the situation. Please return to the table and enjoy your meal.'

As the women collectively cooed, Lorraine gushed, 'We're so lucky to have Gavin with us.'

'I think all the guides are pretty good here. I'm sure they'd all be able to sort out a rogue elephant,' I replied, a touch defensively, receiving a slight dig in the ribs from Cordelia, who smiled at me.

'You know he was a top Ironman triathlete before he became a guide?' Lorraine said. She was watching Gavin's every move as he stood outside the tent issuing instructions.

'That's great,' I lied flatly. Lorraine's enthusiasm for extolling Gavin's virtues was not to be diminished.

'Ironman triathlon – sounds extreme,' Cordelia said innocently.

'It's the peak of physical endurance. You swim nearly three miles, then cycle over a hundred and straight after that you run a marathon,' Lorraine explained. 'You have to be so fit.'

I didn't reply. Voices were raised and Gavin shouted at a couple of porters who were dithering in his way.

Another guide appeared by our table, clutching a rifle and standing beside me with a lop-sided grin. Turning to me, he whispered, 'He does it for effect, you know, loves the drama.'

'Well, I think he's impressing everyone so far.' I laughed. 'Is he going to scare it off with the noise of the vehicles?'

'Ha-ha! You don't know Gavin! This is going to go one of two ways,' he said, in hushed tones. 'Gavin is a nutcase. He has a thing with this elephant. It only bothers us when he's here.'

As the guide talked, I looked on. The headlights of three vehicles all came on and raced round to get in a line in front of the tent. As they did so, a tremendous crashing noise sounded from the bush and a huge male elephant, with only one long tusk, burst into the clearing, trumpeting another piercing challenge.

'Blimey!' I exclaimed as Cordelia's hand suddenly tightened around my arm.

The elephant was about forty feet away, the trucks between us and him, their headlights illuminating his huge form. His gigantic ears fanned out in annoyance. Streaks of wet fluid, rich in testosterone, poured from the temporal glands behind his ears, staining his cheeks, a sure sign that he was in high musth. It signified he was in an aggressive state of heightened sexual activity, unpredictable and dangerous.

'He's got to weigh about ten tonnes,' I murmured, as awestruck by the sight of him as much as I was nervous.

'At least,' the guide said. 'Tusker is the biggest one in this part of the park. They only get into musth when they're over fifteen and I think he's about thirty, in his prime.'

'How long does it last?'

'The madness lasts for about a month each year. It stops the inbreeding in a herd so the less-dominant adult males get a crack at the females because they're driven crazy by desire. If they didn't get into this state then only the most dominant bulls would get to breed because the smaller males would never be able to push their way forward. Tusker here doesn't need it, though – he's dominant already. He can go where he wants any time and the musth just sends him beyond the edge . . . I don't know why Gavin winds him up so much. He is one dangerous animal.'

'Gavin, or the elephant?'

'Both of them, my friend.'

'Will that gun stop him if he gets through the trucks?' I asked.

'If he charges through the trucks, about ten guns will fire at him. The guys are pretty good shots. We should stop him in time.'

'Bit hard to miss, isn't he?' I said.

'If we don't get to his heart or his brain, forget it. We're finished,' the guide replied coolly.

Suddenly a jeep horn blasted into the night air. In reply, the middle vehicle revved loudly and raced forwards. There was not the slightest hesitation in its action – the plan was clearly to drive straight into the elephant.

'What the—' Gary yelled.

Beside me, the guide repositioned his rifle and looked on, open-mouthed, with the rest of us.

Convinced the jeep was about to be destroyed by the bull elephant, the group collectively winced. At the last minute, in what seemed would be an inevitable collision, the elephant wheeled round and ran back into the trees, the jeep chasing him.

'He's so brave!' Lorraine exclaimed.

'He's bloody lucky,' the guide said, looking at me with a grin.

'Is that standard ranger rogue-elephant tactics?' I asked.

'Not exactly,' he replied. 'You're in Gavin's group, aren't you?'

'That's right.'

'Are you the fella who got your vehicle to stop to look at a fish eagle when the leopard cubs were in the tree?'

I nodded dumbly. 'Quite a few about here, aren't there?' I sighed.

'You know your pigeons in Trafalgar Square?' the guide said, his eyes twinkling.

'Come on, this isn't like Trafalgar Square! I was actually pretty pleased with myself,' I said. 'Which is worse.'

'Yeah, Gavin told us about that.' He grinned. 'Are you on honeymoon?' Momentarily, his gaze lingered on Cordelia.

I nodded.

'Well, he likes to impress the ladies, does Gavin, so you should be in for great game drives. Maybe he'll even tell you about his battle scars. And if he talks about his Ironman days, the best time he got was twelve hours on the nose. Don't let him try to convince you otherwise.'

Bidding us goodnight, the guide turned and walked off. As I watched him go, a guilty thought flashed through my mind. If only, I wished, the elephant would turn around and charge the jeep chasing him . . .

The African sun beat down on the hard-baked earth as we drove back to the lodge after another stunning game drive.

'You guys are lucky, eh?' Gavin droned. 'I tell you, you've seen the big five in two days. That is good going.'

'Or good guiding,' Lorraine said, leaning forward slightly. For some reason, both she and Gary had moved further forward in the Land Rover so they were directly behind our 'super-guide', Gavin.

'Good guiding as well,' Gavin replied suavely. 'But that's my job.'

In the back of the truck, I rolled my eyes, receiving a sharp dig in the ribs from Cordelia.

'I say,' Gary exclaimed. 'What is that jeep doing up ahead of us?'

As we rounded the corner of the dusty track, a local guide seemed to be standing in front of a packed safari vehicle, attaching a rope to the bull bars. The vehicle contained ten tourists, crushed together on the raised tiers of seats, all looking on bemusedly as their rangers tried to sort out the predicament.

'Hey, what's going on, *boet*?' Gavin called out.

An older ranger, who was directing things from behind the steering wheel, turned round and replied in Afrikaans, and the two chatted away, presumably about how their vehicle, overloaded with tourists, was stuck fast in the sand.

'*Baas . . . Baas*!' Gavin's local guide hissed at him urgently.

Gavin broke free of his conversation and listened as the guide hastily explained something under his breath and pointed to a dense thicket on the opposite side of the track.

Instantly, Gavin shouted at the other local guide to get back in the jeep and started his engine. Reversing back up the track about fifty metres, he promptly swerved off the road, then drove forwards up a small incline that overlooked the track and the stuck vehicle below. '*Boet*, can you hear me?' he bellowed.

The older man looked up and waved.

'Stay in your vehicle!' Gavin yelled. 'If your man tries to get out, you *klap* him, OK?'

Looking down at the other jeep, I finally understood why.

About fifty metres behind the large thicket Gavin's local guide had pointed to, a pride of eight lions lounged nonchalantly on the dusty ground. The occupants of the stuck vehicle, clearly oblivious to the situation, had no idea of the danger they were in.

'Oh, my goodness!' Lorraine exclaimed, looking down in amazement.

'Do they have a gun?' Gary asked.

'No gun, no radio,' Gavin cursed. 'They're overloaded and poorly driven. This man should know better. I have hunted with him . . . He's much more experienced than this.' Gavin radioed in the details.

'Are those lions going to attack?' Lorraine asked.

'Not at the moment, but you wouldn't want to stroll around there. If they go, they'll just take them right out, no hesitation.'

'Are you going to help them?' Lorraine asked, somehow managing to lower her voice.

Gavin was still for a moment but, true to form, he gave a sombre nod. 'Of course,' he said, flashing Cordelia a smile. 'We can't just wait for the back-up . . .'

That smile needled me. I whispered out of the side of my mouth to Cordelia, 'What's *he* smiling at?'

'Me,' she replied, with a steady gaze.

'You?'

'Me.'

'Right,' I said, not really sure what else to say.

'Don't glower,' she said quietly.

'I am *not* glowering,' I replied, as we descended the hill again. 'But . . . Look, Gavin has just radioed it in, hasn't he? The lions look pretty relaxed. Why not just wait for back-up?'

'Because Gavin is here to save the day,' Cordelia replied, giving my leg a little squeeze.

I sat there as Gavin drove up next to the other tour group's ranger and discussed a plan. In moments, Gavin was out of the truck, walking to the front of the stranded vehicle without a care in the world. Once he was done checking the rope was tied sufficiently, he ambled to the back of our vehicle to secure the other end. There was no doubt about it now: Gavin was positively strutting, loving the attention of all the other tourists.

'Gavin, do be careful!' Lorraine squealed.

'It's like swimming in shark-infested waters,' Gavin said, a little too loudly for my liking. 'You've just got to be in tune with nature, let them be and they'll let you be.'

As I struggled to stop myself retching, Gary, who seemed totally unbothered by his wife's exaggerated concern for our guide, turned to look at me, pointing at a tree. 'Lilac-breasted roller,' he said. 'Such beautiful birds.'

Gavin paused what he was doing to look up at where Gary was pointing. 'Any fish eagles here, Luke?' he said coolly, flicking his gaze back to the ladies in our vehicle.

Lorraine tittered.

'Just a few man-eating lions coming out on the track up there,' I replied.

'Why don't you get out and help him?' Cordelia said quietly.

I shot her a look like daggers, but she only grinned. 'Because he's tying a knot in a piece of rope and it's hard to see how that might need two people,' I replied, unable to stop myself sounding curt.

'OK, *boet*, we're going to pull you out!' Gavin shouted, finishing his knot and casually climbing back into our vehicle.

Gently easing our vehicle forwards, he took up the slack on the rope and we pulled, the other truck's wheels spinning wildly in the sand.

'Could let some air out of the tyres,' I murmured. 'I saw it on Ray Mears. Deflating them means they get more purchase on sand.'

'Be hard to pump them up again out here, though, wouldn't it?' Cordelia replied.

'True,' I murmured. 'But I don't hear anyone else with any handy survival tips.'

'Why don't you tell Gavin?' she asked, a trace of a smile playing round her lips.

I folded my arms firmly. 'He seems to be having a lot of fun with the whole situation.'

'He's very brave, isn't he?'

'Yes, honey,' I said flatly. 'He's my hero.'

'Oh, Gavin!' Lorraine shouted from the front of the vehicle, as the other truck edged forward and we pulled it out of the sandy dip. 'You're saving them!'

Gavin drove about five metres further and hopped out again.

'Why doesn't he drive another few feet?' I said, under my breath. 'He could be even closer to the lions.'

A few minutes later we were back on our way. The excitement had clearly overcome Lorraine, who asked if we could stop once more for a drink of water from the cool box.

We pulled over at the top of a large open hill – and, once Gavin had courageously checked the surroundings and given the all-clear in his manfully commanding way, we spilled out of the vehicle to stretch our legs. Meanwhile, the guides set up a refreshment camp.

As we all admired the African vista below us, I glanced over to see Gary peering at something in the distance through his binoculars. Meanwhile, Lorraine chatted avidly to Gavin.

'I don't believe it!' I said to Cordelia. 'He's taken his shirt off!'

Sure enough, Gavin had removed his safari shirt and was showing Lorraine a large scar that ran across a tanned, muscular chest. 'This is where I was attacked by a leopard.' Gavin's voice was suddenly louder, and now he was walking straight towards us. Behind him, Lorraine was still in a swoon. 'Please don't think I'm being unprofessional in showing you this, ladies and gentlemen,' he continued, coming to a halt beside Cordelia and me. 'I merely want you to appreciate how dangerous these animals are . . .' His eye passed over me and paused just a fraction too long on Cordelia.

'How did you survive?' Gary asked him, coming to stand beside me and peering at the livid scar on display.

'Don't encourage him,' I said, under my breath.

Unfortunately, I didn't say it quietly enough. Gavin heard and fixed me with a wilful stare. 'I drew my knife and stabbed it in the lungs,' he said, with grave mock-sorrow. 'It was an injured leopard we had caught in a trap. It was attacking the livestock on the edge of the park and our plan was to treat it and relocate it but the trap broke at the wrong moment.' He shook his head at the recollection. 'I was lucky to escape with my life.'

I nodded. 'Sounds scary.'

'Yes,' Gavin replied sternly. 'It was scary. Luckily I was incredibly fit at the time. I had just joined the lodge and had been racing internationally in Ironman triathlons – if you are fit, you heal fast. Do you have any scars, Luke?'

'I do now,' I replied. 'The vision of you taking your shirt off on this hilltop will stay in my mind for a long time . . .'

Gavin had the courtesy to smile as he pulled his shirt back on. 'It's living on the edge out here that makes me raw,' he said. 'I can never leave this way of life. It is a part of me. I know every track, every tree, and am in tune with these animals. Never again will I interfere with nature – I have done it once and it was a lesson that almost cost me my life. We let them be and they will let us be. That is my philosophy.'

'What a life!' Lorraine gasped. 'Don't you think, Gary? Wouldn't it be wonderful to be out here?'

'It is not for everyone, Lorraine,' Gavin cut in.

'Every job has its ups and downs,' Gary said diplomatically.

'I bet this one has more ups than downs,' Lorraine said, looking at Gavin.

'I doubt Rocky would like it,' I chipped in, embarrassed for Gary, who seemed utterly oblivious to Lorraine's flirting.

Gavin looked at me questioningly. 'He's Gary and Lorraine's dog,' I said.

Gavin nodded and turned to Cordelia, who was staring at the ground, watching a large beetle roll an enormous piece of desiccated dirt, about ten times its own body size, up the slight incline. 'Dung beetles,' he said, with the same awe he had used when describing his leopard scar. 'Awesome little things, aren't they? You know, they can pull more than one thousand times their own bodyweight. It's said they are the strongest insects in the world.'

'I feel I want to help it,' Cordelia said.

'Let them be and they'll let us be – never interfere with nature,' Gavin said, for what seemed like the fiftieth time. 'Would you like to ride up front in the jeep for the next section?' he asked. 'I can show you the game from a different perspective.'

Cordelia looked up at him, surprised. Beside them, I felt the heat go to my cheeks.

'It is a different world, up in the front with me.'

Involuntarily, my hands became fists.

Finally, Cordelia spoke up. 'I'm fine in the back,' she said. 'Thanks, though.'

'Nonsense!' Gavin declared. 'Look, everyone will get a turn.' He raised his voice to the whole group. 'OK everyone, let's go – we are going to do shifts in the front. My ranger is going in the back and I want you to take it in turns to look for spoor on the road – tracking, we call it. Cordelia, you must come first! Follow me!'

She looked at me – but I could do nothing but shrug. It didn't seem that we had much of an option. Swiftly, everyone started climbing onto the vehicle. The ranger hopped up beside me, gesturing Cordelia into the front.

In moments we were off, our speed increasingly slightly as we raced down the hill. I looked to see Gavin avidly chatting to Cordelia, steering the jeep with one hand and seemingly forgetting the rest of us in the back.

The local ranger looked at me with sharp eyes. He pointed to the tree line on the left. I looked at the blur of green as we flashed past. 'Fish eagle,' he said, and grinned.

Resisting the temptation to kick him over the top of the seat, I grimaced back as we bounced along the road.

As we rounded a gentle corner, Gavin slowed the vehicle and pulled it to a stop, pointing at the track. While the rest of us sat there, wondering what was going on, he simply chatted to Cordelia, lost in his own little world. I knew that feeling well. It was the feeling I'd had when she and I had first met, in the emergency surgery back home.

Finally, Gavin turned. 'Tracks!' he gushed. 'Cordelia has spotted the spoor of an elephant. We're going to follow it for a while, as these footprints are fresh and heading the same way as us – keep your eyes peeled.'

With Gavin's foot firmly on the accelerator, we moved

forwards, everyone peering nervously ahead, into the high bushes that flanked the sandy track.

It was only moments before we heard crashing off to our left.

'OK,' Gavin began. 'Ladies and gentlemen, the elephant is just over there.' We drove on another hundred yards, and the path entered a large clearing. Stopping, we all looked behind us as the elephant materialised from the tree line, only three hundred yards away. The great grey beast paused, registering the jeep. Then, ignoring our intrusion, it slowly walked away.

'OK,' Gavin said, turning to Cordelia and pointing. 'I promised you game from a different perspective so we're going to go in close to this elephant. I want everyone to keep still and quiet. This one is calm and we're just going to get a little nearer.'

'Is that really a good idea?' Gary piped up.

Gavin gave him a look but he was only saying what the rest of us were thinking.

'Oh, don't be a spoilsport, honey!' Lorraine tittered. 'Gavin will look after us.'

Driving forwards, we approached the elephant. Gavin was talking quietly to Cordelia, undoubtedly imparting some amazing story about how he'd single-handedly wrestled a herd of them to the floor one day.

As we came close, the elephant turned to look at us with mild surprise. With studied concentration in its dark eyes, it flapped its ears.

We were only twenty yards away, and even the local ranger to my right was shifting uncomfortably in his seat. Even so, Gavin crept forward intrusively.

'This is a bit close, isn't it?' I murmured to the ranger.

He didn't say anything, his eyes fixed on the elephant.

Casually, she reached out with her trunk, pulled a leafy branch from a tree and noisily thrust it into her mouth. Just as she got to the end of it, another crash emanated from the tree line.

With a huge trumpeting challenge, Tusker burst through the trees and charged directly at the jeep.

In the back of the vehicle, we all froze. My instinct was to be with Cordelia, provide some reassurance and protection, but she was in the front and there was nothing I could do. I was too late to realise that Gavin had had exactly the same idea. I watched him give her hand a quick squeeze of reassurance before leaping into action.

Slamming the vehicle into reverse, he powered us backwards as fast as he could, the elephant gaining over the first few metres, the jeep bouncing uncontrollably over the stumps of trees and through the rough vegetation in the clearing.

Tusker blared angrily and kept coming. It struck me suddenly that if Gavin tipped us over or the truck stopped, we would be done for. For the first time, I was willing those fanciful stories of his to be true. If he pulled this off, I'd forgive him his chest-baring, superman triathlon and leopard wrestling stories. I would even forgive him the way he looked at Cordelia, or took her hand and promised her everything would be all right. I still wouldn't listen to his gibes about fish eagles, but I would, at least, give him hearty thanks . . .

Gradually, we gained some distance. Tusker slowed and so did Gavin. Eventually he was able to swing the vehicle around, slam us into a forward gear and race us out of the clearing.

Not one of us spoke, even as the adrenalin and fear slowly ebbed away. Even the ranger beside me was tight-lipped.

Somewhere in the distance, Tusker let out another anguished trumpet.

At last, we drove into the tented camp and parked. Once there, we shakily dismounted from the vehicle. For the first time, I noticed that Gavin had lost a touch of his swagger.

'I'm sorry, ladies and gentlemen,' he said, as we filed past. 'I didn't see him there. Quite a unique experience . . .'

'I thought you said let them be and they'd let us be,' Gary barked. 'What were you doing? You almost killed us!' His face was purple with rage. By his side, Lorraine was visibly shaken, her face etched and pale.

'It was unexpected,' Gavin began. He threw looks left and right, searching for support, but his efforts were in vain. Even his ranger was walking away, shaking his head. 'That is the nature of the bush,' he went on, as everyone drifted away. 'It's unpredictable.'

It seemed, at the end, that there were only the three of us there – Gavin, Cordelia and I, with the sounds of an African night chiming all around.

'Did you enjoy the excitement, Cordelia?' he asked. 'Are not elephants the most amazing of the animals to see?'

Cords paused. She looked him in the eye and took my hand. 'I prefer fish eagles, myself,' she replied, and we walked into the camp.

8

Born to Fly Pets

'She's broken her leg,' Tony Pines said flatly. 'She did it a couple of weeks ago.'

I looked at the little dog. At least, I supposed, it wasn't one of his man-eating German Shepherds.

'I didn't see this one when I came to do Jake,' I began, running my hand gently over the swollen leg in front of me.

'We keep them in kennels round the back when we're handling the horses, got three of them – believe it or not, they're tougher than the Shepherds! Bracken would have been right in there with Jake and caused all sorts of mischief if she'd been out.'

I laughed.

'How is he, by the way?'

'Still wild as the hills,' Tony replied, watching me closely. 'Hasn't really calmed him down, to be honest, but at least we have a chance of selling him now.'

I kept studying the little dog. 'This happened two weeks ago, you said?'

'About ten days,' Tony replied. 'We bandaged it up and gave her some aspirin, thought it would come good.'

'You should have called me earlier,' I said. 'Aspirin isn't ideal either.'

'I guess we should have done, but I was certain it wasn't a break and that it would get better. What can you do now?'

'It's difficult,' I replied. 'I'm set up as a farm vet so I don't have X-ray equipment or the gear to be able to do this sort of job. Which vet are you normally registered with?'

'Ha-ha! You vets cost far too much. Look, I didn't think there was anything a vet could do, but I thought it worth asking anyway. Now I just want to do the right thing and put her out of her misery if you can't do anything. She's a bit too little to shoot, though – can you put her down for me?'

I looked at him, detecting a hint of remorse in his voice. I had only swooped in to drop off some drugs he'd ordered, not anticipating that his summons was actually a means of getting me to do a consultation on one of his dogs. I also didn't doubt for a second that Tony would have shot Bracken if he'd wanted to, even had she been the size of a mouse. She meant more to him than he was letting on.

'Look,' I replied, 'I can probably fix it but I'll need to X-ray to be sure and that means she'll need to come with me to the emergency service tonight.'

'How much?'

I didn't like the way this was going. 'Depends on the break,' I said apprehensively. 'How much change has occurred around the fracture line and if the muscles have contracted over it. I can keep it down – maybe four hundred pounds.'

That was cheap for a potentially big op, one I shouldn't even be taking on at the emergency service. I knew I'd be pushing my luck to even cover costs but there was no way Tony would take her to a small-animal vet.

Tony scratched his head. 'I don't know,' he said. 'That's pretty steep, maybe we should put her down.'

'Or I could take the leg off,' I protested. 'She'd be fine on three.'

Tony's face twisted. 'I don't want a three-legged dog.' He sighed. 'What good is that to me? Look, Luke, I think it's time . . .'

I looked at the scrap of bandage on the table. It was a pathetic attempt at trying to sort it. Needless to say, it hadn't worked and the leg wasn't even remotely set. 'They do fine,' I persisted. 'She'll still rat.'

'Come on, Luke! You know the deal – it'd be great to fix her, Bracken's a nice dog and an amazing ratter, but I can't afford four hundred quid. And I don't want a three-legged dog about the place.'

I looked at the little dog, who wagged her tail eagerly. There was something really appealing about her expression. I hesitated. None of this sat well with me. I had put hundreds of pets down in my time – it was all part and parcel of the job, and sometimes mercy was the best thing you could do for an animal – but I hated the thought that I was being asked to do this to an otherwise healthy dog just because its owner couldn't afford treatment.

'Look,' I said. 'I'll tell you what. How about I do it for two hundred – literally, I'll go halves with you. I need to practise my orthopaedic surgery and I could do with a case like hers to get my teeth into.' I looked up at Tony, who shook his head.

'You'll make a rubbish businessman.' Tony chuckled, thinking about it. 'Does your new wife know you're a soft touch?'

'Probably,' I nodded, 'but it means your dog will live.'

'OK,' he said with a laugh, holding out his hand to seal the deal. 'Two hundred it is.'

I took his hand. 'Cash,' I replied, grinning back.

That evening, Holly giggled as I walked into the prep room, clutching Bracken in my arms. Sheila, who was helping Bob catheterise a very flat-looking Weimaraner, looked up at me and raised her eyebrows. 'What's wrong with that one?' she asked.

'I've struck an incredibly shrewd deal with one of my farmers to save little Bracken here,' I said proudly.

'Ah,' Sheila said. 'Is this a special deal where you end up paying to do the job and we all work for free without telling anyone you're seeing private small-animal clients at the emergency service?'

'Not quite.' I sighed. 'But almost.'

'Looks pretty bright to me,' Bob commented, straightening his tall lean frame, having threaded the catheter into the vein.

'She looks perfect until she tries to walk,' I replied.

Holly walked up to Bracken and stroked her head. Bracken wagged her tail fiercely.

'She likes you,' I said, as Holly readied the cage and swiftly took Bracken out of my arms.

'I should think so too,' Holly replied indignantly.

'Holly has a way with little wriggling things,' Sheila chipped in.

'Can you give me a hand with her after you've sorted that one?' I asked Bob.

He gave a wry smile, flicking looks between the two nurses. 'What are we doing?'

'We're going to reduce an overriding transverse fracture of the radius and plate it,' I said evenly.

'Ah, old fracture, is it?'

'Ten days or so.'

Bob looked at me, his expression saying more than words ever could.

'It was either this or put her down,' I protested.

Holly put her hand to her mouth in horror and opened Bracken's cage to give her another stroke. 'I only popped in to say hello to Sheila, catch up on the latest news,' she said, talking to Bracken. 'Now I'm going to have to stay to make sure you're OK.'

'That makes two of us,' I told her. 'I'm moonlighting with Pilgrims on-call. Just can't get enough of the healing!'

Holly laughed and looked at my wedding ring. 'You've just had a whole run of nights off!' she exclaimed. 'What are you talking about? You've got lots to make up for after swanning off on your honeymoon. Are you all recovered?'

'Just about – back with a bump.'

We'd been at home for two days, but the adventures of the safari already seemed in the distant past and, having taken the phones back from Rob, I'd been flat out ever since.

'Are you doing small animals as well with Pilgrims now, then?' Holly asked.

'No!' I said.

At that exact moment, my mobile phone rang. I rolled my eyes at Holly, who giggled as I stepped outside to take the call. 'Pilgrims emergency,' I said, my voice echoing down the hallway. 'Luke speaking.'

'Oh, hello,' said a rather posh voice. 'Are you a vet?'

'Yes,' I said, a little bewildered. 'I'm a vet . . .'

'Good. Well, I don't think I need to call you out. I just want some advice, really.'

'OK,' I replied, trying to work out who the caller was. I

couldn't place the voice and, sadly, was unable to flatter myself that I had so many clients I wouldn't normally recognise them in a heartbeat.

'Well, it's my cat. She's seventeen and a half, she's a Siamese and I've been away two weeks and only got back yesterday. I picked her up from the cattery on the way home and stopped *en route* for a luncheon. I probably shouldn't have done, but I didn't think it would be so long, and then I brought her home. She's been fine today – but this evening she went out about five o'clock and had a poo – quite solid – and then, at half six she went out and it was slightly loose. She's just done another and it's very runny.'

'Well, I'm a farm—' I was cut off almost immediately.

'You see, I'm in my sixties and I've had cystitis and I know how quickly old cats can go down and I really want to know if you can give me some advice. Do I keep her in? Should I leave her in the kitchen or take her up to bed? It's silly, really, but I do absolutely dote on her . . .' The voice paused, expectantly. 'You see, I love her.'

'I don't think the diarrhoea—'

'Do you think she'll be all right tonight? I've fed her, you see. You'll laugh, but I gave her some smoked salmon and some prawns and she just isn't herself. I shouldn't have left her in her box for five and a half hours yesterday during the luncheon, but I honestly thought she'd be OK. She might have caught a chill. What do you think? Shall I leave her by the Aga?'

I didn't reply for a moment, trying to get a decent pause in order to say something. The phone crackled in my ear. 'Sorry, who is this, please?' I said.

'Lady Marion Buchanon,' the voice replied, as if it was the most ridiculous question in the world.

'Lady Marion,' I began, an image of Kevin Costner firing arrows dressed as Robin Hood flashing through my mind, 'Pilgrims is a large-animal vet practice.'

'But you treat small animals as well, don't you? Ms Conelson mentioned you at the tennis club the other day, told me all about your animal charity – wonderful, we should talk about that, but you do know about cats and dogs and treat emergencies, don't you?'

'Well, I do, but at night – it's—'

'It's night now, though?'

I looked out of the window. 'Yes, it is,' I had to admit. 'Look, I don't think it's cystitis. Your cat would be straining to urinate rather than having diarrhoea – and, after all, it is only one bout tonight. I think you should keep her in and warm, try not to worry too much and take her to your own vet in the morning for a check over.'

'Oh!' Lady Marion shrilled. 'That *is* good advice! But what time will you be round in the morning? I live at Mainside House, you know. The gate code is four eight seven six. Would ten o'clock be OK?'

'Well, I'm afraid that Pilgrims is a farm practice,' I said. 'I don't really have the facility for small animals.'

This clearly made little sense. 'But it's easy to come to my house,' Lady Buchanon insisted. 'Just like going on a farm call.'

'Well, I . . . It is, but—'

'Right, well, ten o'clock will suit me very well. You have my number on your phone, don't you? Very good of you! Terribly kind!' she carolled. 'I have a couple of beautiful Labradors as well, if you'd look at them. You will? Wonderful! See you tomorrow.'

She hung up.

I stood there, stunned by the conversation. Shaking my head, I wandered back into the prep room. Holly, Sheila and Bob looked at me expectantly.

'Still not doing small animals?' Holly laughed.

'Circumstances change,' I said flatly.

'I don't see why you're laughing,' Sheila said, looking at her friend. 'If he carries on like that, you'll be moving job to work for him.'

Bob chuckled quietly in the background. 'He plans to get us all in the end,' he said.

'Not yet,' I said. 'This small-animal work isn't planned. Cords works at a great vet practice. I'll send Lady Marion there.'

'But what about Bracken?' Sheila enquired, arching an eyebrow. 'Why isn't she at Cords's practice?'

'I sort of didn't have a choice,' I began.

'There's always a choice,' Bob said softly, gesturing to Sheila to help him.

'It all goes on the computer – and that means through the books – even if this is one of your deals, Luke!' Sheila shouted, as she and Bob lifted the Weimaraner off the table.

'I wouldn't exactly call it a deal,' I muttered.

Slowly, Bob approached to take a look at the broken leg. 'This is going to be really difficult,' he said, feeling the line of break. 'The bones overlap a fair way and, even if we reduce it, they're going to need freshening up. We might not get union. It'll take a long time and we might get another emergency in.'

'We've got to give it a go,' I said. 'If something else comes in, well, we'll just have to deal with it.'

'I'll stick around and give you a hand,' Holly said cheerfully. 'I'm not on first responders tonight, anyway. I want to see what happens.'

With no more ado, we got Bracken anaesthetised and took her through for a quick X-ray. Then we prepped her for surgery. Sheila and Holly worked together like times of old, each effortlessly anticipating what would be needed for the operation while ensuring Bracken was comfortable and breathing well.

'You know, I met some interesting people on honeymoon,' I said to Bob, as we started to dissect down to the bone.

'Uh-oh,' Sheila chipped in, much to Holly's amusement. 'Sounds like he's readying for a confession.'

'Not at all,' I said. 'It's just that I think Bob and I should start up a business flying pets.'

Holly and Sheila shared a collective groan. Bob raised his eyes to me. 'It's true what they say about you,' he said.

'What?' I gasped. 'It's a great idea! Hear me out.'

'You're mad,' he said quietly, squinting at the X-ray pinned up in front of us, judging where next to extend the incision.

'I met an airline pilot who was telling me about the business of flying pets – they all go on commercial airliners.'

'You mean the same planes we fly on?' Holly interrupted.

'Exactly,' I continued. 'They're just shoved in the hold in a pet section of the plane. After speaking to this chap on honeymoon—'

'When you should have been focusing on your new wife,' Sheila added sharply.

'I was doing that as well,' I said hastily, 'but the point being, I have this friend—'

'Another one?'

'—Chris. He's a vet at a practice near Heathrow. He helps out with all the sealing work for pet exports . . . and it seems there could be a niche. Lots of people take their pets abroad, but only a few companies arrange it professionally and none of them are run by vets.'

'It sounds more like a removal job than a vet job,' Bob said.

'Well,' I mused, 'it's the welfare of the animals that's key. Most of the pets need permits, health checks, blood tests, import permits . . .'

'Not exactly hardcore healing,' Sheila chipped in.

'No, but we could set up an élite service with the highest welfare standards, take care of the vet side of things and see the jobs through from start to finish. It would be something nobody else does.'

Bob paused and looked at me.

'What?' Bob questioned. 'No vets do this?'

'Not until us,' I said, looking him in the eye.

'How much?' he asked.

'What do you mean?'

'Well,' he said, 'this plan of yours is going to boil down to investment, isn't it? I just want to cut to the chase to see how much you're after.'

'That's not fair!' I said, straining with the effort of repositioning poor Bracken's break. 'It's not just your money I'm after.'

'That's what all the girls say,' Sheila quipped.

'I'm after a partner to explore this exciting business opportunity with,' I added, ignoring her.

'The muscles are quite contracted, aren't they?' Bob commented, adjusting a set of retractors to expose the surface of Bracken's bone. 'We're going to need to go a bit higher to get this plate on properly.'

'We'll need to freshen those edges as well,' I said. 'It won't heal like that.'

Pushing aside thoughts of flying pets for half an hour, Bob and I worked hard to get a plate onto Bracken's leg and bring everything together.

'There,' he said, breathing a sigh of relief as I put in the final stitch.

'The X-ray will prove whether or not you two would be any good at DIY!' Sheila laughed.

We carried Bracken through for a post op X-ray to see if we'd managed to get everything aligned.

'I'll tell you what,' Bob said, 'If we've done this OK, I'll take it as a sign that your crazy idea might be worth looking into. If not, forget it.'

I nodded. It seemed like the best deal I would get.

Nervously, we waited as the X-ray developed. While she was still asleep, Holly took Bracken through to her cage to recover from the anaesthetic.

At last, taking the film out of the processor with a flourish, Sheila held it up to the light. 'My, my!' She laughed. 'Looks like you two might be in the business of flying pets!'

Bob whistled. The X-ray looked perfect. 'I was born for it!' he declared. 'PetAir, here we come!'

We stood together in silence for the longest time, just staring at Bracken's X-ray.

And then:

'Six grand should about cover it,' I said quietly.

9

My Precious

'You can't do that sort of operation here,' Cordelia said.

I paused, the spoon in my hand dangling limply over a bowl of porridge.

'Honey,' I said, 'she's a very persuasive woman. I don't really have a choice. One of her staff will be dropping the dogs off at eight thirty a.m.'

'Her *staff*?' She was incredulous. 'If she can afford staff she can surely afford to go to a proper veterinary surgery.'

'I've told her I'm a large-animal practice a million times. It's impossible to dissuade her and, besides . . .'

'Besides?' Cordelia fixed me with a look.

Before I could humiliate myself further, Leuwen reprieved me with a loud groan. Distracted, I turned to look at him curled up tightly on one half of his bed, while Charlie, a tail-less tortoiseshell that Cordelia had rescued from a drug-addled client a couple of years ago, stretched out beside him, totally oblivious to the huge Ridgeback whose bed she was commandeering.

Cordelia and I had moved into our cottage on return from honeymoon and one of our concerns had been how Leuwen and Charlie would get on. We needn't have worried: Charlie had had Leuwen firmly under control by the end of the first day, and I sensed the house was more protected at night by the firebrand little rescue cat than my huge Ridgeback.

'You know, I love Charlie,' I said, changing the subject as I watched the cat lean back against Leuwen, 'but . . .'

'But?'

'. . . she'd eat me if I turned into a mouse,' I finished.

'Of course she would,' Cordelia said. 'She's pragmatic. If you were a mouse, you'd be no good to anyone.'

'She'd eat you as well,' I said.

'No, she wouldn't,' Cordelia replied firmly.

'Well, I'm not a mouse,' I said, resigned.

'Prove it, and tell Lady Marion that castrating her two Labradors in our garden isn't a good idea.'

When Cordelia put it like that, she almost had me convinced.

I'd visited Lady Marion to have a look at her cat, which had been in perfect health by the next morning, and she had pressed me into castrating her two dogs. For some reason, she had been absolutely insistent I did the job myself, at home, and she wouldn't go to a proper vet hospital. I had tried my best to persuade her but it had been like talking to the wind. 'Honestly, she wouldn't have it,' I said.

'What is she going to say if they die under anaesthetic?'

'They won't,' I said, though of course I couldn't be one hundred per cent certain. 'I've done this under injectable anaesthesia a thousand times. It's only a couple of castrations. I'll have them both done within the hour.'

'With no oxygen, no accurate scales to measure their weight, no back-up, no nurse, no proper facilities, just a blanket on the grass . . . If something goes wrong, you won't forgive yourself! Those dogs would have a better time of it at a proper hospital – you wouldn't want Leuwen operated on in the garden!'

'She won't go to a proper vet's.'

'*You*'re a proper vet – tell her to get it done properly.' Cordelia regarded me patiently.

'She's going to support the charity quite heavily,' I said sheepishly. 'I've done my absolute best to insist she goes to a veterinary surgery but when she asked me how I did it overseas, well, she was quite taken by the rustic approach.'

'So,' Cordelia surmised, '*now* we get to the bottom of it. You're doing this at her whim. These dogs are not tough street dogs, Luke. They're mollycoddled Labradors . . .' She paused, but it didn't mean I'd won her over. 'Have you got any help?'

I swallowed. I'd tried to get either Sheila or Holly to nip over and help me but Sheila had worked all night and Holly was on holiday. I'd even thought of trying to rope Bob in, but considering I had him on a knife-edge with the flying-pets idea, I didn't want to push my luck. Instead, I shook my head and attacked my breakfast.

Cordelia consulted her watch and sighed. Picking up her phone, she walked out of the kitchen. Seconds later, I heard her muffled voice.

I was trying my best to eavesdrop when, suddenly, the doorbell rang.

I cursed, glancing at the clock before peering out of the window. A smartly dressed man stood on the doorstep. In his hand, he held two leather leads, at the ends of which were the Labradors.

I signalled to him to go round the side of the house and headed to the back door to let him in the side gate. Leuwen raised his head questioningly as I dashed across the kitchen. 'He's half an hour early, Leuwen. You can't help me with this one, pal. Stay there and try not to let Charlie totally kick you off the bed,' I cried, hesitating by the back door as I heard Leuwen groan again. 'Exactly how I feel,' I said, taking a deep breath and heading outside.

I had briefly met Lady Marion's man, Peter, on my visit to the house. He had an air of precise efficiency and nodded a polite but curt good morning as I opened the wooden gate.

I stepped back, expecting him to follow me into the garden, but he remained outside the gate. 'I won't be staying for this,' he began, with a tight smile, holding out the leads. 'I don't want to see you getting carried away with whatever you're going to be doing to these two.'

'Right, well, nothing to worry about,' I lied. 'Everything's ready.'

'Great. I'll be back at twelve.' Peter turned on his heel and walked off.

I stood there, momentarily paralysed, as the dogs, equally perplexed as to what was going on, sat down and gazed at me expectantly.

'You may well be confused, boys,' I said. 'I'd love to tell you there's nothing to worry about but I'd be lying. I can, however, promise that you won't feel a thing.'

The two dogs twitched their ears. Then, suddenly, they caught a glimpse of Charlie sauntering across the path behind me. Leaping forward, they pulled me off my feet and the leads slipped out of my hands.

Charlie bolted back towards her cat flap in the kitchen door, the dogs in hot pursuit. All would have been well had I not left the door open in my haste to come out and see Peter. Bursting round the corner, the dogs didn't hesitate in their chase and, seeing the opening, they surged into the kitchen as Charlie raced into the supposed sanctuary of the house. Scrabbling after them, imagining with horror what might be happening, I was suddenly aware of a deep-throated growl that seemed to emanate from the bowels of hell.

Seconds later, the Labradors were bolting back up the garden in panicked retreat. Leuwen burst out of the kitchen, ferociously snarling at the intruders, his paw raking down the back of one of the dogs.

'Leuwen!' I thundered, just about managing to catch hold of him before he got purchase on one of the dogs.

The Labradors, seeing Leuwen was being held at bay, started to bark and snap at him. It took all my strength to haul Leuwen backwards and thrust him into the kitchen. As I slammed the door, I peered through the window – Charlie was cool as a cucumber, curled up in the middle of Leuwen's bed. If I hadn't known better, I might have thought she'd staged the whole thing.

Picking up the leads of my two charges, checking they were both fine, I shook my head and led them to the end of the garden. Catching my breath, I stood there and surveyed my surroundings. I'd stretched a blanket out on the grass and a small box of medicines rested on top of a faded picnic table.

At least it wasn't raining, I thought, tying each lead round a table leg.

The dogs, both in immaculate condition, seemed to have momentarily exhausted themselves and lay down on the grass. Eyeing each of them carefully to judge their weight, I started to draw up the cocktail of drugs I anticipated would be needed for each one, wondering if I should just forget this crazy situation and drive them to the local vet hospital.

Cordelia was absolutely right. This was too cavalier by

far, especially without any back-up. I was – by myself! – performing elective surgery in my garden. I couldn't even monitor the anaesthetic while I was operating. Admittedly, it wasn't a major operation and I'd done many more advanced procedures in even more basic situations, but the point was that there was no need for this. Even overseas, I'd always had another pair of hands, someone to tell me if an animal had stopped breathing or its tongue was turning blue.

The sudden thought hit me: what would my old mentors, Mr Spotswode and Giles, think of me now?

No matter Lady Marion's view on things, there were safer options than my garden and, if something untoward did happen, I would never forgive myself. I knew, with a sudden clarity, that I had been a fool. Lady Marion had money and the attraction was that she would give a load of it to the charity if I impressed her. But it wasn't as if Lady Marion was an old age pensioner and I could persuade myself that, despite the slight risk, I was doing a pensioner an act of human kindness. Effectively, I was putting the animals in danger for the sake of it.

I looked at the two handsome dogs. They returned my gaze with attentive hopefulness, as if I might suddenly whip out a ball or a dog biscuit. They didn't deserve this. I put the syringe down and turned back to the table, rethinking the situation. I would just have to pay for it myself and, if Lady Marion didn't want to support the charity because I had wimped out of castrating her dogs in my garden, then so be it.

The sound of soft footsteps momentarily distracted me and I turned to see Cordelia bending down to stroke the pair.

'You'll be late for work,' I said.

'No, I won't,' she replied. 'All sorted. I'm working

part-time for Pilgrims today. Besides,' she gently went on, 'I may as well get a taste of working with you if you're to branch out into small animals – it's the only way I'm ever going to get to spend time with you the way things are. Come on, let's get these two sorted.'

I could have married her all over again.

'Thank you,' I said. 'I'm going to get things sorted, get the balance right. It's all coming together.'

'We'll see.' Cordelia smiled.

Forty minutes later, the two dogs were sitting up, wondering what had happened. I didn't have the heart to tell them.

'I reckon it's time, poor old chap,' Fred said, reaching forward to scratch the massive head in front of him.

'I remember Bernie's birth,' Louie chipped in reverently, standing beside Fred and also reaching down to pat the bull at their feet.

'So do I, Brother. He was huge! His mother was only a little Angus – never thought he'd make it.'

'Indeed.'

'Backwards he was, pulled him in the nick of time,' Louie finished.

I nodded, filling out the casualty slaughter certificate form as I went. The government scheme for emergency on-farm slaughter was coming to an end, but Bernie was old enough to qualify for government compensation whilst it was still in effect. It meant that although his body would be incinerated, Louie and Fred would receive his worth providing a vet signed a declaration saying he was technically fit for human consumption. While he'd been trying to mount a heifer in the yard, Bernie had slipped and done the splits. Already crippled with arthritis, the injury was too much for him and he would never stand again. As he was such a huge beast, the kindest thing was to put him down where he had fallen.

'Not a bad life, though.' Louie chuckled. 'Living on the farm, endless supply of females to service. Bet you wish you were Bernie, don't you, Brother?'

'I'd be a lot more picky than Bernie!' Fred laughed.

'Even old Mabel – he got her pregnant a few times!'

'Ugliest cow you've ever seen, Luke,' Fred explained to me, wiping a tear of laughter from his eye.

'Bernie didn't think so,' I replied, putting the completed certificate down and stepping forward to peer into Bernie's mouth. 'Beauty's in the eye of the beholder.'

Louie gave me a look. 'Is that how you got married, then?'

I grinned as I placed a hand on Bernie's nose. He snorted at me irritably.

'You've got to check his teeth,' Louie said, coming to help me, the screw in his pierced ear catching the light. 'I forgot you had to do that. Hang on, you'll need a hand, he may throw his head around a bit.'

'Is that a new screw, Louie?' I asked innocently.

'He wishes he had a new screw.' Fred laughed raucously.

'I'm very fond of my screw, I'll have you both know,' Louie said good-naturedly. 'I just polished it. You know, to keep it looking good.'

Louie wrapped a bear-like arm around Bernard's broad nose. As he did so, I slipped my hand into the side of his mouth to grab his tongue and twisted the head up slightly so I could count his incisors. I had to record the number to prove he was of the qualifying age for compensation.

Just as I got hold of it, Bernie let out a low bellow of protest and swung both me and Louie sideways. Louie lost his grip and swung backwards. As soon as he'd let go, Bernie whipped his head the other way and I tripped backwards, falling flat on my back in the muck.

'You don't want to lie down in front of Bernie,' Louie exclaimed, pushing himself to his feet with a grin.

'We've already told him he isn't picky, haven't we?' Fred joined in.

I rolled onto my front and stood up, covered with muck. 'How come I always end up covered in something when I visit you two?' I muttered, as the brothers laughed. 'When's the slaughter man coming?' I asked.

'He'll be here before three,' Fred said. 'Right, I've got to get on, calves to feed. Luke, we'll see you again soon.'

'Yes,' I said, shaking his hand with my own mucky one. 'For another drenching.'

I tore off the top copy of the certificate and handed it to Fred, bidding Bernie and the brothers farewell.

At least Bernie would be spared an arduous trip to the abattoir, I thought, as I left. At least he gets to finish his days in his familiar surroundings with people he knows around him. It wasn't a bad end to his life and not many cattle would be able to say the same.

I remembered a conversation with Phil at Mr David's farm. One of their favourite old cows was barren, we couldn't get her in calf, and it was decided to send her on. I'd arrived at the farm just after she had been loaded onto the abattoir lorry. Phil, one of the toughest, most capable herdsmen I knew, had been silent and thoughtful. 'Wish we could have got her on the scheme, Luke,' was all he'd said to me about it.

I knew what he meant. He'd been with that cow for ten years, milking her twice a day, treating her when she was sick, raising her calves. She'd done him proud, and had been as close to a pet as a farmer could get to one of his cows. She'd never left the farm, never even been on a lorry. There was something uncomfortable about sending her off to her ultimate fate in the back of that truck. But such was the nature of farming, the hard economics of the business. At the end of the day, like every business, commodities had to be cashed in when they were losing value.

'Treat them fair,' Phil had said to me later, when I was washing up. 'Make sure they're free of pain, have a good life and you see them right . . . But the moment you get too soft is the moment you should give up milking.'

I cast a final farewell look back at Bernie, who lay sprawled in the yard. He was chewing his cud contentedly. It was a good end. I smiled to myself and drove off.

Deciding to swoop into the village shop on my way home, I parked and hopped out of the truck to buy some sausages.

Nodding a greeting to the friendly local faces in the shop, all of whom were still getting to know Cordelia and me as we had been in the village only three weeks, I rummaged around the refrigerated selection of local meat until I found what I was looking for.

As I approached the counter, an elderly lady I vaguely recognised as living down the road asked me how we were finding our new house, then enquired about our wedding and honeymoon.

I laughed through the story of Gavin, and as I was handing over my money to pay for the sausages, she asked me if my work prevented me wearing a wedding ring.

It was a strange question.'Of course not!' I answered, holding out my left hand to show the thick band I wore now with pride.

Immediately I felt sick. A cold clammy hand seemed to grip my shrinking stomach. The thought of sausages far from my mind, I stared, open-mouthed, at the ringless finger of my left hand.

The old lady, realising what had happened, murmured something sympathetic but I wasn't listening. In shock, I mumbled my apologies and dashed out of the shop. Flinging open the truck door, I stood stock still, scouring the floor, desperate to see a glint of satinised platinum.

Nothing. Absolutely nothing.

Pulling the contents of the cab out onto the pavement, I searched frantically under the seats, in every corner, crevice and fold I could think of. In the back seat, Leuwen gave a plaintive whimper. 'That's right, buddy,' I said. 'We're in big trouble.'

A passer-by stopped to ask if I was OK, but I couldn't bring myself to answer. They asked again, hands planted firmly on hips, and I muttered something incomprehensible. Leuwen joined in, with a strange sorrowful whimper. After a moment, the passer-by, incensed at my rudeness, walked off, shaking her head melodramatically.

Throwing everything back in the truck, I climbed in and sat there, head in my hands. A wet nose poked in my ear.

'I don't believe this, Leuwen,' I said. 'I've lost it – tell me it has to be here, please . . .'

Taking a deep breath, I got back out of the truck and took everything out again, repeating the process and searching every inch in case the ring had somehow wedged itself into some tiny space I hadn't yet considered.

Still nothing.

Suddenly my phone rang. I looked at it: Rob. Mindlessly, I pressed the button and held it to my ear.

'I've lost my wedding ring,' I blurted out.

At the other end, Rob reeled. 'Three weeks,' he said. 'Not bad going.'

'I mean really lost it!' I snapped. 'I have no idea where it is. A lady was talking to me in the village shop when I realised it had gone. I had it on this morning, I'm sure.' I paused, trying to remember when I had last registered it on my finger. Everything seemed a blur.

'Do you take it off to operate?' Rob said.

'Yes,' I replied. 'I did an LDA this morning.' First thing, I'd done an operation on a cow at Mr David's. The cow had had a left displaced abomasum, LDA for short: one of his four stomachs had moved out of position. It had required an operation to put it right and I'd rolled him onto his back before operating to fix it in place. I remembered taking my ring off before I'd scrubbed up.

'OK,' Rob began. 'So you definitely had it on this morning. It has to be between then and now. Where have you been?'

I groaned. I thought hard about my visits. After Mr David's, I'd been to Mr Hootle's to drop off some milking tubes. Then I had nipped back home to my makeshift office in the garage to get the forms for the casualty slaughter certificate before heading over to see Fred and Louie.

'Three places – no, four,' I said. 'I have to look at home as well.'

'If it makes you feel any better, I lost my wallet for a couple of days once.'

I let the silence hang in the air as what Rob had said sank in. 'It doesn't. Three weeks we've been married. Most important thing I own. I'm hardly at home with my new wife as it is and now I've lost my wedding ring.'

'Right, well, good to catch up – let me know how it goes,' Rob said. 'I'll see you next week for a beer or two if you don't flog yourself to death.'

'You don't want to help?' I said.

In reply, the phone went dead.

I looked at Leuwen. At least *he* seemed to be sharing in my predicament. 'Best get on with this, mate.'

Gunning the engine, I turned the truck around and roared off to Highmoor Farm.

As I leapt out of the truck and ran to where I had done the operation earlier, Mr David was in the yard talking to Phil. The nausea hadn't abated and I looked forlornly at the deep bed of straw in front of me.

'Hello, Luke,' Mr David said, in cheerful greeting.

'Mr David,' I replied, not looking up, my eyes still fixed on the straw.

'Everything OK, Luke?' Phil enquired.

'Well, not really, actually.' I dropped to my knees, and started hopelessly sifting through the straw. 'I've lost my wedding ring. Do you remember the operation this morning, Phil? Did you see me put it back on after I washed up?'

'Can't say I do, Luke,' Phil replied, looming over my shoulder.

'What operation was that?' Mr David asked, joining us and peering at the thick layer of straw.

'LDA,' Phil began. 'Luke does them a different way to the others, rolls them on their back and does a paramedian incision to deflate and stitch them on. Seems to work pretty well.' Phil went on to describe the different techniques of performing the operation, Mr David listening intently.

As they chattered away, I continued my fruitless, tormented

search. I was close to panic when the futility of trying to find a ring in so much straw dawned on me.

I needed to think – fast. I tried to block out the chatter, and my mind spooled through the morning. I saw it in flashes of colour, like a movie on fast forward.

My normal routine had been to take the ring off and roll it up in the top of my sock. That way it couldn't fall out of a pocket and was always in my boot. Normally, it was the safest place I could think of. I recalled placing it in my sock for the operation – and, every time I did that, I religiously put it back on afterwards. I just couldn't remember having done so that morning. Maybe it had somehow got out of the sock and fallen out of my welly as I'd scrabbled around on the floor with the cow.

'Hang on,' Phil said.

I looked up, wild-eyed.

'You had it in your sock,' he went on. 'I remember you fishing it out because I wondered what you were doing after you'd washed up.'

A wave of relief washed over me. Phil offered me a huge grin and then dropped it for a fraction. 'I'm ninety-nine per cent sure anyway.'

I must have looked like a helpless puppy because Mr David pulled out his radio. 'Will?' he called.

The line crackled.

'Dad?' came the reply.

'Can you get over to the yard with your metal detector, please?'

The line went static for second, before Will came back on. 'Why's that, Dad?'

'Just do it, Will. The vet's lost his wedding ring.'

I felt myself flush slightly. It seemed that every time I had a crisis Mr David was somehow dragged into helping me sort it out. And, in turn, that meant his son was roped in to do something tedious – whether it was heading out in the early hours of the morning in a thunderstorm to help me jumpstart the car or, now, to comb a deep-straw yard with a metal detector.

'Probably won't find anything, Luke,' Mr David smiled, 'but Will can take a look.'

I nodded my thanks. 'Better check the next farm,' I said and, without pausing to say more, ran back to the truck and sped off.

Mr Hootle was equally bemused to see me. Upon retracing my steps, I could find no sign of the ring, but he promised to scour the ground and I left to go home and check the office.

The place was a tip and, as I tried to picture my movements, I glanced at the clock. The hours were swiftly marching by; it was already two. At that realisation, something dawned on me – Bernie was due to be picked up from Fred and Louie's farm at three. If the ring had slipped off my finger there, I had only an hour to find it before the whole area was walked over and disturbed.

I ran back to the truck. Leuwen, used to my dashing around, was fast asleep. 'Big help you are,' I said, and kicked the engine into gear.

I reached the farm in what must have been world-record time. Slamming the brakes into a deep, muddy skid, I leapt out and barrelled across the yard. 'Fred!' I yelled, slobbering like a madman. 'Fred!'

Fred's face appeared round the corner of a barn.

'Is Bernie still here?' I called.

'Just about,' Fred replied calmly, lifting his flat cap to

scratch his head as he regarded me with a confused expression. 'What's this all about, Luke?'

'I've lost my wedding ring,' I floundered. 'I think it must have slipped off my finger during the visits today and I need to check around Bernie. Might have happened when I fell over.'

Fred nodded and I charged past him into the yard, only to see Bernie lying there with two men near his head.

Louie turned from the big man by his side to watch me as I approached, my eyes fervently scanning the ground.

'Vet's got rabies,' Louie said to his huge companion. 'Clearly gone mad.'

'Lost my wedding ring,' I said, dropping to my hands and knees and probing the thin layer of wet muck that lay over the concrete.

'Was it on your finger or round your neck?' Louie asked, the big man beside him silent and watchful.

'Finger,' I replied breathlessly. 'I never wear it round my neck.'

'Not the finger that you grabbed Bernie's tongue with, by any chance?' Louie chirped.

I froze and looked at Bernie. It wasn't possible, was it? The ring couldn't have slipped off my finger when I'd put my hand into the bull's mouth, could it? Was my wedding ring – the symbol of my devotion to Cordelia, to our new life, the most precious thing I owned – hidden inside old Bernie's guts?

'No,' I gasped, rooted to the spot, looking from Bernie to Louie and back again.

Fred came to stand beside me and scratched his head again.

'Well,' he said pragmatically, 'first things first. We need to make sure it definitely isn't lying around here, don't we?'

The four of us started slowly walking around Bernie, who seemed not in the least concerned by the events taking place. Even the big man was pacing backwards and forwards, staring at the concrete yard.

I clawed hopelessly in the muck and, after ten minutes, I sank back on my heels and looked up at the farmers.

'You've gone over that patch at least six times,' Louie said.

'I know.'

'I reckon it's in Bernie's gut,' Fred said. 'What do you think, Brother?'

Louie tipped his chin up. 'I reckon so.'

I felt wretched. I didn't say anything, just looked at Bernie, who was quietly chewing his cud, oblivious to the accusations being levelled in his direction.

'Do you want to cut him open?' the big man asked abruptly.

In a daze, I raised my eyes and looked up at him. It was the first time I registered the gun in his hand and, kneeling at his feet, I fleetingly wondered if it would be such a bad thing if he could just put me out of my misery.

'Cut him open?' I parroted.

He nodded curtly. 'I'll shoot him, you slice him open and have a look. Just don't tell the boss. I'm due another pick-up in half an hour. I'll say the lorry was playing up.' He offered me what I guessed was supposed to be a reassuring smile but, with his heavily scarred face and missing front teeth, was more like a terrifying snarl.

Louie and Fred both nodded.

'It's fine, Luke,' Fred said sympathetically. 'You have to do what you have to do.'

'What about the weight?' I asked. I knew that Bernie would be weighed before his body was incinerated and that the farmers would be paid a price based on that.

If I cut into him, significant financial loss would be involved.

Fred gave me a gentle smile. 'Don't worry about that,' he said. 'You need to find that ring of yours.'

I nodded dumbly, and went to fetch my kit. Returning, the full realisation of what was about to happen dawned on me. I was going to sift through Bernie's guts to find my wedding ring. How I was going to explain this to Cordelia when I got home, I had no idea.

Almost in slow motion, the big man stepped forward and shot an oblivious Bernie right in the middle of his huge forehead. Although I'd known what was going to happen, having done it plenty of times myself, I still jumped at the sudden crack. Then I galvanised myself into action, silently willing Bernie's spirit to forgive me for desecrating his body.

Slicing into his rumen, I started to empty his stomach contents into a wheelbarrow, which Louie had brought over. Piling the contents into a heap, we all started to sift through it, desperately hoping for a sign of the ring. The warm smell of partially digested silage wafting over us, we set to work. Four wheelbarrows later, we were still going.

'It won't have moved down that far,' I said, exasperated. 'It hasn't been long enough.' I drew myself up, the seething mass of entrails spilling out all over me as I pulled away, covered with stomach contents.

Fred wrinkled his nose at me. 'Do you think Louie would do this if a cow ate his screw?' he said.

'I most certainly would, Brother!' Louie laughed. 'I'd do it to *you* if you ate my screw.'

I looked at the brothers, their sleeves rolled up, and felt a wave of gratitude. They weren't fussed about the money it was costing them, or the time they were spending when they had a million other things to do. Even the slaughterman seemed genuinely concerned and was still pacing about, trying to see if the ring was still in the yard.

I looked miserably at the empty stomach and the huge pile of contents we had removed. 'Right,' I said to the men. 'Let's face it, it's not here.'

Fred, Louie and the slaughterman shook their heads. The loss of my wedding ring seemed to be weighing heavily on their minds. Guiltily, I looked at Bernie's lifeless head – his demise had almost gone unnoticed with the focus of my hunt.

'Thanks very much for all your help,' I managed, the words tasting bitter as I realised the time had long passed to halt the search.

I was determined that Louie and Fred shouldn't lose out. I took up a shovel and, piece by piece, began to shovel the contents of Bernie's stomachs back into him. Silently, I worked.

'Do you think we'll see you again?' Louie asked, watching me work.

'What do you mean?' I asked. A lump of silage spilt back out of Bernie's rumen and I stopped it with my boot.

'Well, when you get home, explaining this to your new missus is going to be a bit of a job, isn't it?' Fred said. 'If I were you, I'd climb into Bernie and stitch yourself inside, spare yourself the trouble and let Steve here take you off!'

Louie laughed, trying to break the mood.

'Could be worse, Luke,' Fred went on, contemplating the scenario.

'How could it be worse?' I said flatly.

'Well, you could have been married to Louie's missus.'

I arrived home exhausted, stinking and utterly depressed. I paused in the driveway, defeated by the day's events. Louie,

Fred and the slaughter man had all been so patient and kind in trying to help me find the ring, but the volume of Bernie's intestines had overwhelmed us and we just hadn't been able to find it. I didn't know how I was going to break the news to Cordelia.

Leuwen, sensing my mood, gave me a solid wag of his tail as I let him out of the truck and slowly led the way to the back door. Peering inside, I saw Cordelia sitting at the kitchen table with Abe, her older brother, who had come to visit the new house.

'Hi there,' I said, trying not to sound too wretched as I stepped through the door.

Cordelia and Abe turned, surprised, their eyes open wide. I couldn't blame them. I must have looked worse than a drowned rat.

'What's happened to you?' Abe beamed, rising from his chair but preferring not to shake my hand. 'You look like you've been for a swim in a sewer.'

'Well, sort of,' I said. 'More like a cow's stomach, truth be told.'

'Shower. Now,' Cordelia said, wrinkling her nose in my direction.

'I've got some bad news,' I said, unable to contain myself a moment longer. 'I've lost my wedding ring. I'm so sorry, honey. It must have slipped off and I've looked literally everywhere I could think of.'

Cordelia came forward and planted a kiss on my disgusting face. 'I wondered how long it would last,' she said. 'Just as well I put it on the house insurance.'

I hesitated, wanting to hug her. The only reason I didn't fling my arms around her at that second was the thick layer of cow muck between us. If she had been understanding about the wedding ring, she'd be less so about that.

She smiled. 'Now,' she said, as Leuwen's head appeared between us, 'get into that shower so we can talk about setting up a proper small-animal practice in the village . . . and Abe can show you these websites he's been working on.'

With Abe grinning at me, I dashed to the shower with an overwhelming sense of relief.

Sheila arched an eyebrow as she joined Bob and me at the table in the emergency-hospital staffroom. I stretched out the papers in front of me and outlined my plan to get the pet travel business literally flying.

The last few weeks had passed in a blur. Abe had not only revamped the charity website, but – for the token trade of a box of fine ale – he'd knocked up one for Pilgrims and a template for PetAir. Having a brother-in-law who also happened to be a technical whiz definitely had its plus points.

The other big development had been a serious discussion with Cordelia about the direction in which to take the practice. After the Labrador castrations, Lady Marion had not only made a generous donation to the charity but had also told her well-to-do friends that I was open for business. The result was that I'd received a deluge of calls to vaccinate and treat various dogs and cats locally and, it seemed, there was definitely an opportunity to expand things.

Deciding against any more operations in the garden, Cordelia had started looking at premises in the local village where we might be able to open a surgery – and we now had plans afoot to convert the old village shop into a one-room practice.

Although it was early days, and much still had to be approved, leases signed and building work started, the rough idea was that Cordelia would give up her job and come to help me with Pilgrims, driving on the small-animal side of things while I was out on farm visits.

After that, the next step would be to try to twist Holly's arm into coming in as our vet nurse. She would have jumped at the opportunity only six months ago, but she had just landed a job at another practice not too far away and they had a solid reputation for looking after their staff well. I phoned to tell her what we were up to, but without being able to offer her a firm job, it was a difficult situation.

I swooped into the emergency service to catch up with Bob and Sheila. Things were moving on all fronts and it was time to get Bob to commit to having a go at the flying-pets business with me.

'Nice new wedding ring you have there,' Bob commented, glancing at my left hand.

'Very tight fit, this one,' I replied.

'Three weeks!' Sheila said, shaking her head. 'Luke, even for you . . .'

'I know, I feel bad – but this one is pretty much welded on, so no messing about . . .'

'A bull really swallowed it?' Sheila asked.

I nodded.

'And you cut it open to try to find the ring?'

'It was being shot anyway,' I quickly added, 'so it didn't suffer on my account.'

'The journey of the ring – Frodo will be phoning you up before you know it,' Bob said, with a smile. Clearing his throat, he pointed to the table.

'So, you have this website that Abe designed, you've got a business plan, and your friend Chris is convinced this is a winner. So much so that he's helped you get the idea off the ground.' Bob flicked through the papers. 'But, for some reason, he isn't going to do it with you.'

'He's applied for a job with a pharmaceutical company,' I replied defensively. 'I think if he didn't have that in the pipeline, he'd join us.'

'Us?'

'You and me.'

'Right,' Bob said steadily, contemplating the figures I had jotted down.

The plan basically revolved around us getting accredited with a major airline, setting up an account that would let us export live cargo, finding a carpenter who would make us airline-approved dog and cat crates and advertising to fly pets.

'This is as madcap as it sounds, isn't it?' he said, after a moment.

'We've already had some enquiries,' I replied.

'Seriously?' Bob asked, disbelieving. 'Who would trust us to fly their pets when we've never done it before?'

'See? You're already coming round to the *us* concept!' I exclaimed. 'This is my point – we're vets, we know pets, we can do this, and once we've done a few, we'll be away.'

'And if I put in six thousand pounds and you put in the same – which neither of us has – then you think that will be enough buffer to get us airborne?'

Naturally I nodded. 'We have to give half of it to the airline as a guaranteed bond. Then they'll sponsor us as exporters.'

'Small-scale exporters,' Bob said. 'To the tune of six thousand, I imagine.'

'There's a lady who wants us to fly her two Tibetan Terriers to the south of Spain next week,' I said. 'Well within budget.'

Bob looked at me pensively. We both knew the regulations

for pet travel within Europe weren't complicated. The dogs basically needed us to sign a fitness-to-fly document, and that was that. The hard bit would be making the crates to the right dimensions and working out how to make an airway bill for live-animal export.

'Look, Luke,' Bob began, 'I'm working here for the next five nights.'

'So you've got plenty of time in the day,' I said, with a grin.

After a moment's deliberation, Bob regretfully nodded. 'OK,' he muttered. 'Let's do it.'

'Sucker.' Sheila coughed from the other side of the room.

10

Expect the Unexpected

'Rabbits?' I said into the phone, the surprise in my voice making the caller chuckle.

'Bit like cows in a lot of ways,' the voice replied, the accent more Southend than deepest Dorset. 'They eat grass, they don't say much and we've got hundreds of them. We want you to take us on.'

'But Pilgrims is just a farm vet practice . . .' I began.

'That's not what I heard,' said the voice, betraying another laugh. 'Arcn't you opcning a surgcry in Cranbornc soon?'

'It's a plan,' I replied, 'but we're a long way from being there yet. I'm not geared up for rabbits – truth be told, I'm not an amazing rabbit vet.'

'Look,' the voice said, 'we want to be treated like a farm. That's what we are, really – we farm rabbits. We breed them and sell them to pet shops. We need a vet to accredit us and treat us like a business, rather than a pet owner.'

I hesitated. The whole idea repelled me. Being a vet for a wholesaler who supplied animals to pet shops had never been on my list of things to do. 'Look,' I said, a hint of frustration creeping into my voice, 'I'm not a good vet for you. I run an animal charity. I'm not being rude, but I'm not the man you're looking for. I don't like the idea of farming animals for the pet-shop industry.'

'That's exactly why you're the man to look round us,' the voice replied. 'Look, I'll be honest with you. I've done it all, been in the business twenty years. I've seen things that turned my stomach in this line of work and there isn't much that can do that – but I've got this contract, it's a big one, and I need to be the best, squeaky clean. Come over, have a look, and if you don't like it, tell me so. Can't say fairer than that. I'll pay you normal farm rates.'

'Why won't your usual vet do it?'

'Honestly, it's because he'll charge me through the roof. I don't mind paying, but I'm not getting robbed. You do this, I'll pay you the prices you advertise and no messing about.'

I let the silence hang in the air for a moment. 'A farm visit, like a herd-health plan.'

'Exactly,' he replied. 'Biosecurity, disease control, isolation procedures – we've got all that, and I want you to look at it and write what you think.'

'I won't like it. I'm telling you, I'll hate it.'

There was a moment of pure silence. 'Steady on! You've got to see our set-up first. We'll surprise you. If we're doing badly, you can say so.'

The voice had me stumped. I'd pretty much told him that I would damn his business in trading live animals and he still wanted me to visit. 'I'm not a rabbit vet,' I insisted.

'You will be if you take us on.' He laughed again. 'Come on, you can't knock something if you don't know anything about it. Come and see us and let's have a chat.'

He had a point and I had to confess part of me was intrigued now. I'd never come across a large-scale provider for the pet industry. I'd seen lots of small-time breeders, some good, some bad, but never a wholesaler of rabbits.

'Fine,' I said. 'I can come this afternoon.'

'Right,' he said. 'See you about four, then. Kettle will be on.' And, with that, the line cut off.

I swung into an unmarked yard and parked next to a gleaming new BMW with tinted windows and what looked like a large warehouse to my left. I had no idea if this was the right place, but a few cars were parked outside and the directions had been very straightforward: turn left at the junction, first drive on the right and park in front of the big warehouse. There were also no other buildings even remotely near, so I supposed it had to be right.

A sudden grating sound echoed out as a large grey door slid sideways and a thick-set man in his mid-forties swaggered out. 'All right there?' he called.

'All good, thanks,' I answered, climbing out of the truck to shake a strong, calloused hand.

He didn't look like a typical rabbit owner by any stretch. Quick eyes seemed to weigh me up in seconds and he offered me an easy, well-practised smile. 'Call me Tim,' he began. 'Tim Muntford. Thanks for coming along.'

'No problem,' I said warily, 'but this still might not work out.'

'Sure, but you won't have ever seen anything like this – so come on inside and let's have a chat.'

Tim Muntford turned and headed back through the door. With a fleeting glimpse at Leuwen, who was sitting up in the back seat of the truck, I gripped my medicine box and followed him into the barn.

What confronted me literally took my breath away.

The warehouse was vast, about the size of a football pitch, and it was subdivided into about fourteen aisles, each with a ladder and a raised platform at one end. Each aisle stretched back like those in a giant supermarket and each was comprised of a wooden frame running up from the floor to about eight foot in height. It took me a second to realise that what I was actually looking at were rows upon rows of wooden rabbit hutches.

My mouth dropped a fraction and Tim, not missing a trick, let out a hearty laugh. 'Welcome to the rabbit-breeding business.'

'How many have you got?' I asked, unable to hide the amazement in my voice.

'Not counting babies, we've got about five hundred breeding does. But if you count the rats, mice, guinea pigs, gerbils and hamsters, there are several thousand breeding animals here. We had to put in the second floor to keep up with demand last summer.' As he spoke, there was a gleam of pride in his eye.

'And if you count the babies as well?'

'Multiply that by at least ten.' He chuckled.

'Who do you supply?' I asked, starting to walk down one of the aisles, looking at the rabbits to either side of me.

'Who don't we supply? I cover all the big pet shops in the south. You think of a big chain and we'll be their number-one supplier. Anyone asks them where they get their animals from – this is where. We're the best in the business and proud of it.'

'No one would know you're here,' I said. 'I mean, I never even thought about where all the animals in pet shops come from.'

'Well, if we put a big sign up, we could have a situation on our hands, couldn't we? This line of work doesn't appeal to everyone's sensitivities, but everyone likes a baby bunny rabbit and they've got to come from somewhere. That was the idea.'

'And it pays,' I said, unable to help myself, overwhelmed at the scale of the enterprise.

'It does now, Luke, but it didn't to start with.' Tim's gold necklace sparkled in the warehouse light. 'Took me twenty years to build it up. But just imagine, one outbreak of disease going through this lot, and we'd be ruined. This is big business we're talking about. Sure, the mark-up on some of these rabbits is three hundred per cent by the time they get sold on the shop floor – but multiply my base line by a thousand and you can work out what that means. With all the regulations and that, I've got a lot of papers that need to be signed. Imagine what trouble I'd be in if anything ended up contaminating a shop floor.'

I nodded dumbly, pausing outside one of the hutches. A pretty brown and white doe looked back at me dolefully. She had plenty of space, she could turn around and even had a nesting box for her litter, but it was a sterile, soulless existence. Her whole purpose was to breed – and when she couldn't . . .

'How long do you keep the breeding does for?' I asked.

Tim caught my expression. He'd got to where he was partly by being able to read people in seconds and know what to say. 'Luke, I'm not running a charity,' he began. 'This isn't Watership Down. But they're clean, fed, watered, free of disease, and they get to do what nature intended. They last a few years and then I have to get rid of them. I'm licensed. You know how it works. I'm not here to pull the wool over your eyes. It's the real world. It isn't battery farming as such, they do it worse in many places, but it's intensive and they aren't pets.'

'It *is* battery farming,' I countered, looking him squarely in the eye.

'Well, they aren't on wire,' Tim went on. 'All these hutches are much bigger than any RSPCA welfare regulations you care to find. Just compare these conditions to what many of the pet rabbits you see at your surgery have to live in. I'm telling you – this place is the best in the business.'

I shook my head. 'I already told you, Tim. I'm a farm vet. I don't see pet rabbits at the moment.'

'But you did and you will do again – or so I heard . . .' He was wearing a winning smile, and I wasn't sure I liked it.

'Maybe,' I began, 'but what's your point?'

'The people who get a baby rabbit when it's all sweet and cute, they give it to their little daughter, who then loves it for a few years. What happens when that child grows up? Rabbits become boring. Those animals languish – what? About eight years? Stuck in little dark wooden boxes in people's sheds. No company, no stimulation, no life. I'm not painting roses around what I do, but that rabbit you're looking at there, number 164, according to the tag, is fine. It won't get myxomatosis, it won't languish in a shed and it always has fresh food and water.'

'That's not exactly the rabbit idyll,' I replied.

'Life is hard. Welcome to the real world,' Tim replied, an edge to his voice. 'Look at those tower blocks next time you get the train to London. Bet you half of those people would rather be this rabbit.'

I let the comment hang in the air, unsure how to respond. Part of what Tim was trying to say rang true; I thought of intensive pig farming, chicken farming, all sorts of practices across the world that abused animals. All the same, bringing people into it was a cheap emotional trick.

'They have choice,' I said, angry frustration welling up inside me.

'What choice? Live in a council flat with their three kids or move out onto the streets?'

'Your rabbit doesn't have a street,' I replied.

Tim stepped forward and unlatched the hutch. The door swung open and the poor animal looked terrified, hunching into itself.

'That's a five-foot drop,' I said. 'It's like giving those people the option to escape by jumping off their balconies.'

Tim laughed, closing the door with a smile. 'All right,' he said, 'you win. But the thing is, I wouldn't let that rabbit jump out of there because I care about it. I want it to breed, I want it to live, and if I didn't get to it in time and it broke its leg, I'd put it down.'

I looked at him calmly. 'How?'

'Neck,' he quickly replied. 'It would be dead before you drew up your injection.'

I sighed and flicked the plastic piping on the outside of the hutch.

'Automatic water feeders – they never run out of water. They're clean, fresh and custom made.'

I nodded and walked on down the line. Rabbit after rabbit sat there, a few hopping forwards out of curiosity. They all looked in good, glossy condition, bright-eyed, with clean noses, every hutch nicely bedded up with clean shavings.

'How many deaths do you get a week?' I asked, unaware I was even formulating the question.

'Between five and ten,' Tim replied. 'It's between one and

two per cent, better than any other intensive farming system I can think of.'

'Intensive bull beef might disagree,' I said quickly.

'Not the calf units,' Tim replied just as swiftly.

There was a moment of silence. Then, because I couldn't stop myself: 'I hate it,' I said simply.

Tim nodded. He had been expecting this. 'All the same, you know it's a good set-up. No one does it better – and I do care about them.'

I looked back at the rows of hutches. I had never had a huge affinity with rabbits; Cordelia had had one as a child and spoke about it fondly, but for me they had always been the target of farmers in more ways than conversation. Despite my fairly neutral feelings, my heart went out to the animals around me. It was a grim life to be a breeding machine – but, despite that, they were as Tim had said. They were free from disease, free from hunger and thirst, free from fear and pain, free to express some natural behaviour – not all of it, of course, they couldn't dig or burrow or interact, except with a buck at allocated times, but still . . . I thought of the pigs and chickens, sheep and calves that I regularly treated. Did they really have it any better?

'What am I doing here?' I asked tightly.

'You're signing a welfare report,' he replied candidly. 'Making comments and answering the questions on the form to the best of your ability.'

Despite Tim's wheeler-dealer nature, there was something very honest about his business with me. Nothing was hidden. No question I asked was too probing. It was almost a challenge for him to get the approval with everything on display.

I trudged upstairs. Plastic tubs, a little larger than

ice-cream boxes, were stacked several feet high, each one seething with Russian hamsters.

'I used to do birds,' Tim said quietly. 'You think these are bad, you should have been here when a lorry arrived from Belgium with its imports.'

'Imports?'

'Birds come from Africa, get shipped to Belgium, and then they're driven all over Europe. Put a couple of parrots in the middle of a lorry, send it through on a Sunday night, no problem. Sometimes they even still have the glue on their claws from the glue traps.'

'Glue traps?' I asked.

'It all goes on,' Tim said, with a wry laugh. 'They're supposed to be captive bred in the UK – but do you know how to identify a parrot that's been captive bred in the UK?'

I looked at him blankly.

'A metal ring round its leg. Not that hard to put one of them on, is it?'

I imagined a large African Grey, the size of its beak and the fact that one bite could potentially nip a little finger off. Not that easy, I thought, but I suspected there were a few tricks I probably didn't know.

I shook my head in disbelief at the world I had just entered. Never in a million years had I considered the UK pet industry and how it worked. 'Why did you stop doing birds?' I asked, unable to stop my fascination with learning more.

'Dodgy business,' Tim explained. 'Big mark-ups, lots of middle men, beak and feather disease.'

I smiled. Beak and feather was a disease that would be latent in a lot of birds that carried it, only to appear maybe six or seven years later. An owner of a bird would have no idea that their pet had had it when they'd picked it up. I doubted any were ever tested, and although it would be impossible to prove so long after purchase, fingers would be pointed at whoever had supplied the bird.

'They belong free,' I said, cringing as I realised I sounded like a twelve-year-old animal-rights activist.

'You've met plenty of pet parrots that have brilliant lives,' Tim said, a hint of admonishment in his tone. 'Come on, it's like everything – depends on the owners.'

To my shame, I had to admit that he was right. I had met some parrots that were in peak health and had a fantastic quality of life.

We walked back down the stairs and Tim guided me to his office at the far end of the building. 'Luke,' he said, 'I just want you to write whatever you think. The truth about the welfare of these rabbits. The businesses I sell to don't care about the ethics of free-range rabbits. All they care about is that I don't sell them diseased stock – and you can look anywhere you want. I just want your opinion on the set-up. Take the report away and let me know.'

He gestured for me to open the door. Ducking inside, I looked up to see a hard-faced blonde girl in her mid-twenties and a lean, heavily tattooed man, about the same age, standing behind the desk.

'Luke, meet Leanne and Guy.'

I smiled a hello. They nodded back at me, giving away nothing.

'Leanne's my daughter and Guy is her man. They run the workshop,' Tim said.

'Workshop?'

'We don't just sell the rabbits, Luke. We also sell the pens. You see all those hutches out there? Imagine how much that would cost us to have them made. Leanne and Guy here run the show on the manufacturing department. When we took on this building, it was just a shell.'

'You made all those hutches?' I asked incredulously.

Leanne allowed herself a smile and squeezed Guy's arm. 'We can make a rabbit hutch in about half an hour,' she said.

I looked again at the constructions behind me. They were really just glorified crates. 'Tim,' I said, 'I run an animal charity. I'm absolutely gobsmacked by your set-up. You're right – I've never seen anything like it. I can't deny you run a tight ship but it bothers me that these rabbits will never see natural light and so on.'

Tim nodded. 'Well, you put that down and give me some solutions. I'll work with you. But you have to admit, it is indeed a tight ship.'

I felt as if he were running me around in circles, like a fox with a rabbit. 'Yes,' I had to admit, 'it is a tight ship and the rabbits do look healthy, it's just . . .'

Tim smiled. 'Not your thing?'

'That and the fact I'm your hardest critic.'

'No, Luke,' he said. 'You're my credibility. Just tell it straight.'

I felt as if I had ten thousand pairs of rabbit eyes boring into my back. 'Only thing I can promise is to write the report objectively,' I said, 'but I'd be a terrible vet if I didn't empathise with the animals you have here.'

'That's fine by me,' Tim replied. 'I'm not in this business for popularity – but surely it's better I do this with you, rather than doing it like all those people who breed hundreds of flea-ridden rabbits in their garden sheds.'

I nodded and turned to leave, pausing at the door. 'Just one last thing, if you don't mind me asking,' I said, looking past Tim to Leanne and Guy.

The three of them looked at me blankly, waiting. 'Would you be interested in making me some wooden dog crates?'

'Take Rob instead!' Sam exclaimed.

'I need Rob to cover Pilgrims,' I replied, looking over my pint at Sam, who started to shake his head from side to side.

'This trip is really worth doing,' I said firmly.

'They're all really worth doing!' Sam bleated and raised his eyes at me.

'What about spending time with your wife? You're mental. Stop coming up with these plans to save the world.'

'This trip will really make a huge difference, animal welfare for human welfare – it's unique,' I continued.

'Why do I bother being your friend? It's just constant give.'

'I'm offering you a chance to be out and about – normally something that would require a licence if the authorities knew you properly.'

'Seriously, what about Cords?' Sam protested. 'Why not take her? At least you'd be spending time as a married couple for once.'

'She's still working for the practice in town,' I explained. 'If we manage to get Pilgrims its own premises, it'll be a different story – I'll hopefully take on some help, Cords will be running the small-animal side and this sort of thing will be a lot easier. We'll go on trips together, and with Bob taking on the nights at the emergency service, I'll be home all the time.'

'Dreamer,' Sam said.

'It's going to happen,' I said.

'No, I don't doubt that,' Sam went on. 'You peck away relentlessly and Lord Cranborne will give you the premises to shut you up. The problem is that it won't get easier – you'll still be roping me and Rob in to bail you out.'

'Friendship is for ever,' I declared.

'No,' Sam chipped in. 'That's something else you need to talk about at a clinic.'

'Look, this trip is an absolute winner. It'll be the making of the charity.'

'You said that about India.'

'And it was! This is another making. We've had a couple of big donations – one from Lady Marion and another from a benefactor known only as Steve.'

'Mysterious Steve – now that's the way to give to charity.'

'Mysterious Steve sounds like a pretty great guy,' I said. 'He basically judged us on what we'd done and is now testing us with a donation to run a proper trip.'

'So the other trips weren't proper?' Sam blurted in mock outrage.

'This will be our first disaster-response trip,' I explained. 'It's a landmark mission and it's a situation we're uniquely placed to help with.'

'"Uniquely placed", in that no one else will do it?' he enquired, lifting his glass to his lips.

'Look, there's been a lot of political unrest in Kenya. Tribal wars have resulted in more than half a million people being displaced, and at least a thousand killed.'

'And in come Luke and Sam with a packet of cat wormer to sort things out,' Sam interjected.

'The thing is, the displaced people have all fled to refugee camps,' I said, deciding to carry on, regardless.

'Can't be a refugee in your own country,' Sam interrupted.

I tried to ignore him. 'They're all pastoralists,' I went on. 'Families have fled to the sanctuary of these—'

'Internally Displaced Person camps, or IDPs,' he interrupted, smiling.

'—OK, IDPs, bringing with them the few cows, goats or sheep upon which they depend for their livelihood and survival, and that's how we can help them.'

'They're going to need food, water and money, not antibiotic for their cows,' Sam said, looking at me hard.

'There's a big risk of disease,' I explained. 'Huge herds are being formed from groups of three or four cows coming from different regions. They're bringing disease with them and parasites are on the increase – but we can run vaccination campaigns at each camp, drench and spray all the animals against parasites and promote animal welfare for human welfare.' I stopped and took a long swig of beer. It was a tough pitch and I could see Sam thinking hard about it.

'How on earth are you and I going to get into an IDP camp to vaccinate cows?' he blurted out. 'Have you even considered the logistics of this? Permissions coming out of your ears and with big humanitarian issues . . . we'll be a joke! It'll sink the charity, not make it. Save the cats? People are dying in those places through starvation every hour. Who cares about the cats, cows, sheep, goats and donkeys?'

'The animals are key in these places – we help them, we help the people.'

'You are certifiably, absolutely mental! Refugee, IDP or whatever-you-call-it camp. It isn't going to be fun. This is going to be . . . bloody sad, I expect.'

I clinked my glass against Sam's, our recurring signal for another drink.

'Mate,' I said, 'I need your help. An African charity has put out a request for aid, the Kenyan Vet Department supports the project and they have a proposal in place. They need money and vets – and WVS can do it.'

'Why not a much bigger and better-resourced charity?' Sam asked.

'No one will go,' I said. 'No international animal NGOs are geared up for this sort of thing.'

'Except for WVS, of course, thanks to Lady Marion and Mysterious Steve.' Despite his reluctance, I could tell that Sam's resistance was waning. 'Jane is going to take some persuading,' he said. 'How are you going to broach this one with Cords?'

'Leave that to me,' I said. 'We can do something special here.'

Sam nodded wearily. At last, he had agreed.

'My round,' I said, and headed to the bar before he could change his mind.

'You're going to Kenya?' Sheila asked, with an arched eyebrow.

'I am,' I replied, focusing hard on my final stitch.

'And Pilgrims?'

'Rob,' I said simply.

I had spoken to Rob on the phone after managing to convince Sam. He'd agreed, but as a trustee, he'd also expressed concern about people's perception of the charity. The deal was that I had to do the trip properly, explain publicly to our members and supporters exactly why I was going to such a desperate place to help animals. The key, he had said, was to ensure WVS had a PR campaign built around the mission to ensure no opportunity was wasted and that it did the charity some actual good in getting us more members.

'Dare I ask you about how you broached this with Cordelia?' Sheila said.

'Carefully. I've booked us tickets for a concert when I get back and I've got a whole romantic campaign lined up.' I laughed.

'Sounds intriguing,' Sheila baited me.

'And that's the way it will stay,' I said. There was no way I was telling anyone what concert I was planning to take Cordelia to – if word of that ever got out, all my credibility as a male would go out the window.

I stroked the dog on the table and stepped back to assess my surgery. He was a black Miniature Schnauzer called George, and had been in a fight with his 'brother'. The other dog had bitten his throat, ripping the skin to within a millimetre of the pulsating jugular below. It was the third time one of the dogs had been down to the emergency service in as many months.

'It can't go on like this,' Sheila said, moving forward to clean around the op site, half an eye on the dog as he started to come round. 'One of these two needs to get rehomed.'

'The owners messed up,' I replied. 'They got them both neutered – that was the mistake. They should have got the less dominant one done and left the other intact. They must be ripping their hair out.'

'Like Bob will, when you tell him you're going away again.' Sheila laughed as she gently lifted the dog to the recovery cage. 'How's he going to take the news that he now not only has to keep an eye on this place as well as your pet-flying activities?'

'Well, he's got you to run this place,' I said cheekily, 'and once we get our first dog flight under our belt tomorrow, we'll be away.'

'So tomorrow's the big day?'

'Our first job. Take-off!' I declared. 'Two little dogs to Spain. Bob is picking them up at a.m. two and bringing them here for the fit-to-fly, so we can go over the paperwork together. Then it's just a quick drive to Gatwick and we're sorted.'

Sheila's eyes narrowed suspiciously. 'Gatwick?' she said. 'So you'll be leaving me at what time?'

'Don't worry,' I said – though perhaps there was a note of worry in my voice. 'Cords is going to cover me for a couple of hours while I drive to the airport with Bob.'

Sheila nodded. 'And when you go on this Kenya trip you were mentioning, Bob will have to work here *and* do the drives to the airport?'

'There's only one other dog booked for this month,' I said. 'It's a Belgian Shepherd going to New Zealand. By the time we've got these two little ones on their way tomorrow, we'll have the hang of it.' I glanced up at the clock. It had just gone midnight.

'Right,' I said. 'I'm going to phone George's owners and tell them to pick him up in the morning. They'll be waiting for the call. Then, hopefully, I'll grab a few hours' kip before Bob arrives.'

It was the kiss-of-death statement: no sooner had I finished speaking than the phone rang. Sheila looked at me crossly. 'You cursed it!' she said accusingly, lifting the receiver.

I sighed and listened as she took the details, her face breaking into a smile.

'Excuse me a moment, the vet is right beside me. It may be best if you speak to him directly.' Her eyes sparkled as she passed me the receiver.

'Who is it?' I mouthed.

Sheila shook her head, clearly enjoying the moment. She tossed the phone to me and I had no choice but to reach out obligingly.

'Hello,' I began. 'Luke speaking, one of the vets, how can I help?'

'My snake!' a squeaky voice replied.

'Your snake?'

'Yes, my snake!' the caller persisted. 'It's not right.'

I waited for the titters of laughter that were sure to follow down the line as I replied tiredly, 'What's wrong with your snake?'

Student practical jokes happened towards the end of term – last week we'd had a caller phone at dead of night to tell us that his ducks had all flown away.

'I think it's constipated,' continued the voice. 'Is that a problem?'

'Your snake's constipated, is it?' I repeated, mainly for the benefit of Sheila, who was busy laughing and presumably texting Holly with the latest news.

'Yes, very constipated,' replied the caller.

'Well, that sounds like a critical emergency,' I said, still waiting for the explosion of laughter that was sure to follow. 'I'm afraid it's going to be quite expensive but anyone with a constipated snake needs urgent veterinary help. If you can get down here within twenty minutes, I'll be able to see you – but I'll need two hundred pounds in cash before I get hands-on.'

'You're used to handling a big snake?' asked the voice.

This was going too far. I took a deep breath and then calmed myself; it was only a bit of fun by a drunken student. I was almost definitely on a loudspeaker in some flat somewhere. 'Yes,' I said. 'I'm used to handling a big snake, if that's what you want to hear.'

No laughter, no audible sniggering. I frowned. The line went dead.

'A constipated snake!' Sheila laughed, wiping a tear from her eye. 'That was worth a midnight call.'

'You know what?' I said pensively. 'Normally they burst out laughing, but this time she just hung up. What if it was real?'

'You can't be serious!' Sheila exclaimed. 'Who phones the vet at midnight to say their snake is constipated? That was the best prank call yet, if you ask me. Even better, you seem to be falling for it!'

Unable to help myself, I smiled. It was ridiculous; of course it was a joke. Shaking my head, I mumbled goodnight to Sheila, and with a quick last-minute check on the dog, I turned to leave and catch a couple of hours sleep.

Just as I did so, the doorbell rang.

'Who could this be?' Sheila said, a hint of exasperation in her voice. 'Unless their animal is literally gasping its last, they're about to get short shrift for not phoning us first.' Calmly, she headed off to answer the door.

Partly curious, and partly to make sure Sheila wasn't about to be confronted by our drunken practical jokers, I followed her along the corridor, slowing to listen as she answered the door.

'Are you the nurse for the vet I was just speaking to a few minutes ago?' said a familiar voice.

My stomach lurched.

'I've brought my snake,' she said. 'And I've got your money too. I only live round the corner and, since you said it was critical, I dashed over here as quickly as I could.'

I heard Sheila swing the door open wider.

'Of course,' she said. 'I'm Sheila, the nurse. Please come in and I'll get the vet for you immediately.'

Fighting the urge to turn and run upstairs, lock the door and pretend to be invisible, I waited for Sheila to return down the corridor, an expression of horror on her face. 'It's huge!' she mouthed at me, passing me a consent form as she did so.

There was no escape. Bracing myself, I walked into the consulting room and opened the door.

The snake was about four feet long and was draped around the neck of a grey-haired lady, who regarded me from the other side of the waiting room with a worried expression. Dressed completely in black, her appearance was striking, to say the least. I beckoned her into the room.

'Hello,' I said apologetically. 'I, er, thought you were joking on the phone just now.'

'Joking?' the lady replied, clearly a bit agitated as she took a seat.

I fumbled mentally with how to deal with the emergency in front of me. 'Yes, we don't get emergency calls like that every day.' I smiled.

'She's in a terrible way!' the lady replied, clearly too bereft to acknowledge my hopeless attempt at small-talk. 'I really think she needs urgent help.'

I glanced down at the consent form Sheila had given me.

'Miss Trehin,' I began, 'I can see Pansy is a Royal Python, but what's the problem exactly?'

'Oh, it's wonderful you know what sort of snake she is – every other vet I've seen insists she's a Rock Python. What a relief.' For the first time, Miss Trehin's thin lips spread in a smile.

Too late, I realised I'd got myself into potentially deep water. I knew what type of snake Pansy was only because I had lived with Sam at university and he had gone through a snake-keeping phase, owning about ten baby Royal Pythons at one stage. I had picked one up in the past, but my veterinary knowledge was sketchy to say the least.

Carefully lifting Pansy from around her neck, Miss Trehin held her out towards me. Gingerly, I reached forward with both hands and the snake immediately twisted round to look at me.

'She's very aggressive at the moment,' I heard Miss Trehin say. 'That's why I think something's stuck.'

I nodded, just as Pansy seemingly realised she was no longer coiled around Miss Trehin's neck. Suddenly she tightened around my arms and, as my eyes widened in surprise at her strength, her head lifted up to look at me and coiled back in a classic strike pose. While python bites aren't poisonous, they can still give a nasty 'suck'. Helpless, I stood there, transfixed, silent and bracing myself for the bite that was about to happen – desperately hoping it wouldn't be on the face.

'Are you hypnotising her?' Miss Trehin said.

I said nothing. Pansy remained poised. Miss Trehin looked on and, out of the corner of my eye, I saw her expression soften.

'My goodness, she already looks more relaxed,' I heard her say.

Unable to move, I was vaguely aware of Sheila entering the room behind me, gasping.

'This is the brightest Pansy has been for days!' Miss Trehin gleefully declared. 'I've been worried to death, but she's really come alive.'

'He's very good with snakes,' Sheila said, edging around me and moving to stand next to Miss Trehin. Meanwhile, I locked eyes with Pansy, knowing any sudden movement would trigger her to strike.

My arms were aching where the snake had bound them together. Without a hand free, I was unable to do anything about the situation.

'Has she eaten recently?' Sheila asked.

'She had a frozen mouse about ten days ago and I've been worried that it was stuck as she hasn't shown any interest in anything since. That's why I thought she was constipated – until now. But she seems to have got her appetite back! Look at her – she looks hungry, doesn't she?'

'She does look hungry. Don't they get active at night?' Sheila asked.

'Oh, yes,' Miss Trehin replied. 'Now is the time they hunt. To be honest, I haven't had her that long – maybe that's part of the problem. Look how alive she is! It's all a bit of a learning curve, I guess.'

'How long have you owned her?' Sheila asked suddenly.

'Oh, she was my brother's – but he moved to Australia and I took her on.'

'Every two weeks . . .' I whispered, out of the corner of my mouth.

'What was that, Luke?' Sheila said, looking at me.

'Feed an adult every two weeks,' I hissed. 'She wasn't eating before because she wasn't hungry.' I paused. 'Now she's hungry.'

Pansy, sensing the nervousness in my voice, seemed to tense and lifted her head fractionally higher, looking me straight in the eye.

'Oh – you mean I was trying to feed her too soon after her last meal!' Miss Trehin exclaimed.

I didn't trust myself to nod. My arms were burning and the snake was still on the edge of striking me.

'I'll take her home and feed her then. Maybe tonight's the

night. But, whatever you've done, it's made all the difference to her. Thank you so much.'

With a grateful smile, Miss Trehin held out her arms to take Pansy.

My eyes darted to Sheila, who was standing back against the wall. She offered me a warm smile but, understandably, made no move to help. I twitched. Certain that Pansy was about to lunge, I let out a deep sigh when Miss Trehin's hands enclosed her neck and eased her away.

'She's wrapped round your arms quite tightly, isn't she?' Miss Trehin said, struggling to take hold of her snake.

Pansy, as bewildered as I was, suddenly relaxed. She allowed herself to be slung around Miss Trehin's neck and frog-marched out of the room. As Sheila went to let her out of the building, I took a deep breath of fresh air.

'Miss Trehin!' I shouted.

Too late, I heard the front door slam.

'Miss Trehin!' I called, clattering through the surgery doors and racing into the dark.

'Yes?' a voice called back from across the road.

'Might not be a plan to wrap Pansy around your neck!' I cried.

That was the last I saw of Miss Trehin. After that, she just faded into the night.

The early-morning light feebly penetrated some heavy clouds as Bob and I sat in the car and waited for signs of activity within the large warehouse that loomed in front of us.

'You never said the dogs needed to be checked in four hours before the flight,' Bob said quietly.

'Only found out a couple of days ago,' I answered softly, the heavy feeling of fatigue numbing my conversation skills. 'Bit of a pain, isn't it?'

A moment's silence. There were no signs of life, the parking bays all empty.

'It'll be better weather than this in Spain,' Bob said, peering out of the window.

'Providing we're in the right place,' I replied.

Bob turned to look at me blankly before twisting round to glance at our passengers. The two Tibetan Terriers, sweet little dogs, were curled up on their vet beds in overly large crates, fast asleep on the back seat. They'd been no trouble and seemed more than content to have been boxed up and driven to the airport.

'If they don't make the flight, then I guess we're responsible for them until we find another flight to take them,' I said.

The pain of booking the flight had taken hours. Not knowing how the process worked, we'd had to phone repeatedly for advice on getting every detail right. I glanced down at the file on my lap. It was bulging with papers. 'Never thought this much paperwork would go into it,' I replied.

Bob had arrived at the surgery at four, having picked the dogs up from their owners at just after two. Sheila had been right: another emergency had come in for me at one o'clock, so both Bob and I were dribbling with exhaustion. With the help of a couple of super-strength cups of coffee, we'd done the fitness-to-fly examinations, checking each terrier thoroughly, and done our utmost to ensure they were comfortable in the crates. It had been something of an ordeal.

'Shall we take them out for a wee?' I asked.

'We did that half an hour ago, I think. A bit like me, they just want to kip.'

On our arrival at the live-animal export centre at Gatwick, we'd found no sign of life. No one answered the door and no other pet shippers had turned up. It was as if we'd found the most remote building in the airport complex and were just loitering outside.

'Different at Heathrow,' I said.

'Really?'

'Yep. I met up with Chris and he showed me. They have a huge animal reception centre, a super-organised team. Twenty-four-hour on-site staff, big place, very efficient.'

'Why is it so different at Gatwick, then?'

'No idea,' I replied, shifting in my seat uncomfortably.

'We're in the wrong place, aren't we?' Bob said, after a moment's pause.

I sat there, willing the fatigue to wash away. I had a huge day on after the dog delivery and had never envisaged it would be so emotionally draining. Both Bob and I had worried about the dogs every second since we'd picked them up. With the client heading to Spain on the same flight, if we didn't get the dogs aboard, there would be chaos.

Literally a moment before I suggested to Bob that we should recheck the directions for the twentieth time, a door swung open in front of us. Almost simultaneously, five vans appeared around us. Within minutes, what had been an empty parking bay was turned into a hive of activity. Crates, pets and people appeared from everywhere. Almost overwhelmed by the sudden burst of activity, Bob and I heaved ourselves from the car to unload our charges.

Amazingly, we were at the back of the queue. Gradually, we inched forwards, the two little dogs now awake and looking very bemused about the whole business. Twenty minutes later, we faced a red-faced, overweight Customs official, who glowered at us. 'Cutting it fine, aren't you?' he asked, reaching out a fat hand to take the file from me. 'Check in for pets was seven a.m.'

'We've been in the queue,' I responded wearily.

'Blimey, what's all this, then?' he said, leafing through the paperwork. 'Al!' he shouted.

A lanky figure sauntered up and peered at the papers. Bob and I both seemed to be holding our breath, dreading what might come next.

'New to this, are you?' Al said, out of the corner of his mouth, his eyes flickering across each page.

'Yes,' Bob said, his six foot three frame tensing defensively.

Something about his tone made the man look up. 'You've photocopied everything. You don't need half of this – you're wasting everyone's time,' he said, craning around us to look at our dog crates. 'Huge crates, over-bedded, total waste of money,' he sneered. 'You'll fold within the month. Mark my words.'

'The crates are all exactly on the button with International Air Transport Regulations,' I chipped in.

Bob looked at me. 'Are those rabbit IATA regulations?' he muttered, under his breath.

Al didn't seem to hear, just flicked through the papers before bending down to squint at the two little dogs. 'Sure they are,' Al tutted. 'Just far too big.'

As Bob and I waited for him to stamp the paperwork, another man came up behind us and started to load the crates onto a trolley.

'Hold on!' I protested. 'What are you doing?'

The man gave me a perplexed look. 'Well, they aren't going to walk onto the plane, are they?'

'Don't tip them – you'll spill the water!'

Bob nudged me 'What do you think happens when the plane takes off?' he asked. 'I only half filled the water containers – it's OK. When they tip it won't spill.'

'Genius,' I replied, bidding farewell to the two little dogs as they were wheeled airside, ready to be loaded.

'You'll make sure they go next to each other, will you?' I asked Al.

Al looked up at me, handing me the clipboard. 'Sensitive soul, are you?' he asked.

'Sensitive enough to get upset if you don't look after those dogs,' I said.

Bob stepped forward. 'If they could go next to each other, we'd really appreciate it,' he said, much more calmly than I might have managed.

Al looked from Bob to me and back again, shaking his head. 'Yeah, they'll go together,' he muttered. 'We're not ogres, you know.' He turned, dismissing us with a wave of the hand. 'Still be amazed if you don't go bust, though.' And, with that, he turned away and the door slammed.

Bob and I stood outside the once-again-deserted warehouse. 'They don't muck about with this, do they?' he said quietly, as we walked back to the car.

'No,' I replied.

'You say it's different at Heathrow?'

'Well, we've got the Belgian Shepherd due to fly in a couple of weeks from there,' I replied. 'You'll have to let me know.'

I was almost back at the car when I realised Bob hadn't followed. I looked over my shoulder. He was simply standing there, looking at me with his hands on his hips.

'What do you mean, let you know?' he asked. 'You're coming along, aren't you?'

'Bob,' I said, 'there's something I've been meaning to tell you.'

He inched closer to me. Some sixth sense told me to make sure I kept the car between him and me.

'What?' he asked.

'Well,' I said, 'have you ever heard of a country called Kenya?'

11
Mission Kenya

'Volcano eruptions would be hard,' Sam said, as we hunkered down in the Nairobi guesthouse.

Having flown in earlier that day, the two of us squeezed our legs under a battered round table and waited for Henry, the head Kenyan vet who was co-ordinating the veterinary-disaster response team.

'Volcanoes would indeed be tricky,' I said. 'So would nuclear disasters. But I don't think vets would be top of the list for an emergency response in those situations.'

Sam squinted. 'Now we're officially WVS Disaster Emergency Response,' he began, 'I want my own special badge and a list of emergencies you say we can and cannot do – otherwise I'll be all over the place. How about forest fires?'

'Are you taking this seriously?'

'Of course!' Sam exclaimed, earnestly. 'You've now dragged me to Kenya during a period of incredible political and civil unrest just to help you inject some cows. How can I not be serious? I seriously need help.'

I tried to ignore him. If he didn't want to come, he didn't

have to come. There was just something in him that propelled him into it. There was only one thing Sam loved more than helping animals and that was whingeing about helping animals.

'I thought about what Rob said,' I began, swiftly changing the subject.

'Which bit? The bit when you were out of the room and he told me to try and find an African witchdoctor who would clear your head of all the crazy voices that keep making us do stupid adventures?'

'No,' I said. 'About a fundraiser for WVS on the back of this trip. Something to really drive on the PR and flag up awareness. I'm going to do an Ironman triathlon . . .'

Sam rolled his eyes. 'Ironman?' he asked. 'Why not Steelman? Or Superman, for that matter? Or Batman? You fancy yourself as a bit of a hero, don't you?'

'A quick swim, a short cycle and a little jog,' I replied. 'Nothing to it. When we were on honeymoon, our safari guide was into them. I can nail it.'

Sam shook his head sadly. 'Let me get this straight,' he began. 'You confess that you run like a duck, and in all the time I've known you – the best part of ten years – you've probably never cycled more than five miles in one go.'

That much was true, but I didn't much care for what Sam was saying.

'I can ride a bike,' I said. 'And I like swimming. I also know I can run a marathon.' I passed him a bit of paper with the specifics of what the Ironman involved.

Clearing his throat, Sam read out: '"An Ironman triathlon is one of a series of long-distance triathlon races organised by the World Triathlon Corporation, consisting of a two-point-four-mile swim, a hundred-and-twelve-mile bike ride and a marathon run, raced in that order and without a break. There is usually a strict time limit of seventeen hours to complete the race, and all finishers must complete their marathon by midnight."'

He looked at me. 'Seriously,' he said, and for the first time I thought he was genuinely concerned, 'there are loads of tiny muscles in your back for cycling and we aren't talking about going down the road to the shops. Your safari guide was probably quite a fit bloke. You, my friend, are not. Ducks are not allowed in this sort of competition.'

'Well, I'm going to do it,' I muttered, snatching the paper back. 'We need something to get WVS some attention.'

'You've never even done a triathlon! What about spending time with your new wife?'

'I'm taking Cords to a concert when we get back from Kenya,' I replied.

'Wow, you romantic, you! What sort of concert?' Sam asked.

'Doesn't matter,' I replied, a bit too quickly. 'The point is, I have a plan to balance everything.'

'Does your plan allow for breakages and spillages? You won't be able to balance trying to train for an Ironman triathlon. You need to practise sweating – a lot.'

'This trip is good training,' I replied, feigning confidence. 'It's going to be endurance.'

'Endurance vaccinating cows and dogs?' Sam spluttered.

'And camels and goats,' I corrected.

'Camels?' Sam breathed, just as the door swung open and a friendly face beamed at us.

I ignored him and turned to meet the new arrival. 'Henry?' I asked, standing and returning the warm greeting.

'Luke, it is good to meet you. This must be Sam?'

'My goodness, you're being nice to me from the off! What's going on?' Sam asked.

Henry looked at him, a little confused.

'Henry, thank you for all your help,' I said quickly, as we sat down and a waiter brought over a tall glass of Coke.

'Not a problem at all, Luke.' Henry smiled. 'Thank *you* both for coming. Your help is very much welcomed and we can do a lot of good. I think this is fantastic. We can really get cracking up there.'

'Oh, no.' Sam groaned. 'Henry's an African version of *you*!'

Henry had just come from a meeting with Jean and Jos, who represented two large animal-protection charities based in Nairobi, the Kenyan Society for the Protection of Animals, the KSPCA, and the Africa Network for Animal Welfare or ANAW for short. Both charities, he explained, were very much supporting this venture and Jos's charity, ANAW, would be sending vehicles with us.

'I'll be coming from the university and the government minister for animal welfare is also coming along. Quite a convoy!' Henry laughed.

'Quite a convoy for the WVS Disaster Emergency Response team of two,' Sam said quietly.

I nudged him under the table. 'Here's a copy of our plan,' I said, spreading out the paperwork on the table. 'Quite action-packed, I think you'll agree.'

Sam took one look at it and blanched. On the paper was a list of the twelve IDP/resettlement camps we were planning to visit. Over his shoulder, Henry scrutinised it seriously. 'We should try to get to all these camps,' he said. 'It's important to spread our aid. Otherwise, it won't be perceived well by all the other agencies who have to distribute their help.'

'How many people are in these camps?' Sam blurted. 'And do they really need vets?'

Henry seemed to understand the question. 'We're about to find out for sure,' he calmly replied. 'But, yes, they need vets. I've visited the camps during the preparations and there are a lot of animals. Diseases are spreading. There are lots of humanitarian aid agencies – all struggling – but no veterinary help.'

In brief, the formation of the IDP camps was a direct result of the eruptions of violence during post-election unrest – warring tribes had fought over land redistribution issues dating back to Kenyan independence in 1963, neighbours turned on each other, and normally peaceful communities had erupted into vicious and violent battlegrounds. In the previous three months, more than twelve hundred people had been killed, and property worth billions of Kenyan shillings had been destroyed. At least 350,000 people had been displaced from their homes. Hundreds of thousands had fled to the sanctuary of camps run by the Red Cross, manned and protected by the Kenyan Army and the UN. All of this in a country normally viewed as a bastion of economic and political stability in a volatile part of Africa.

The camps were getting bigger; managing such a mass of people was proving overwhelming for all concerned. Three months on, no one in the camps felt safe enough to go home and the Kenyan government was generally perceived to be sitting on the fence as to whether the instigators of the violence had committed a punishable crime.

Jos's charity had said that the animal-welfare crisis was a flashpoint. Many cattle had been stolen and, since the people in the camps were mainly from pastoral communities, they depended on their farms and livestock for their livelihood. Without them, they had absolutely nothing – and those animals that remained were all corralled in the camps. They were the only things keeping some families from starvation. Disease was a huge anxiety: an outbreak of Foot and Mouth would wreak absolute devastation among the remaining animal population.

'So, you two will be the first foreign vets granted permission to work here since independence in 1963,' Henry declared suddenly.

'Is that for ever?' Sam said, with a smile.

'No, just while you are in the IDPs.' He laughed. 'But it makes life easier to get in the camps.' He paused. 'I don't mean to pry, but how did you find the funding for this?'

I took a deep breath. 'Things have happened at breakneck speed, Henry. WVS has had a couple of very generous benefactors who believe in us enough to fund a team. They trust us not to squander any resources.'

'Basically, one of Luke's mad clients coughed up,' Sam added helpfully. 'And, of course, a mysterious philanthropist called Steve.'

'We're under a bit of pressure not to let our supporters down – they have gone out on a limb of blind trust to support us in this and we need to ensure we do some good rather than end up performing a PR stunt that will make us look ridiculous,' I added.

'You won't look ridiculous,' Henry said firmly. He pulled a map of Kenya from the pile of papers and pointed at a large red dot in the centre. Concentric circles emanated from it. 'The epicentre of this unrest is Eldoret,' he began. 'This is right in the heart of the Rift Valley province, and more than a hundred and twenty thousand people have been displaced in this region alone. This is where we're going, right into the heart of things. We'll set up a mobile outreach clinic and treat as many animals as we can. I promise you, it will be very well received.'

'It's been months since the unrest, though,' Sam said, rubbing his eyes with fatigue. 'Surely people are starting to go home now.'

Henry shook his head sadly. 'They're just too scared,' he replied. 'It's neighbours turning on neighbours simply because their names say they belong to a different tribe. The government is trying to establish the resettlement camps as halfway houses to allow people to stay in a secure compound at night, yet return to their farms in the day to try to rebuild their lives. They're all still at capacity.'

'So we're going to the camps and then we can still assist with the Pokot problem?' I asked, casting a quick glance towards Sam. He didn't know about the extra trip I had tacked onto the end of our visit to help a tribe in northern Kenya that was suffering an outbreak of goat plague.

'Hang on!' Sam snapped. 'You mean you have another plan for us in addition to the camps?'

Henry laughed and looked at Sam with a smile. 'Your friend is quite spunky, isn't he?' he said to me.

'Oh, yes, he's my spunky friend – never leave home without one,' I replied. Much to Sam's chagrin, Henry laughed louder.

'And so it begins,' Sam muttered.

'Yes,' Henry exclaimed, still wearing a thick smile. 'After the camps, we'll go to the East Pokot district and assist with the goat vaccination project – but only for two days at the end of our work here.' Pausing, he pulled out yet another piece of paper. 'Here is the internal memo that has been circulated within my department,' he said, turning it towards us:

Internal Memo – Kenyan Veterinary Disaster Response Team

WVS Disaster Response Collaboration

Specifically pastoral communities comprise the IDPs where livestock and working equines are key assets to said affected communities on which they have complete economic dependence. The purpose of the Kenyan Veterinary Disaster Response Unit is to collaborate with International Veterinary NGOs, namely Worldwide Veterinary Service, to set up and provide a sustainable aid programme to affected areas.

Whilst appreciating that this programme has to be approached with a grounded perspective and clear sensitivity to the fact we are attempting to promote animal welfare issues in areas of extreme human plight and suffering, initial talks with several humanitarian aid agencies as well as preliminary visit to the areas, including meetings with Local Veterinary Inspectorates, has indicated veterinary response teams could be of use. Specifically, Eldoret refugee camps where large concentrations of people and animals have been brought together in confined situations due to displacement through conflict.

The collaborative team will also target the East Pokot District to initiate a 5000-goat vaccination programme against goat plague.

Sam and I scanned the memo.

'We'll pick up the vaccines tomorrow morning,' Henry said. 'Then we drive there and set up the clinic.' He eyeballed us with a gleeful look. 'We leave at dawn. And don't forget to pack all your things. We won't be back here until the end of your trip – we have fifteen hundred miles to cover before then.'

Before he had finished speaking, Henry was almost out of the door.

'Wait!' Sam called, halting him in his tracks. 'Where will we be staying when we get to Eldoret?'

'I don't know yet,' Henry admitted. 'But we'll find somewhere.' With a wave, he left us.

In his wake, Sam looked at me accusingly. 'Tell me you aren't booking us into a refugee camp for ten days.'

His face was a picture.

'Get some sleep, pal,' I replied, elusively. 'A comfy bed is going to be the last of our concerns with this one.'

Henry arrived at six a.m. on the dot, clutching several oranges and bottles of water, which he handed to us once we'd loaded up the vehicles. ANAW had organised a convoy of jeeps. Sam and I warily eyed the green machine we were directed to.

'We will go first to pick up the vaccines and supplies I have ordered through the university,' Henry said, as we clambered in. 'Then we go on.'

'It's got three doors,' Sam said to me, as we scrambled inside. 'Never been in a car with three doors.'

'It's a custom,' I replied. 'Regard yourself as privileged.'

The owners of the vehicle, deciding they didn't like the conventional two-door version, had put an extra door at the back on the left for easy access. The whole jeep had been welded together, piece by piece, and even the windows weren't properly aligned.

'Does this jeep have suspension?' Sam wondered, as we began to bounce around. Even I was darkly aware that this was only the start of an eight-hour journey on unmade roads.

'It's a custom, remember!' shouted Henry from the front, with a broad grin.

Heading north-west from Nairobi, I gazed out the window at the breadbasket of Africa. The Rift Valley, one of the world's largest battle scars seen from space, stretches from Ethiopia to Mozambique, and I marvelled at the lush fertile plains, the sweeping escarpments and the stunning views as we drove past Lake Nakuru and beyond, towards Eldoret and the Ugandan border. The basin of the valley was home to some of Africa's most spectacular wildlife: flamingos lined the famous freshwater lakes, and the forested slopes were home to rhinos, giraffes and other large mammals.

Out in the rural countryside, it was difficult to appreciate the turmoil the nation was in, the hardships of the people, all of whom seemed to look at us with smiling faces, their heads piled high with fruit or clothes, babies wrapped on their backs in bright sarongs and scarves.

It was only as we started to approach the city that the real signs of the recent unrest became apparent. As the convoy pulled over for a rest stop, Sam and I climbed out of the jeep. While Sam wandered off to stretch his legs, I turned to look a hundred yards up the road in the opposite direction. A burnt-out truck half blocked one lane, its blackened shell a symbol of the recent struggles and violence.

'They started to throw things at it,' Henry said, following my gaze and coming to stand beside me, 'so the man at the wheel tried to drive away.'

'What happened?' I asked quietly.

'They threw spikes to burst the tyres. Then they torched it.'

'Why?'

Henry's voice betrayed little emotion. 'The driver was from the wrong tribe in the wrong place.'

'Did he escape?'

Henry shook his head. 'Nowhere to run,' he said. 'It was a mob.'

I shook my head in disbelief.

'It could have been worse,' Henry said. 'He could have had his family with him in the truck – they often do. But, according to the people who told me this, he was alone.'

'Such a terrible death,' I said.

'You will hear many sad stories where we are going, Luke. This is a sad place.'

We stood in silence for a long time. Somewhere, Sam was idling in circles. I was beginning to wonder what I had taken us into.

'How far to go?' I asked, suddenly apprehensive.

'The camp is close,' Henry replied. 'It is in an old football stadium, and this one has eight thousand people. But, according to Jos, there is another a bit further on – smaller, only five thousand or so. We may go there first – they have all the animals ready for us.'

'Ready for us?'

'Oh, yes, they will all be ready for us. Two of Jos's workers, Isaac and Frank, have gone ahead to liaise with the camp managers and the headmen. If we are to do any work today, it must be a fast job. We cannot stay in the camps after it gets dark. It's just too dangerous. Those people with nothing have nothing to lose. We'll never get through all the animals at Eldoret in one afternoon.'

We climbed back into the vehicles and travelled for another half-hour. Throngs of people lined the streets, many clustered in groups who turned sullenly to watch our small convoy drive past. The other vehicles on the road were invariably humanitarian aid agency trucks, and Sam and I felt a sense of apprehension that perhaps we had got things terribly out of perspective by coming out here to help as vets.

'What are you going to say to the camp manager?' Sam asked me, in all seriousness, as we drove through the first wave of guarded barriers to pull up outside the office of the first IDP. Getting out of the jeep to follow Henry to the administration centre, I didn't know how to answer.

As we wove between Red Cross and Médecins Sans Frontières vehicles, I floundered for a suitable response. I contemplated the situation. I'd pretty much frog-marched Sam on a mission to the camps in an effort to launch the first WVS Emergency Disaster Response team. While it had seemed a great idea in principle, now that we were here, it was fairly clear that the people around us had slightly more pressing matters on their minds than worming the camp dogs and vaccinating their cows.

I glanced at a sea of UNICEF tents that stretched into the distance through the wire fence, preparing myself to fake some sort of spectacular collapse. When the camp manager asked me what on earth we hoped to achieve, arriving at this crush of desperate humanity with a stethoscope and bottle of pen:strep, I was all set to reply, 'I'm here to save the cats,' and then to start wheezing and staggering.

Instead, the man inside the makeshift office rose and held out a hand in friendly greeting. We crowded around his ramshackle desk, each shaking his hand in turn.

As Henry and the camp manager chatted in Shona, I looked at the map and pie charts pinned up on the walls. My eyes were drawn to one in particular. It depicted the main causes of death within the camp – malaria, worms and dental disease accounted for what appeared to result in over 95 per cent of mortality.

Seemingly pleased to meet us, the camp manager radioed ahead, then led us back out into the compound. He beckoned Henry, Sam and me to walk with him, while the rest of our team drove through the second set of barriers. Once there, they were directed to drive round the back of the tents to the other side of the camp.

'We're not driving?' Sam asked.

'The manager thought we'd like to see the camp,' Henry replied, 'so he's walking us through the middle to the other side. The cattle enclosure, the *boma*, is over there.'

Nudging through a queue of starving women and babies, all patiently waiting to be weighed and measured to see if they qualified for extra food rations, was something I never imagined myself doing. I had seen such scenes on TV, with news reports of famine and devastation, but had never imagined I'd witness one at first hand. The whole perspective of what we were doing crashed around me and I shared a tight-lipped look with Sam.

'These tents look big,' Henry told us, 'but they're subdivided inside – one end for one family, a sheet in the middle, and another family at the other end.'

'How many in a tent?' I asked.

The camp manager grinned at me, understanding my

question. 'We suggest a maximum of five,' he said. 'You can just about get five in with nothing else. But there are often many more.'

Small cooking areas were neatly defined outside each tent, all of which were in long rows with channels crudely dug for drainage.

'Sanitation is our biggest problem,' the camp manager explained. 'There's also a lot of crime at night – rape is a big problem. The children are very vulnerable.'

These were all words I didn't want to hear, but I couldn't block them out. This was the reality of life here, where the people had no help, no aid and little protection.

'No one reports anything,' the camp manager went on. 'We can't risk it. We do what we can, but it is hard to deal with it.'

Small children began to flock around us, clutching at our hands and beaming up at us with big bold smiles. Thick clots of snot hung under their eyes. They had stick-thin arms, were barefoot and dressed in rags – the only clothing they possessed in the world.

Gone were the sweeping vistas and sun-baked soil of magical Africa. Instead, we had arrived at some sort of human hell. The people in the camp truly had lost everything. It was hopeless to attempt to contemplate how they would rebuild their lives, given that their own communities and friends had turned against them.

'We had bad rains a few days ago,' the camp manager said, a hint of apology in his voice. 'The *boma* got a little flooded.'

'It's not a problem,' I croaked, still wrestling with the ludicrous situation in which Sam and I had arrived.

'Wait until you see it,' Henry said quietly.

A long block of tents indicated the periphery of the other

side of the camp. Our vehicles were parked adjacent to them and Frank and Isaac were unloading our equipment. Drench guns and water were being brought from somewhere to make up the tick sprays.

'The toilet block,' Henry said. 'The *boma* is behind it.'

Sam looked at me, about to make a quip, but changed his mind and, instead, smiled at one of the children who had trailed us all the way across the IDP.

It was the end of the rainy season, which meant that there were still showers that came down hard and fast. The driving rain could stab bullets of water into the skin and drench everyone in seconds. Rivers of mud would suddenly ravage the camps as drainage channels overflowed and the camp manager was apologising, not for the mud we were about to wade through but because it was clear that the toilet block had flooded the *boma*.

A thick mixture of mud and excrement had pooled at the edges of the toilet block as we trudged around it to look at the animals we had come to treat. Expecting to find ten or twenty, I was seething with myself for being so misguided; all that energy, effort and money raised into getting medicines to help a few sheep, goats and cattle when there were literally thousands of desperate people who needed so much help. I could have kicked myself, but managed to rein myself in.

I looked across at the children and adults who had gathered into a small crowd around us, all oblivious to the filth we were walking in. Suddenly, I felt ashamed – I was concerned about the muck but at least I had boots on.

It wasn't until we got right round to the other side of the tents that things seemed like they might change. Our efforts suddenly seemed like they might have a valid purpose.

Instead of the three or four sheep I'd half expected to be aimlessly wandering around, there were suddenly hundreds of cattle, all corralled into a large, makeshift *boma*, patiently awaiting our arrival. Goats and sheep were tethered to wooden stakes around the edges, with their owners clamouring for us to ensure their animals had their drench, pour-on and vaccinations.

In spite of everything, I felt a deep wave of relief. Suddenly we were in the zone and could do something useful.

Sam and I looked at each other with grins that could split our faces. The ever-stoical Sam, whose least favourite discipline was working with livestock, had suddenly come alive. As he laughed, all the children surrounding him laughed and clapped.

With big smiles, we knuckled down and got on with the job. Five hundred animals awaited us, and we powered on with the work, a huge weight of doubt about the ethics of the trip seemingly lifted from our shoulders. Our plan was to vaccinate all the animals within the camps against diseases such as Foot and Mouth and lumpy skin disease, which threatened to spread within the enclosures. The animals flooding in and out of the camps were at significant risk to the spread of disease among a population that was normally spread out over miles and suddenly crammed together in giant herds.

Tick-borne diseases were rife, so we treated active cases, as well as drenching and spraying every animal we could find to get rid of all internal and external parasites. Dogs were caught up, flea and tick prevention applied and rabies vaccination administered. We similarly wormed and vaccinated any cats, and the donkeys had some foot attention and dewormer.

Although with Henry we were only three vets, our role was as much about the organisation of the people as it was about treating the animals. After the first couple of camps, we had the hang of it. Sick animals needing veterinary attention were directed to an area where one of us would be stationed, leaving another to manage and oversee the deworming, drenching, spraying and vaccinating; the third ran a small-animal clinic, treating and vaccinating the dogs and cats. There were twelve in our party, so Sam and I always had at least one, if not two, interpreters with us, who also assisted with treatments. Isaac and Frank worked tirelessly, going ahead of us to each camp to ensure the animals had been rounded up before we got there.

With only the best part of a couple of weeks to get through all the camps, we needed to be as efficient as possible and, by getting the headmen on-side, we invariably had more help than we could handle. Before we could blink, helping hands were pushing animals through makeshift races, assisting with spraying, ticking and vaccinating.

Working with the government made it easy to obtain the necessary permits to enter the camps and, as word spread between camp managers about our visits, we were welcomed everywhere we went. With little on-site amusement, huge crowds of children gathered round to watch us at work, cheering wildly and good-naturedly when a cow misbehaved or one of us tripped or dropped something.

'We're the hundred and nineteenth most dangerous country in the world out of a hundred and forty at the moment,' said a voice, as I fished in the coolbox for another 500-dose bottle of lumpy skin vaccine. I turned and looked up at an elderly man with a kind, patient face who had wandered over to see what we were up to. We were at the Endebess camp, which held approximately 6,500 people. Beyond him I could see Mount Elgon and the Ugandan border in the far distance.

'Better than a hundred and twentieth,' I replied, in a friendly tone.

'I think my flock have lost their way somewhat.' He smiled.

'Your flock?' I asked, casting my eyes around for an aberrant group of sheep that must have escaped the corral.

He laughed. 'No,' he said, shaking my hand. 'I am a pastor. My name is Fredrick. I meant my flock who came to my church.'

'What happened?' I heard myself say.

Fredrick's story was typical of those displaced during the political unrest. A local pastor in his village, where the Luhya and Sabaot tribes resided, Fredrick had regarded his community as interwoven and settled. In recent years, though, this had changed. Tensions surrounding a fifty-year-old government land-distribution law at the time of Kenyan independence had resurfaced and, suddenly, members of Fredrick's tribe, the Luhya, had found themselves victim to their Sabaot neighbours, who argued that the Luhya had no right to their ancestral village land.

There was no anger in Fredrick's voice, no hint of hatred for the people who had done this to him and other members of his tribe, just great sadness as he told me what had happened on that fateful day. A group had entered the village, a mob who were a faction of organised militia called the Sabaot Land Defence Force. They had shouted their intentions and stirred up passions so that the Sabaot residents had suddenly been encouraged to turn on their Luhya neighbours. Those siding with the mob were spared; those who didn't were at risk of attack, and anyone from the Luhya tribe was declared outcast and subsequently hunted, robbed, beaten or killed.

Everyone knew that Fredrick and his next-door neighbour were Luhya. His neighbour was targeted immediately and the mob, rapidly losing control and whipped up into a frenzy, had burst through the wall of Fredrick's hut as they ravaged the street. While the mob had begun stealing all of his belongings, Fredrick had herded his wife and eight children out of their home as quickly as possible. Collecting his three cows, they had fled the chaos as night descended.

'But we made it,' he said. 'We are safe. We are lucky.'

'How far away were you?'

'We ran fifteen kilometres. Some chased us – they even fired arrows at us. Miraculously, they missed. God was watching.'

'They fired arrows at you?' I asked, incredulous. It was like a story from the Dark Ages.

Fredrick nodded. 'Next week, I will take my three eldest children with me and try again.'

'You'll go back?' I asked, horrified.

Fredrick spread his hands wide. 'Where else?'

'The people who looted and robbed you – won't some of them still be in the village? Won't they just attack you again?'

It was, of course, something Fredrick had spent long hours deliberating. 'They'll all be in the village,' he said calmly. 'They'll still come to my church. I know them, I know their families, they will look at me with shame . . . but it was a difficult time.' He paused. 'When it is safe, I will send for my wife and my other children.'

I struggled to appreciate what Fredrick had been through, what he was planning to do and how he was coping. I felt ashamed that I had ever worried about anything. Compared to Fredrick and the people around me, I didn't even know what a problem was.

My look must have been dumbfounded, because he stepped forward and placed his hand on my arm. 'God forgives,' he said quietly, looking into my eyes.

I could do nothing but stand there in silence.

'You are doing good things here,' he said. 'It is very helpful. I wanted to thank you for treating and protecting my cows.'

I didn't know what to say. With a wave, Fredrick wandered back towards the tents from which he had come. I could only stand up, speechless, and watch him shuffle back. Elderly, limping and stick-thin, he had an inspiring strength and depth of character that I knew I would never forget. I felt choked by his gratitude to me for having just vaccinated his three cows. It had taken less than a minute.

Out of nowhere, Sam's voice broke into my reverie: 'Are you daydreaming again?'

'There aren't many animals at this one, are there?' I replied.

'No,' Sam said, wrinkling his nose. 'And the tents are a bit shabby. I reckon I'd go for that one we went to the other day, the one up on the hill. I like those dome tents, bit better ventilation, great view . . . If you get a pitch up the top of the slope you've got less worry about what could run into your tent.'

'They're partitioned, though,' I replied, our inane chat about what type of refugee tent would be best taking our minds off the situation around us. 'You've got a serious crowding issue. At least, with these ones, you have a tent per family. Give me USAID ones every time.'

'Depends if you get a tent,' Henry said, walking over to us. 'This one, at its peak, was very overcrowded. I'm afraid the likes of you would be on the ground. I'd go for the one we went to yesterday. Best toilets, lowest violence.'

'That was the one where they had the cannibalistic pigs, though,' Sam said.

One of the camps had had a small pigpen, crammed with pigs that were kept in their own filth and fed whatever was passed through the bamboo bars. Starving, squalid and hungry, they had started devouring each other through vicious tail biting. It was the grimmest animal-welfare case any of us had seen to date, most of the animals having been kept as carefully as possible until then by their desperate owners.

'The man was mortified by your concern for the pigs,' Henry said. 'He'll do something about the situation for sure. But, yes, that was the camp I would choose.'

It had been so difficult to berate a man who was living in conditions almost as bad as the pigs. He was already giving them half of his own rations in an attempt to keep them alive.

'Those animals weren't long for this world,' I said. 'The man knew he couldn't keep them like that. He was going to slaughter them, I think.'

Henry nodded, thoughtfully. He had found it as difficult as we had. Nothing could have prepared any of us for the experience of working in the camps.

'What's next?' Sam asked.

Henry cleared his throat. 'This is why I came to talk to you,' he said. 'Our next stop is the Pokot tribe to vaccinate the goats, but we have a request from the Eldoret camp manager. He wants us to run a dog vaccination programme. As people are leaving the camp in the day and coming back at night, they are being harassed by local dogs so, because there are not so many animals here, I was thinking we might vaccinate all the dogs this afternoon and go to the Pokot tomorrow.'

'You mean dogs outside the camps, in the town?' I asked.

Henry nodded.

'Run a clinic for the Sabaot?' I asked. I wasn't sure how I felt. 'The tribe that put a lot of these people in the IDP camps in the first place?'

Sam flickered a look between Henry and myself.

'It isn't just the Sabaot,' Henry explained. 'There are many tribes. It is much more complicated.' He hesitated. 'But, yes, we will run the clinic in the community of the warring tribes, the ones who controlled the mobs. It enforces our neutral aid position. The minister who is with us will approve of this very much. Politically, we should do this.'

Sam looked dubious.

'Come on, Sam,' I murmured. 'It'll be a change from all the livestock and, I suppose, vaccinating the dogs helps everyone.'

Henry walked forward and slapped him on the shoulder, laughing. 'Yes, come on, Sam! It will be as big a challenge as working here – those dogs will be a handful.'

'I'm trapped between a UK Luke and an African Henry.' Sam sighed. 'Resistance is futile.'

And, with that, we packed up the equipment and headed off.

'So, we need to find the headman for these guys first and then they'll bring all the dogs to us?' I asked Henry, as we jarred along a crowded street. The jeep's appalling suspension had totally given up the ghost a couple of days ago, and the going was rough.

'Yes,' Henry replied. 'The headman is the community leader. All the tribes function in the same way, but these people are somewhat more . . . forceful.' He was obviously choosing his words carefully.

'Where can we find him?' Sam piped up.

'He's right there.' Henry exclaimed, pointing out of the window at a rangy man who was leaning against the truck in front. 'He's talking to Isaac. They know all about us.'

Sam and I craned our heads to see. The man looked to be in his late twenties, with big goofy teeth. He was dressed in a Manchester United shirt. 'The UK football clubs get around, don't they?' Sam commented.

'English Premier League is bigger here than it is in England,' Henry laughed. 'Everyone here is either Manchester United or Arsenal at the moment.'

'A lot of Africans have played for Arsenal,' Sam said.

Henry and I turned to him, surprised.

'What?' I said.

'Vieira was born in Dakar, even though he played for France. Kanu was from Nigeria, Toure from Ivory Coast, and Adebayor is from Togo.'

Henry and I shared blank expressions and Sam sighed. 'Adebayor, Adebayor . . . Give him the ball, and he will score!' he chanted.

'*Mastermind*, here we come!' I grinned.

There was a sudden rap at the window. Sam and I jumped. Henry wound down his window and the rangy man poked his head in to say hello. He looked at us with yellow eyes and dazzling white teeth.

As he chatted to Henry about the mobile clinic we were going to set up, I cast my eyes around. Throngs of people walked past us, and shops – all dilapidated, with flaking paint – lined each side of the street. They were open for business, and the contrast with the IDP camps only just down the road couldn't have been more marked. We weren't in the city centre but in a suburb that linked up to the IDP and, although clusters of people were standing around doing nothing, there was a sense of purpose about the community that was lacking in the places we'd been immersed in for the last week. In the IDPs, the atmosphere had been of beaten despair; here, there was tension. A community on the edge of normality, an unpredictability hanging in the air – anything could happen at a moment's notice.

'Funny not seeing any security. I'm used to pitching up to these clinics through eight-foot wire with armed guards at the gates,' Sam said, echoing my thoughts.

'There are no police or army here,' Henry said quietly. 'That would cause trouble. It is like the Wild West at the moment.'

The headman stepped back and offered us a lopsided grin. Henry said something to him in parting, then drove forward to park in a big open square. Our little convoy formed a neat line and, as we unfolded ourselves from the vehicles and began to set up the clinic, the headman returned. Clutching a megaphone, he proceeded to announce who we were and what we were doing. He seemed to be making jokes between his announcements.

'He's a bit familiar on the megaphone, isn't he, Henry?' Sam said.

Henry frowned. 'He is a very young headman,' was all he said.

It was agreed that Henry would run the sick-animal station while Sam and I would take control of vaccination and deworming. Dogs quickly began to filter towards us; Frank and Isaac recorded people's names and directed them to one of the two lines. Within ten minutes, a huge queue of people curled down the street in front of me and Sam. Frantically, we tried to keep pace with the dogs presented.

Whatever the headman was or wasn't saying to the community, it was doing the job. The stream was constant and we were swamped with dogs, all of them dragged by chains, bits of wire and even old power cables. There was no joking, no children clapping. This was clean, methodical business – and, not only did we only have a few hundred vaccines, but time was against us to finish before dark.

'Henry!' I called across the crowd.

He bobbed up from a sea of dogs and people and gave me a cheerful wave.

'We're running low,' I shouted. 'I reckon only about fifty vaccines left.'

Henry's face twisted. 'I'm running low on meds too – a lot of these guys have wounds. We should get going in about half an hour, I think. I don't know where all these dogs are coming from.' He paused, darkly. 'They are not all from this community.'

Within moments, the headman was back on his megaphone and there was a sudden stirring in the crowd.

'What did he just say?' Sam looked up sharply. About six feet away from us a fight was erupting, two men jostling for position in the queue.

'No idea,' I said. 'But people are extra keen all of a sudden.'

Voices were raised all around us, as Frank, Isaac and a few of our team tried to calm things down. I felt a tap on my shoulder and looked around. Henry stood behind me, a worried expression on his face. 'The headman has told everyone we are leaving now,' he said, with a note of steel. 'They are shouting because they want their dogs vaccinated. I think we will need to do as many as we can.' He surveyed the crowd. 'But be ready to leave on my command. The mood is getting worse.'

'I thought we were leaving in half an hour,' I replied.

'I did not tell him to say this,' Henry said. 'He is quite impetuous, this fellow.'

Suddenly there were urgent shouts. Hands grappled out and plucked at my arms. Standing on my toes, I peered at the front of the queue. In the middle of a crowd, I could just about make out the shape of a dog lying in the dirt.

'Luke, be careful,' I heard Henry call out behind me as I pushed forward, clutching my stethoscope. 'Luke, it is frothing at the mouth.'

Sure enough, as the crowd widened I could see that the dog was convulsing on the dirt, a thin wire round its neck, as the owner stood nonchalantly beside it. Froth was spilling from the animal's mouth and, as I stepped closer, I could see its pupils begin to dilate. When I was only metres away, it gasped an agonised breath and convulsed violently in death.

I bent down to the dog, scruffing it. Careful not to spill any saliva, I gently lifted it and carried it through the crowd to our work station. Sam had appeared at my shoulder and gave me a worried look.

'They think it has rabies,' Henry said, as we approached.

'Maybe, but it was on a lead,' I said, bending down to see if there was any chance of reviving the poor animal. 'It must have been fine for them to bring it to us, and sudden frothing followed by death within the space of ten minutes doesn't fit with the disease.'

'Um, Luke . . .' Sam whispered, as a shadow fell over us.

'Has it got rabies?' the headman asked, poised to issue the news down his megaphone to the expectant crowd.

'It has died,' I replied. 'But I'm . . .'

Too late, the headman was blaring out the news that the

dog had died. I looked at the faces around us. The dog's owner was watching us intently.

Grabbing Henry, I asked him to talk to the owner and find out a bit of the dog's history.

'Headman,' I said. 'This dog didn't die of rabies. Please tell everyone not to panic.'

The headman looked at me with glazed eyes and raised his megaphone as Henry returned.

'He choked it,' Henry said.

'What?' Sam and I replied in unison.

'He is the brother of the man who owns the dog,' he explained. 'He tied it to the back of his bicycle and dragged it here. He choked it – that is why it was frothing. He has just told me. He pulled the dog because he thought we were leaving and he was told by his brother to get it treated for fleas.'

As the headman chatted away behind us, I shook my head in despair. The poor dog had been killed for free flea treatment. The brother of the dog's owner stood there, a neutral expression on his face, his hands in his pockets.

A chorus of cries had broken out in the crowd and I looked up to see Frank and Isaac hurriedly carrying the tables back to the jeeps and loading everything up in a hurry.

'I think you should go now,' the headman said, then switched to Shona to talk to Henry. Neither Sam nor I could understand his words, but there was no mistaking the urgency in his voice.

Henry cast me a fevered look. 'They are shouting that we killed the dog,' he breathed. 'That it had been treated by us and died as a result. There are some shouts that we are actually here to kill the dogs for the government.'

'Can't the headman tell them what happened?' I said dumbly.

I twisted round to see him prancing about, shouting again into his megaphone and waving his hands in the air. No one was listening and the atmosphere in the crowd had suddenly turned.

'He doesn't have the authority,' Henry said firmly. 'We have to leave *now*.'

The government minister, who had been observing the clinic from the edge of the square, was being escorted back to the jeeps by Frank and Isaac, a crowd of people around them shaking their fists, screaming unintelligible curses.

'This is insane!' I cried, feeling a swell of anger myself. 'Just tell them what happened! Can't the man who choked it tell them?'

'Quickly, Luke!'

Already at the door of the jeep, Sam gave me a jagged look. 'Luke, get your backside into that jeep. This lot are seriously unhappy.'

I stood stock still.

'If we dash off, doesn't that make us look guilty?' I protested.

Henry marched towards me, pulled my arm and dragged me towards the vehicles. 'We must not run, just keep moving,' he said. Up ahead, the first of our convoy was leaving. People clamoured at its sides. I watched as hands banged on the vehicle. Slowly, it forced its way through the crowd.

'If we aren't quick, they won't let us through,' Sam said.

Throwing the last couple of bags into the jeep, Sam and I climbed in. Up front, Henry started the engine. Before the door had fully closed, we were moving. Henry's hand hovered over the horn.

There was a sudden crack. A sudden smash. Fists slammed on the roof and the windows, angry faces loomed above us.

A stone whipped against the door, and I felt the dull thud where it struck the metal.

'Brilliant,' Sam muttered. 'We get to experience our very own mob. You don't get this on your standard African safari package.'

Suddenly a clump of people were in front of the car. There looked to be no way through. I took a quick look at Sam. 'Sorry, pal,' I said.

'Jane's going to kill you.'

'If Cords doesn't get there first . . .'

The crowd had us penned in – but just when it seemed inevitable that Henry would need to slow down, there erupted some deep, throaty shouting. The crowd froze for a second. It was long enough for us to nudge through the deadlock, find some empty space and accelerate away.

'What went on there?' I asked. 'I thought they had us.'

Henry was clearly shaken. He risked a look in the mirror – and only when he was satisfied that we were clear did he take a moment to answer. 'I think they were militia telling them to let us through,' he said. 'Politically, killing you would cause them many problems. For once, we were lucky that they were there.'

'Saved by the baddies,' Sam said, and closed his eyes.

'Wow! I guess we won't be going back in a hurry.' I laughed, the relief flooding through me.

A deep grin erupted on Henry's face. 'I think we have done our political bit now – and we still vaccinated several hundred dogs, so the mission was a success. We'll go off tomorrow to see the Pokot. This will be an adventure.'

'They're out of all this, aren't they?' Sam chipped in.

'The Pokot?' Henry chuckled. 'The Pokot are a warring tribe, for sure – but they aren't armed like these tribes. They don't use arrows and stones.'

'Now, that is the magical Kenya we all know and love,' Sam said. 'Proper friendly African tribes out in the bush.'

'Indeed,' Henry said, with a twinkling laugh. 'They all have AK47 machine guns instead.'

It was a quiet journey back to the guesthouse.

12
Hard to Handle

An elderly Pokot man, hard-faced and wearing a green hat with a feather tucked into it, whistled at me while signalling with his hands, clearly frustrated that I couldn't understand.

'I don't know what he means,' Henry said apologetically. 'He's speaking Pokot.'

'Guess that makes sense for a member of the Pokot tribe,' Sam commented.

I looked around for inspiration. The three of us stood among a sea of goats we had just vaccinated. The animals crowded around us, then began to bleat as two young girls in red vests, with the lines of tribal scars down their backs, herded them away. I glanced to our left, where a group of women stood in a small group, huge, thick-beaded necklaces adorning them, offset by six or seven gold rings dangling loosely from elongated ear lobes. They chuckled to themselves as they watched us.

'This region is Africa's most remote frontier,' I heard Henry tell Sam.

He was right. We had driven for ten hours to the

north-west border of Kenya where the situation we had got into was almost worse than the dog-vaccination programme we had tried to run for the Sabaot in Eldoret.

Lured in, under the impression we were helping an impoverished remote tribe fight an outbreak of goat plague, we had been surprised when an army convoy had rendezvoused with us for the final two-hour leg of the journey. Henry had tried to tell us it was routine when travelling so close to the border, but when pressed, he had been forced to admit that he had been kept in the dark as to how volatile the region was. It seemed that his joke from the previous afternoon had been in poor taste, and the Pokot really did have automatic weapons.

We had travelled from the frying pan into the fire. The Pokot, it transpired, were a nomadic tribe, depending utterly on the survival of their cattle and goats for their own existence. In an area where there were absolutely no schools, medical facilities or tarmac roads, the lawless land was rife with cattle and goat rustling. The goat plague that was ravaging the population wasn't the result of an endemic disease flaring up – more the fact that the Pokot had crossed the Sudanese border, killed some goat herders and stolen their goats, thus introducing goat plague to their own herds. Having brought the animals back, they now had a crisis on their hands, especially as the recent rainy season had bypassed the region so water was a huge issue for the plants, animals and people of the area. The drought had brought everyone together into several key spots – which meant that the plague could flourish.

The old Pokot man gestured again. Unsure what else to do, I nodded sympathetically.

It seemed to be the signal the man was after because he

turned and waved for me to follow him. Casting a sideways glance at Henry and Sam, I shrugged and moved forwards.

As I did so, my phone rang loudly. Its piercing noise made everyone jump and the elderly man spun to look at me. Even the chattering women stopped talking. As I looked down at my phone, I felt tens of pairs of eyes fix on me.

'You phoned Cords last night and didn't switch it off, didn't you?' Sam sighed.

'Incredible where you get reception, isn't it?' I said, nodding to Sam as I instinctively pushed the green button to answer the call.

'That is going to cost you a fortune!' Sam hissed.

'Hello,' I said.

The voice at the other end of the line was not my wife's.

'Hello, Luke,' it began. 'It's Judy Conelson. I have a problem with one of my ducks. I wonder if you could help me?'

I looked up: sand and scrub, goats and Pokot. I was as far away from troublesome pet ducks as I could imagine.

'Hi,' I began. 'You won't believe this but I'm actually talking to you from Kenya. The phone should have been on divert to my friend Rob, who is covering the practice, but I forgot to switch it off last night. I'm currently surrounded by thousands of goats who belong to the Pokot tribe right up on the north-western border of the country.'

Ms Conelson, oddly, did not seem in the least surprised. She barely even chuckled. 'Oh, really? That's lovely! Do they look like Masai?'

'There are a few similarities,' I replied, catching Sam rolling his eyes. 'They have the long ear lobes.'

'That's fascinating, Luke, just fascinating!' She sounded thrilled. 'While I've got you, though, I was wondering if you might be able to give some advice about a duck. It has a split beak, you see, right on the underside. It can get some food in but it just keeps falling out. The problem is that its lower beak has a huge gap in it, like a split down the middle.'

As Ms Conelson spoke, I could hear the blare of the television in the background and the familiar grunting of a tennis match in mid-flow. 'I'm worried this call will be costing you a fortune,' I said.

'Oh, not to worry, dear! I'll look forward to hearing all about your adventure when you're back – but I am very concerned about my duck.'

I lifted a hand at Sam and Henry to tell them I'd only be a minute. From the looks on their faces, neither of them really believed me.

'How long has it had a split beak?' I asked.

'To be honest with you, I don't know. It's quite a young duck – but I only noticed it because I saw her having a drink and wondered why the water was pouring out the bottom of her bill.'

I scratched my head; a few goats ran around me and the Pokot people stood there, fascinated by my call.

'Bit surreal this, Luke,' Sam chipped in. 'Can we at least move while you chat about a duck?'

I started to walk slowly onwards as Sam and Henry moved up to stand on either side of me. The elderly Pokot man gave a shrug as he resumed leading the way.

'We can try to repair it,' I said, into the phone.

'Well, the trouble is that she's so thin. She needs feeding and she can't manage it herself right now. Her beak just isn't letting her do it.' Ms Conelson paused. 'When are you back, Luke, because I'm going away myself tonight.'

'Tonight! Ms Conelson, I'm in Kenya.'

'Who's covering you over the next couple of days? Can they take the duck on?'

I thought about what Rob would say if I asked him to syringe-feed a duck with a split beak over the weekend. I winced at the response I knew he would give me.

'Give me a minute,' I said. 'Let me come up with a plan and I'll call you back.'

With that, I rang off.

We'd walked a long way from the goat corral and our silent guide showed no sign of slowing. I turned to look at Sam.

'Duck with a split beak?' I asked Sam.

'Roast duck,' he replied, with a grin.

'You're predictable,' I said. 'That's what Rob would do as well. Can't you fix them with wire?'

'You can try to glue them,' Sam began, at last being constructive. 'Wire them or stitch them, but it's a long shot, I think. Never done it, of course – only mad people in the New Forest would operate on their pet ducks.'

'Ducks can be great pets,' I protested, scrolling through the contacts on my phone, then editing a number to enable an international call.

'Who are you phoning now?' Sam said with a laugh. 'International duck rescue?'

I ignored him as I waited for the phone to be answered.

'Holly!' I exclaimed, just as we rounded a thick acacia bush – and immediately leapt back as a huge head swung towards me. 'Wooooah!' I yelped. In front of me, an enormous camel let out a large bellow in protest at our sudden appearance.

'Luke? Luke? Is that you?' I just about heard Holly say as I regained my composure. 'You're in Africa, aren't you?'

'Hi, Holly,' I said, still aware of the camel's flaring nostrils. 'It's me, yes. Sorry – I just walked round this bush and stumbled on a huge camel.'

The phone went silent. I listened hard, my eyes warily watching the camel. The Pokot man stood off to one side and quietly chatted to a young man, who was crouched beside the recumbent beast, one of his hands loosely resting on its neck.

'Holly?' I said again.

I pushed the headset to my ear and could just about make out a wheezing sound. For the briefest second I was worried; then I realised Holly was collecting her breath between bouts of laughter.

'She's having hysterics,' I said to Sam, by way of explanation.

He and Henry stared at me, bemused.

'He wants you to look at his camel's eye, I think,' Henry began. 'But it looks like a very angry camel, so you'd best be careful.'

I gestured to Sam.

'I've already explained to Henry about your experience with eyes and exotics,' Sam said. 'He's very impressed. A great chance for Henry and the local Pokot to see the master in action!' Sam pointed behind him as the Pokot women, who had been watching us vaccinate the goats, filed around the camel to observe the proceedings.

I shook my head; Sam was setting me up again.

'Holly,' I said, turning back to the phone, 'I need a huge favour, I was wondering if you fancied looking after a duck with a split beak this weekend. Ms Conelson's—'

The shriek of laughter that emanated from the phone was audible metres away; even the camel pricked its ears.

'Can I text you Ms Conelson's number to pick it up?' I yelled, my words drowned by another bellow from the camel.

Thirty seconds later – and after a bit more coercion – Holly agreed to take on the duck and phone Ms Conelson.

'All sorted,' I said with a smile, sending the text. 'Technology – amazing stuff!' I paused. 'Right, how are we going to treat this camel?'

'No idea how you're going to do it,' Sam replied cheerily, 'but I have a ringside seat.'

'Thanks,' I said, looking at the elderly Pokot man and gesturing at my eye.

He nodded enthusiastically and said something loudly to the younger man, who promptly stood up and barked a command at the camel.

Whatever the young man instructed the camel to do, the camel didn't like it one bit. Instantly, it gave another barking roar and swung its head towards its handler in protest. As it did so, I saw the problem. Its right eye had a large suppurating ulcer right in the middle.

'I reckon it's stuck its eye with a thorn off one of those acacia bushes,' Sam shouted.

'Could be.' I nodded. 'Looks a bit like nasty New Forest Eye in cattle.'

New Forest Eye was a condition with which I was very familiar. Back home it was the result of bacteria that invaded the surface of an eye and was spread by flies. The infection resulted in painful ulcers and it was mainly seen during the summer months in young stock and yearlings. The condition the camel was suffering from looked identical. I doubted it was the same bug as the one back home, but whatever had caused the original ulcer, the result was the same. There was no doubt that the eye was infected, and the camel needed antibiotics to get it back on track.

Our medical kit didn't contain expensive eye ointments for conditions such as this, but I had packed a large box of dry cow milking tubes. These tubes, used on cows about six weeks before they are due to calve, are designed to be inserted into the four teats of a heavily pregnant cow when the animal is dried off from the milking herd. Once taken out of the herd, the pregnant cows spend their last few weeks before giving birth gaining strength and condition for the year ahead. During this time, particularly the first two weeks after they leave the milking herd and the last two weeks just before they give birth, their udders can be prone to picking up infections, which can cause a nasty mastitis. To prevent this, many dairy farmers use dry-cow tubes. Containing a long acting antibiotic in a thick paste, they can stay in the udder for as long as fifty-six days, and prevent infection when the animal calves.

They were also a staple part of my kit when I was travelling overseas – not for preventing infection in cows' udders, of course, but for packing wounds in animals with deep injuries. I wasn't the only one to use them out of context, though; as they are much cheaper than a tube of eye ointment, farmers back home also use them to treat New Forest Eye in their cattle. It was the latter use that sprang to my mind.

'I reckon we should get a tube into that eye,' I said. 'We'll never hold it still enough to inject it.'

The ideal would probably have been to inject the eye in the subconjunctiva – but that would have required the camel to remain absolutely still. Getting the antibiotic into the eye as a cream would be hard enough.

'You could give it a jab of long-acting into its muscle,' Sam suggested. 'That, and some pain killer combined with the eye cream, is as good as we're going to get.'

'If you don't treat this it will go blind,' Henry added.

'How am I supposed to get near its eye with its head swinging around like that?' I asked, hesitating to move forward.

'Luke, this camel can bite you very badly,' Henry said. 'It is very much in pain, I think.'

'That's helpful, Henry, thanks.'

'"Fear is the true opiate of combat,"' Sam chipped in.

I looked at the two of them and shook my head in mock despair. In front of us, the young Pokot camel handler managed to grab the rope high up under the beast's halter and looked at me expectantly.

I moved forward, leaning towards the eye. Tentatively reaching out, I lifted the eyelids and, satisfied that the only injury was the large ulcer, I asked Sam to pass me the things I needed from the medicine box.

I couldn't hear his response because the camel gave another loud bellow and the Pokot man tensed his grip on the rope.

'Don't make any sudden movements, Luke,' said Henry. 'This isn't a very well-trained camel. It is only young.'

'Do they often bite?' I asked stupidly.

In response, there was only Henry's laughter.

'A bull camel with a bad eye,' I said. 'What a day!'

Suddenly Sam reappeared, holding out the things I'd requested. He stood at a distance, eyeing me with more suspicion than the camel.

'I can't reach them from here,' I said with a smile.

'It's going to spit at me if I come near you. Can't you stretch?'

I held out my hand and Sam reluctantly walked within spitting range to hand me the medicines.

'Do you want to stay and help hold its head?' I asked innocently.

Sam grinned at me and retreated to sit next to Henry. 'Ringside seat,' he said.

I indicated to the young Pokot to hold the head tightly. At first he was as reluctant as Sam – but then the elderly Pokot man barked at him. When he reached even further up the rope to tighten his grip, I made my move.

Pushing the eyelids apart, I squirted the antibiotic into the eye. The camel made another huge bellow and flung its head wildly around as I grappled to get my syringes and inject it. Quickly sticking the needles deep into the neck muscle, I got the antibiotic in fine, and just about managed to depress the second plunger of the pain killer. At that exact moment, the camel decided that enough was enough. Rearing forwards, it heaved itself upwards, throwing the young Pokot handler off balance.

The effect was instant. All the Pokot women and the elderly man fled as quickly as they could. Even Sam and Henry were on their feet, looking worried.

The camel lurched round to face me and bellowed angrily. It seemed disorientated and spun round to face the other way.

'It can't see you,' Henry commented.

'Probably because I've just stuck a load of cream in its eye,' I replied, skipping out of the way.

As the three of us retreated, we watched the young camel handler bravely step forward and take hold of the rope again. Then he barked commands at the camel to settle.

'Five thousand goats, a duck and a camel – saving lives today, aren't we?' Sam cheered.

I didn't have time to laugh, because just then my phone rang again.

'Are you a sucker for huge phone bills?' Sam said, nudging Henry. 'What is it with you today? Are we and the Pokot not company enough?'

I pulled out my phone, about to switch it off – one sick duck was enough for today and, in any case, Rob was back home handling things – but as I glanced at the display, I hesitated. 'Hold on,' I said, a look of consternation on my face.

Walking a little away from the others, I pressed the 'receive' key and listened hard to the caller. About five minutes passed before I returned.

'Looking serious there,' Sam said. 'What's happened? Has someone found a chicken with a limp?'

'No,' I replied, suddenly serious. 'Bit worse than that. We've lost a dog.'

'A lost dog?' Sam exclaimed, prompting Henry to a fit of deep laughter. 'Well, it sure won't be around here!'

'No, not through Pilgrims,' I replied, a faint sense of panic welling in the pit of my stomach. 'You know the flying-pets thing I set up with Bob? PetAir UK?'

Henry looked confused, but Sam nodded.

'Well, we had our second ever export this morning – a Belgian Shepherd going to New Zealand.' I realised I was speaking with a calm I didn't feel.

'And?' Sam asked.

'And it's lost,' I said quietly.

'What do you mean *lost*? It ran away before you could pick it up from the owners' house?'

'I mean lost!' I cursed. 'It escaped. Not from their house . . . It escaped at the airport. Someone let it out of its crate.'

I kicked at the ground, racking my brains for what on earth I could do to help from Kenya.

'It'll turn up, surely. The airport is fenced?' Henry asked.

'That's the problem,' I replied. 'It bolted through an open door, got over a fence and ran like the wind to get away from them. It's only our second export and it's missed the flight – a complete disaster.'

'Not going to be hard to find a huge dog like that, is it, though?' Sam ventured. 'Someone will spot it?'

'Bob doesn't think so,' I said. 'Apparently it got into the scrub around Terminal 4. It's a massive belt of land with warehouses, property developments, council estates, main roads. There are a million places it could hide.'

'Well, we're heading home soon enough. It'll probably have been found by then – nothing you can do about it now,' Sam said. 'You need to get a search party on the ground to try to find it.'

'That's part of the problem,' I replied. 'I'm the other half of the search party.'

'When are you taking your new wife to that romantic concert you won't tell me anything about?'

'Four days after we get back,' I replied.

'Well, come hell or high water, you'd better find it by then,' Sam said, with a wicked twinkle in his eye.

The grey drizzle of the afternoon turned to a steady rain as I stepped off the plane and walked with Sam to Baggage Reclaim. It had been an epic and incredibly successful trip. With Henry and the team, we'd vaccinated and treated more than nine thousand animals in eleven working days – far more than we'd ever imagined we'd be able to see – and had returned with a definite spring in our step.

That spring soon disappeared, though, as we cleared Customs and I clicked on my mobile. Several messages from Bob awaited me but, disappointingly, none of them indicated that the dog, Moses, had been found. Grabbing my bags and saying farewell to Sam, I phoned Cordelia to tell her it would still be a little while before I got home.

The Animal Reception Centre at Heathrow was close to Terminal 4 and it took about twenty minutes to get over there and rendezvous with Bob. As I walked into the car park, his lean frame looked bone tired and he offered me a faded smile.

'Nice van,' I said, looking at the hired vehicle parked behind him.

'Had to extend the rental,' he said, obviously exhausted. 'It's about the only vehicle that can fit a crate big enough for a dog of that size.'

'So,' I ventured, 'better tell me the story, get it over with . . .'

'I checked Moses in, no problem,' Bob told me. 'The Animal Reception team at Heathrow were brilliant and super-efficient, just as you said. Moses was about to clear Customs with the other live-animal exports for the afternoon but, just as they were going to go through, while we were still in the reception area, one of the other pet shippers realised his paperwork was in a muddle. He was supposed to be exporting a dog – almost identical to Moses – to the States. His crate and ours were adjacent to each other, and there was a discrepancy on his forms with regard to the microchip number. For some unknown reason he decided to scan his dog in the reception area to double check – even though the door was open and it was idiotically risky to let a dog out of a crate there. The shipper pushed forward to prove a point about the chip, and before anyone could stop him, he opened the door to Moses's crate instead of the one belonging to him. That's when Moses disappeared.'

I could hardly believe it. 'What!?' I exclaimed.

'I know. The two crates didn't even look the same. The guy just opened Moses's and it was too late. Moses just knocked him back, like we would bat away a fly.'

'You were there?'

'I turned when I heard the commotion, saw the clown bend down to Moses's crate and shouted at him. He ignored me totally – he was stressed because he'd messed up his own export job. The Animal Reception Centre staff who were behind their desk also tried to stop him opening the crate, but he just flicked the catches. Moses bolted into the forecourt and ran towards the fence over there,' Bob said, pointing to a wire mesh fence.

'No!' I said, open mouthed. 'I don't believe it . . .'

'I swear you've never seen anything like it. Moses was just impossible to contain.'

I looked at Bob. My expression must have said it all. 'That fence is about seven feet high!' I sighed, scanning the fence where Bob pointed.

'Straight over it, took him seconds. Twenty feet wouldn't have contained that dog.'

'And the other pet exporter?'

'He's in a lot of trouble. He'll lose his registration – he's even been cautioned by the airport police for threatening staff. He was super-aggressive when everyone got angry with him – but, ultimately, Moses was our export. We're the ones that will carry the can for this.'

I was silent for a moment as I digested the whole horrible story. Then I said, 'How could he get the two crates confused?'

'The guy was a cowboy. He was flying a Belgian Shepherd that looked like Moses. He was flustered, his paperwork was a shambles and he wasn't thinking.'

'It's not our fault,' I said quietly.

'No,' Bob said flatly. 'But who's going to see it that way?'

I looked up as another figure came round the corner. At first, I had no idea who it was. Then, familiarity dawned. It was Cordelia's younger brother. I was bewildered as he marched over and shook my hand. 'Ed!' I said, surprised. 'What are you doing here?'

'Bob phoned Cords to find out exactly when you were back and if you were coming home first before heading over here. I thought I'd pile down and give you a hand.'

I couldn't help grinning. Once again, family were riding to my rescue.

'I also roped in Debbie and a few of the nurses from my old practice yesterday,' Bob said. 'The staff at the Animal Reception Centre have been amazing. It's absolutely nothing to do with them but they've all come out in their breaks to help. Your brother-in-law, Matt, also drove down. We've looked everywhere. It's been a long two days.'

'Matt?'

'Long story,' Bob explained. 'Your sister's dog was sick and came to the emergency when I was working. I fixed it and told your sister what was going on. Matt phoned to offer his help. He's been brilliant.'

I shook my head, flabbergasted – my whole extended family seemed to have roped themselves into this while I'd been away. 'You didn't phone my mum or any of my cousins, then?' I asked.

'My dad, my brother and his girlfriend have been down, if that makes you feel any better,' Bob replied, pointedly.

'Any posters?'

'They're being printed, should be delivered to the Animal Reception Centre in the next half-hour. I've put a reward on there, but it's just such a vast area – there are a million places where Moses could be hiding.' Bob wiped his brow, obviously fighting exhaustion. 'Let's have a coffee and make a plan – I've got some bad news as well.'

He began to tramp away, but I remained still.

'You mean *this* isn't the bad news?' I asked.

He stopped and turned around. 'You remember Moses belonged to a lady who had to relocate because of her fiancé's work?'

I nodded.

'Well, turns out the fiancé's Israeli, an ex-commando, and as it happens, the dog is actually his . . .'

'So?' I asked, perplexed where this was leading.

'Well, his parents are coming down to meet us in about twenty minutes. They've been on holiday in France and got back this morning. I spoke to the dad on the phone.' Bob's face was etched with worry. 'He's pretty upset and said something about the dog being quite difficult to handle. We're also in the press.' Bob produced a copy of the local paper and handed it over. A picture of Moses was on the front page with the headline: *Dog takes off!*

'Good pun,' I said quietly. 'At least it's good for our advertising problem . . .'

'Not the best launch for a new business in pet travel,' Bob replied. 'Our name is all over that article.'

Bob, Ed and I went inside for a coffee and Bob spread out a map, marked into different zones for searching. I could see the areas they'd already covered – but there were no guarantees, of course, that the dog hadn't backtracked and returned to one.

'I've been down here eighteen hours for the last couple of days trying to get a glimpse of it,' Bob said, pointing out all the various landmarks. 'We had some rain and I think it must have gone into these big yards here. Many of them are warehouses, but there's a scrapyard, a gypsy camp, office blocks, a nursery, stables and some scrubland, which backs onto this massive, sprawling estate.'

'OK,' I said. 'It's probably gone to ground, if there haven't been any sightings. Poor thing must be hungry, so it must be about ready to go on the prowl for food.'

'It'll probably be seen in someone's garden going through the bins,' Ed said.

'Probably,' Bob added, rubbing his eyes. 'But they won't go near it – he's massive. Moses is more like a wolf than a Belgian Shepherd.'

'At least he won't be picked up by someone, and if the fiancé's dad said Moses was a bit tricky, it's probably no bad thing they don't try to catch it. All we need is for someone to get bitten by an escaped dog that's our responsibility,' I said tiredly.

'No – you'd lock the doors if you saw this dog in your garden . . .' Bob paused. 'There's a canine tracking unit I've phoned. They reckon their dogs might be able to sniff him out if we let them scent his crate and bedding.' He produced a scrap of paper. 'Here's their number,' he said. 'Luke, this dog isn't skittish – it wasn't terrified when it bolted. It seemed very switched on, if you know what I mean. It's a really smart dog. It was just very determined to escape.'

Bob handed me a card and looked at his watch. 'I hate to do this,' he said. 'I can be back tomorrow, but I'm on duty tonight at the emergency service. I've got to get back and get ready.'

'You're kidding me!' I replied, realising, for the first time, that Bob was leaving.

'Over to you, I'm afraid. How was Africa by the way?'

'Rapidly fading into distant memory,' I said.

Bob nodded. Then, looking from me to Ed, he rose from the table. 'Keep me posted,' he said. 'I'll be on the phone.' He walked off.

I looked at Ed. 'Thanks for coming down,' I said, glad that I wasn't the only one there.

'No problem,' he replied. 'I've got a sound recording on Friday, but until then I can lend a hand.'

I smiled my thanks. Ed was a drummer and singer in a rock band in his spare time. It had been a main focus during his student days in Glasgow, but now he kept it ticking over while he worked for an accountancy firm in Bournemouth.

'If we don't find it by Thursday night, it's really bad news,' I said.

'Why?'

'I promised to take Cords to a concert and she's really looking forward to it. I've been neglecting her a bit with all the night work and the charity trips . . . not ideal.'

'She'll be cool,' Ed said casually.

I nodded silently. It was more than just a concert, though: it was a planned date focusing on us and, with me being all over the shop, it was something we badly needed.

Seeing my expression, Ed slapped me on the shoulder. 'We'll find it, don't worry. We'd better get started if we want to cover some ground before it gets dark.' He took the map and drew a line perpendicular to the Animal Reception Centre. 'Posters will be here any second and we can start putting them up.'

At that moment, a shadow fell across the table. I looked up, into the darkness.

'Are you from the pet travel company who lost my son's dog?' a heavily accented voice demanded.

A stocky, muscular figure with a bald head and very dark eyes looked down at me. Although he was in his fifties, the man looked like he could outrun someone half his age. His physique suggested he was no stranger to spending lots of time in the gym.

Behind him stood three other people – I guessed they were his wife and two of his other sons, judging from the physical similarities between them. As a family, it wouldn't have surprised me to find out that they chewed glass for breakfast every morning.

'Yes,' I said, standing and holding out my hand. 'I'm one of the directors. I'm incredibly sorry about this. My name is Luke Gamble, and we're going to move heaven and earth to find Moses.'

The man ignored my hand and gestured with his head that we should step outside. I motioned for Ed to stay and followed the family to the car park.

'I don't know what game you're playing, young man,' he said, 'but I want to know why this has happened and what you are doing about it.'

'The dog was picked up, brought here, ready to go on his flight. He was comfortable in the crate we had made for him. Another pet exporter confused Moses's crate with one of his own and let him out.' Even as I spoke, I couldn't help cringing. It sounded so incompetent.

'You were contracted to export Moses!' the man barked. 'Don't try to blame a third party for your incompetence.'

'I know,' I said. 'I can only say how sorry we are. It truly wasn't our fault – but we are doing everything we can to find him.'

'But he did escape, and you have been paid to fly him to New Zealand. It is completely amateur! What have you done? How many of you are here looking for him now?'

I swallowed, despite myself. 'We have two of us here at the moment,' I replied.

'Two?' the man snorted. He leant in a little towards me as he spoke in a lowered voice. 'I will tell you this straight. You had better find this dog. You will spare no expense. If you don't find it, I will make it my personal mission to destroy your company. Do you understand that?'

I could feel the warmth of his anger all over me – or, possibly, it was his breath. 'I don't think threatening me is going to help me find the dog,' I replied, forcing myself to meet his stare. 'We're doing everything we can. I appreciate that what has happened is unacceptable, and I'm incredibly sorry about it – but that doesn't change the fact that the dog has escaped. It would be great if you could help us look.'

The man looked at me, slightly stunned. 'You expect us to look for this dog?' he balked. 'No, you do not understand. *You* will find this dog. I want to be updated every morning and afternoon as to your progress.'

I sighed. This was going from bad to worse.

His wife appeared from behind him. 'Have you done posters?' she demanded.

'Of course,' I replied, still trying not to cringe. 'In fact, they're due to be here within the next ten minutes or so. I'm about to start putting them up.'

'Have you a picture of the dog on them?' she said.

I hesitated. I had no idea what Bob had put on the posters. In fact, I had very little idea about the situation at all, other than that we had lost a dog at the airport and now had the angriest family in the world to answer to.

'Yes,' I replied, trusting to Bob. 'Of course there would be a picture of the dog – it would be pointless otherwise.'

'How much reward have you offered?'

I gulped. There was no way I was going to admit that I hadn't seen the posters and hadn't even been in the country for the last two days – but, equally, I felt that it was a fair enough question. 'We've had to be very careful with that,' I replied, evasively. 'Too much and people might hold the dog for ransom, too little and they won't bother to get in touch. As soon as they are here, I will send you a copy so you can see what we're doing.'

'You do know that this was my son's dog when he was in the Oketz Unit of the Israeli Special Forces, don't you?' the man snapped. 'This is no ordinary dog. You were told this!'

I was wrong, things could get worse. 'Is Moses dangerous?' I said, hesitantly.

'Dangerous?' the man gasped, as if I were a simpleton. 'Don't you understand this? He was used to track down and attack kidnappers!'

There had to be a silver lining in this somewhere. I grappled to find it. 'Surely he's highly trained, though – won't he come to call? Surely Special Forces don't let their attack dogs retire as pets,' I said hopefully.

The man was flabbergasted, his eyes opening wide, seemingly at my stupidity. 'He is still in work. It is complicated and not your business and, no, he won't come to calls. He is trained to *ignore* calls from people he doesn't know! These dogs would be easy to kill if they answered anyone!'

'We were thinking about using a dog tracking firm to help us find him,' I said. 'It's a huge area with a lot of scrubland.'

'Moses will kill tracking dogs if they get close to him.'

I sighed. 'He responds to your son and his fiancée, though?'

'Yes,' the lady replied. 'But you, young man, are missing the point. My son and his fiancée are both in New Zealand.'

I could see there was no easy way out of this. I would have to treat it like the IDP camps: one little step at a time.

'Look,' I began, 'I have to get these posters up before dark. In the worst case scenario, your son may need to fly back to help us. It sounds as if it really isn't safe for Moses to be out there – what happens if some children stumble on him?'

'If they are no threat, he will leave them. It is more adults you need to be concerned with,' the man said. 'Make no mistake about this – if anything bad were to happen, it would be *your* fault. I do not accept you passing the blame onto anyone else.' The man fixed his eyes on me and spread his hands expansively.

I nodded.

'You will phone us later,' the lady said, turning to leave.

I nodded again. 'Absolutely.'

As the family got back into their car, all giving me hard stares, I went back inside to tell Ed the good news with nausea welling in the pit of my stomach.

'You let the paper take a picture of you holding a net?' Bob said, holding a copy of the local paper up in front of us.

'Ed's holding the net,' I replied. 'I'm just standing by him.'

'It's a trained attack dog – not a fish!' Bob said.

'Look,' I replied, wincing. 'It draws attention to the situation. There's a picture of the dog below and it shows we're doing all we can to try to catch it. Positive spin.'

'Why are you wincing?'

The truth was that I had a blister the size of a tennis ball on the sole of my foot, having walked around the outside of Terminal 4 for about eighteen hours the previous day – but there was no way I was going to tell that to Bob. 'I'm just frustrated,' I replied.

'What do you think, Ed?' Bob asked.

'I liked the net,' he began. 'Just a shame they wouldn't let us keep it. Amazing, the props these papers have, isn't it?' He leant against the van, sipping a cup of coffee, gazing out at a long field of scrubland about a mile away from the Animal Reception Centre. Remarkably, he had kept a cheerful demeanour throughout, not once resenting his idiotic brother-in-law for dragging him into this situation.

I rubbed my face with my hand. It was Wednesday and three days had passed since I'd arrived back from Kenya. Bob was doing nights at the emergency service and Rob had thankfully agreed to keep covering Pilgrims for me while I looked for the dog.

'You tried the tracker dogs?' Bob asked, looking upwards for some sort of divine help.

'Yes,' I replied. 'Total failure.'

The tracker dogs had been field champions, four manic Springer Spaniels who scented the crate, then bounded off, leading us on a merry chase for a good five miles, only to do a huge circle and end up back at the Animal Reception Centre.

'They had fun, though, didn't they? One of them had a great swim!' Ed said, grinning.

One of the dogs had gone for a swim in a river; another had spent twenty minutes rooting about in a bramble bush to retrieve a discarded slipper. It had been a phenomenal waste of an afternoon. Needless to say, I hadn't reported that to the owner's father.

'We're going to have to fly the owners back, you know. We're not going to find this dog. I'm going to miss taking Cords to the concert tomorrow night. I feel like going for a one-way swim myself at the moment.'

As the words escaped my mouth, Ed suddenly straightened.

'That's the dog!' he said, pointing frantically ahead of him.

The effect of those words was like an electric shock. Both Bob and I jolted upright, straining our eyes in the direction Ed was pointing.

I wasn't certain. Out there, in the scrub, a dark shape danced. It could even have been a mirage. We were, for sure, like three parched souls wandering through a desert.

'That *is* Moses!' Bob exclaimed. Maybe his eyes were better than mine, or maybe he was just a little more tired and ready to accept the mirage. 'Quick, let's go! He's only trotting – we can catch him.'

Without waiting for any form of acknowledgement, Bob vaulted a flimsy barbed-wire fence in front of us and started to run, his long legs carrying his lean frame over the ground in massive strides. In seconds he was closing the distance between us and the dark shape.

Like a duck with blisters all over its webbed feet, I, too, started to run. I was vaguely aware of Ed calmly opening the door of the van, but I was too focused on following Bob to pay much attention.

By the time I was halfway across the scrub, still trailing Bob by many yards, the mirage resolved itself. This was no phantom, no ghost dog mindlessly stalking a blasted heath. This was – without a shadow of a doubt – Moses himself.

Once the certainty sank in, it seemed as if my blisters disappeared. Suddenly I could run – not like a duck but like an Olympic athlete. I quickly closed the gap on Bob, and we raced on together.

Initially, we gained on Moses. He gambolled in his own little world, seemingly unaware of our pursuit. Then, his ears pricked. He stopped, turned and looked at us. Both Bob and I slowed and stopped as well. There were only about twenty yards between the dog and us.

'He's huge – have you got a lead?' I wheezed, the run having been the quickest four hundred metres I had ever done in my life. The thought that my training for the Ironman had officially begun crossed my mind.

Bob shook his head, his chest heaving.

'Moses, *SIT*!' I said, as commandingly and sharply as possible.

Bob just looked at me.

'Worth a shot, show no fear and sound confident,' I said, shrugging.

Moses just watched us, immobile.

'He's not looking bad, given four days on the run,' Bob said, walking forwards.

'Be careful, Bob,' I said quietly, sensing Moses's building irritation at our presence. 'He's not looking too friendly.'

'Nonsense,' Bob replied, taking another step. 'He's going to be fine.'

As he came near, a deep growl emanated from Moses's throat and his ears twitched backwards.

'Oh dear,' said Bob.

Moses dipped his head and fixed him with a stare.

'Hang on,' I said, frantically pulling my phone out of my pocket and pushing the buttons. 'Don't move and don't look Moses in the eye!'

'Who are you ringing?' Bob said, frozen to the spot.

'My new best friend – the owner's father,' I blurted, pressing the phone to my ear, waiting for an answer.

'Yes?' came the blunt voice.

'We've found Moses,' I said.

'Well, it's about damn time. Where is he?'

'He's in the middle of a field of scrubland and about ten feet away from us. He isn't running. In fact, he's in some sort of attack position. I wondered if there is a command we can use to relax him.'

The line went silent for a moment.

'If you stand still, he won't attack you without a command.'

'We can't get close enough to get hold of him,' I replied. 'He's looking like he might bite us.'

The owner's father laughed. 'If he goes for you, he won't bite you. He'll savage you until he is called off or you kill him.'

'Comforting,' I said, casting a very nervous glance at Bob, whose eyes were fixed on the ground.

'You don't look like a kidnapper, do you?' the man guffawed. 'I wouldn't worry, if not. A barking dog rarely bites.'

'Moses is completely silent now,' I replied steadily.

The phone went quiet again for a moment.

'Did you chase him?'

'Yes, for about half a mile,' I said quickly.

The owner's father grunted. 'That means you're a threat to him,' he breathed.

'I think it would be fair to say he's thinking along those lines,' I replied.

'You must keep your hands by your sides,' he said. For the first time, he sounded serious, not like he was having a joke at our expense. 'Does your phone have a speaker function?' he asked.

'Bob, keep your hands by your sides,' I hissed, holding down one of the buttons for about a second and waiting for a thin beep to sound from the handset.

'Moses, *artza*!'

Moses's ears twitched at the faint Hebrew command. His eyes momentarily left Bob and flickered to the phone.

The owner's father shouted again and the tinny voice echoed out of the speaker. Instantly Moses gave a wag of his tail.

'He wagged his tail,' I whispered into the handset.

'Okay. You must approach him confidently and click your fingers.'

I started to walk forwards. Moses looked up at me, a little confused.

'Good boy,' I said.

As soon as the words left my mouth, I realised my mistake. Having forgotten to click my fingers, and by uttering pleasantries, I'd broken the spell of what Moses had heard down the phone. With a quick look at me, Moses turned and ran.

'No!' I gasped.

'What's happened?' the tinny voice said.

I picked the phone up, watching Moses lope away across the field. Bob and I looked at each other, a wretched look on our faces. 'He's run off,' I said quietly, lowering the phone and hanging up. A mouthful of angry abuse was the last thing I needed.

'Come on,' I said to Bob. 'We can't let him out of sight, even if we drop dead trying . . .'

In concert, we started to trot after Moses's rapidly disappearing form.

'He's gone through the fence at the other end,' Bob said, exhausted. 'Can you see him? I can't.'

'Lads!' came a faint cry across the field.

We stopped. There was nothing in sight: just endless, endless scrub. Moses had escaped for the second time in only a week. I could have cried.

'Bob, Luke, over here!' the voice called again.

Bob and I scanned the horizon. Just beyond the fence line, we could make out the roof of the van.

'It's Ed,' I said, quickening my pace.

As we approached, I saw that Ed was wearing a grin big enough to split his face.

'We didn't get him, Ed,' I said. 'He bolted again.'

'I know you didn't,' Ed replied. 'But that's okay.'

I had loved Ed's nonchalance, his steadfastness, throughout the whole débâcle – but this was too much. Nothing about this whole situation was okay.

'How can it be okay?' Bob exploded. 'The blasted dog's legged it, we have no idea where it's gone – and it could be another four days before we see it again! Also – we can't get near it. It's a killer attack dog that seems to respond only to commands in Hebrew.' He paused for a second, but only to catch his breath. 'And last time I checked – none of us can speak Hebrew.'

'It *is* okay,' Ed said calmly. 'You haven't cancelled your concert tickets, have you, Luke?'

Both Bob and I looked at him. We might have been about to tear his head off, more viciously than Moses could ever have done.

'How is it okay?' I asked.

'Because while you two great lugs have been enjoying your little jog across the scrubland, I caught him.'

We froze.

'What?' I gasped.

'It's quite simple.' Ed smiled. 'I saw Moses come through the fence. I clicked my fingers to get his attention and he came straight up to me. I opened the door of the van and he hopped into the crate. Job done. He's in there.'

We clamoured past him and peered through the window of the van. Sure enough, the massive shadow of Moses could be seen inside the crate in the back.

I stepped back in amazement. It was over. All of it was over – and all Ed had done was click his forefinger and thumb.

'Ed,' I said, 'I love you – but don't tell your sister!'

13

Always Be Prepared

'So you got the dog back to them?' Rob said with a broad smile.

We were standing in my driveway, Rob helping me unload the kit from the truck so we could restock it and inventory what needed to be ordered.

'Yes,' I said, allowing myself to grin.

'And now you're good to take back Pilgrims?'

'I'm all set and raring to go,' I replied. 'You're going to miss it. Don't tell me you haven't enjoyed getting back to your roots for the last couple of weeks.'

'I'll enjoy it more once I cash your cheque. Been quite busy – you're building up a few clients here. Seems like it's going well.'

'Absolutely – all eyes intact.'

'Well,' Rob said. 'Almost. I saw a dog with cataracts, which I've recommended for phacoemulsification – hope that's okay?'

'What do you mean?' I asked, confused.

'You told me you aren't doing small animals yet, but I had at least a couple of calls a day to see a dog or a cat – I'm not sure what little club you've got yourself into, but Lady Marion and her pals love the one-to-one, don't they?'

'No . . .' I stumbled. 'I mean *yes*, they love the one-to-one, but what are you talking about with the cataracts?'

'Ah – laser surgery!' Rob exclaimed. 'I can do it now at Bristol. I can remove cataracts the same way as they do for people. Really amazing. Not sure the client'll go for it, though, bit rough and ready – Tony Pines was his name.'

'He won't go for it – absolutely no chance, I'm afraid.' I wondered what Tony would make of such a procedure. 'But what were you doing there?'

'Dropping off some medicines and picking up this little one,' Rob said, opening the door of the vehicle. 'He said to bring her back to you and you'd do what had to be done. Didn't sound promising – but he isn't the sort of chap to debate things with, is he?'

'Tony doesn't muck about,' I replied, reaching forward to stroke a very excited Bracken.

I picked her up and felt around the back leg; it was hanging limp and my heart sank. From just feeling it, I could tell that the bone had rebroken and the plate had come loose.

'Apparently she got out and jumped off the edge of a patio – a six-foot drop,' Rob said, seeing the disappointment in my face. 'She was doing well until then. Annoying, isn't it, when you've bust a gut to fix something?'

'Yep,' I replied, the word thick in my mouth. I knew what Tony wanted and I was all out of options. I stroked Bracken again – she was so bright and happy, despite all she'd been through.

'So, what's next with your grand plans?' Rob asked, trying to steer the conversation away from little Bracken, who was wriggling to get down and hobble about on her three legs.

'Cords is trying to secure the lease for the practice,' I began, 'so we'll move in there and the big project will be to kit it out and get the doors open a.s.a.p. We need a base where Lady Marion and her friends can come and visit for a change,' I paused. 'I've also got to nail this triathlon. All your fault, of course.'

'My fault?' Rob said.

'As a trustee of WVS, you told me to ensure I did a fundraiser off the back of the Kenya trip. Drive the PR bus forwards and all that.'

'Of course,' Rob said. 'But *Ironman*? One of my cousins has done that. He said it was hell and he's as fit as a fiddle. I suppose the good news for me is that it's only one day of cover I'll have to do for you. The bad news for you is that it's going to be a pretty awful one.'

'It'll be fine.'

'Have you ever cycled a hundred and twelve miles?'

'You know I haven't.'

'Have you ever swum two point eight miles in open water?'

'No – but I float well.'

'You do realise there's a time limit on the run? You'll kill yourself.'

'Can't be a patch on the Marathon des Sables,' I said confidently.

'Glad you're in a strong state of mind.' Rob laughed.

'Well, I've taken your advice. It's the best time to bring awareness to the charity. I'll have the Kenya report ready to be published the same weekend as I do the race. Got a few months yet, so I can definitely manage it. I'm determined to take Tess on full time too – and that means I've got to make sure we get enough in to cover her salary . . . and we're going to make WVS huge.'

'Talking of huge,' Rob said, 'a bike arrived by courier for you today. Would hate to see the invoice for it.'

'Brilliant!' I smiled, feeling like a schoolboy all of a sudden. 'Where is it?'

'Well, it's blue and shiny – certainly looks the part. I put it in the hall, but you might want to check it out. You'll need some extras.'

'Yep – I'll get a helmet and stuff, don't worry. Soon I'll be flying along, no problem.'

'Talking of flying – what about your PetAir project?'

'Bob and I are having a chat about that later. It was a heck of a few days. It's a difficult business to get into.'

'At least the dog's back with its owners. Are they still going to take it to New Zealand?'

'Well, that's the thing – they've asked us to help with it,' I said.

'What? You aren't going to take it on, are you?'

'Well,' I said, with a hint of pride, 'it *is* fantastic for the launch of the company – couldn't be more high profile in the pet-travel world at the moment! They're telling everyone that they really trust us, which, after what happened, says a lot. Now they've finally accepted it wasn't anything to do with us, I think they feel a bit bad.'

'Haven't you got enough on your plate?' Rob said, arching an eyebrow.

'Yes,' I replied, 'but that's why Bob and I need to have a good chat. It's really up to him. He'll be the one to drive it on and make it be all it can be. I can help, but I have to build up Pilgrims for a while and focus on home life a bit more.'

'You mean spend more time with your wife?' Rob said.

'Yes, I've been away a lot. It's a bit rubbish. Neither of us planned it like that, I've just been a bit carried away with the various projects,' I admitted quietly.

'Concert tonight, though?' Rob said.

'If you don't mind one more night on the phones?'

'You've been building up to this concert and I know Cords is looking forward to it. How could I stand in the way of true love, even though you've already made me do three days more than we agreed?' Rob quipped.

'You're earning serious Brownie points,' I said.

'I'm earning money,' Rob replied with a laugh.

'That too,' I said.

Rob nodded and looked at me, scratching his head.

'What are you going to say?' I asked, wondering what was on my friend's mind.

'The phones tonight are no problem – just switch them over before you leave. It's Bracken. I should have dealt with her. I'm sorry, Luke. I knew what Tony meant, but I just bottled it. She's a cracker, isn't she? Let's do it together and get it over with.'

We stood in silence.

'No, it's okay,' I finally said. 'I'll take care of her. Thanks, pal.'

Rob and I said our goodbyes and I put Bracken in the kitchen to scamper around with Leuwen, wondering what to do. Charlie, seeing the terrier, wisely disappeared upstairs as Bracken and Leuwen started to jump on each other. Despite her broken leg and being an eighth the size of her new friend, the little dog was more than holding her own.

There was something special about Bracken. She was such a character – a broken leg shouldn't mean she had to die.

Walking through the hallway, I looked at the shiny bike I

had recklessly bought. No going back now, I thought, looking at the expensive bit of kit.

Suddenly I realised what Rob had been talking about. The bike had come – but it didn't have any pedals! I dug out my phone and rang the bike shop. The sales assistant thought I was winding her up, and only then did it dawn on me that professional bikes didn't come with pedals – that was a whole different ball game. Feeling every inch the amateur, I placed an order for the cheapest ones they had in stock and sighed. Never mind, I thought. The bike training could wait until next week.

Making a cup of coffee, I went through the diary, delaying what I knew had to be done. Seeing what Rob had been up to and which cases needed following up took my mind off the dilemma for a moment. It had been a busy couple of weeks – there had been an outbreak of sudden death at a smallholder's pig farm among his weaners, several horses with sarcoids that had needed treating, the normal herd fertility routines on the farms, and Mr Hootle had had a bull with an abscess in its foot. Flicking over the pages, I totted up the small-animal cases – Rob had been right, there had been almost one a day: a dog with sore ears, a cat with fleas, a coughing terrier, another with diarrhoea. The list went on. I smiled: it boded well for the practice. It was a big step to take on a surgery premises and all the overheads that went with it, but it was essential if we were to make a go of things and build the practice up.

I sighed and picked up the phone. 'Tony,' I said, 'it's Luke. How are you?'

'Luke, hi, fine, thanks. Was Kenya good?' Tony replied succinctly.

'Not bad – but I've just caught up with Rob. I'm so disappointed about Bracken.'

'I know,' Tony said, more than a hint of frustration in his voice. 'Such a shame after all that – she was a cracker.'

'She was doing so well before I left,' I ventured.

'These working dogs, they don't do with all this fancy surgery. I know I shouldn't have let her out, but you know what she was like, all over the place, impossible to keep still. She just wasn't happy in that cage.'

'She jumped off the patio or something?' I asked.

'Yes, that's when it went. There was no stopping her. Would have been kinder to do it straight away than have to kill her now. I should have shot her – but thought you should see what happened. No chance it was going to come good after that, was there?'

'It's another full break,' I said. 'It'll be impossible to repair now.'

'You mean you haven't put her down yet?' Tony said, surprised.

'Well, this is the thing,' I began, 'I wondered if you'd sign her over to me. I'll take her leg off and get her a home.'

The silence didn't last long this time.

'No,' Tony said simply. 'Put her down, Luke. She's an outside dog. She doesn't like the pampered life and she won't do on three legs. Let's not go over this again.'

'Tony,' I said, 'she'll be fine and it won't cost you a thing. If I put her down then I'll charge you.'

There was a pause at the end of the line.

'I'd have shot her here if I'd known. How much?'

'A hundred pounds,' I replied.

'A hundred pounds!' Tony exploded. 'That's ridiculous! I'm not paying that!'

'Then I'm not putting her down.'

'I'll come and get her and I'll shoot her at your house.'

'Tony, if you were going to shoot her, you'd have done it already.' I could feel the receiver trembling in my hands. 'I know the plating didn't work and thank you for giving it a try – but we would have had her fixed if she hadn't jumped off the patio. The same would happen to a human if they tried that after surgery for a broken leg. She's a great little dog. I can get her a home that'll look after her.'

'She chases cats, Luke! She's a farm dog! If you rehome her, like as not they'll have her put down once she misbehaves. It's just not fair to her.'

'If I can get her a home lined up that you're happy with in the next twenty-four hours, will you sign her over, let me do the surgery and not charge you a penny?'

Tony sighed.

'Come on, Tony! I'd be a rubbish vet if I didn't try.'

'Twenty-four hours, Luke – but if I'm not happy, I want your word that you'll put her down and not charge me a penny.'

'Tony,' I said, 'the clock starts now.'

Without waiting for another word, I rang off.

I stood up and walked back to the kitchen. Leuwen and Bracken had stopped jumping on each other and were lying on Leuwen's bed. Bracken opened her eyes and her little stump of a tail starting to beat feverishly as I bent down to give her a stroke.

'Twenty-four hours, Bracken,' I whispered. 'Twenty-four hours to get you a home.'

Totally oblivious, she licked my hand and wagged her tail even harder. At that moment, I heard Cordelia's car swoop into the driveway. I flicked on the kettle again and, once Cordelia had come inside, I introduced her to the intruder in our kitchen and explained Bracken's predicament.

'We're going to need a nurse as soon as we open the surgery, Luke.'

I nodded, unsure where this was going.

'I had the contract back today,' she said. 'We're really close. There'll be a bit of building work we need to do to get it all set up as a surgery – build a consulting room, for example – but the planning permission has come through for change of use and the building regs are all on board.' She paused, a smile playing on her lips. 'I mean, we should think about taking someone on in about six weeks.'

'I know,' I said, unsure where this was going. 'But that doesn't help Bracken, does it?'

'Well, it might,' Cordelia replied, waiting for me to catch up.

My face broke into a broad grin. 'Yes, it might indeed,' I said, and reached for the phone. Two seconds later, I pushed the handset to my ear. 'Holly,' I began, 'how's the duck? Quacking well, I hope?'

'Ha ha!' Holly giggled. 'Yes, I named her Polo and she's doing great. Rob stitched the beak back together and, so far, it seems to be holding.'

'Holly, that's brilliant! . . .' I paused. 'Look, Holly,' I went on, unsure how to slide into this, 'you know how your current job won't allow you to have pets?'

'Yes,' Holly said.

'Well, you remember Bracken?'

'That little Jack Russell you and Bob plated?'

'The exact same one. Well, she's feeling a bit lonely and wondered if you'd join her as head nurse at Pilgrims Veterinary Practice in about six weeks.'

A long silence.

'Does Bracken pay well?' Holly asked, obviously thrilled.

'Better than Polo,' I replied.

Holly laughed, and I almost held my breath while she responded.

'I've been thinking about it for a long time,' she said. 'It's a lovely job here, they're great people . . . but I do like the idea of working with Bracken. Can I think about it some more and get back to you tomorrow?'

'As long as it's within the next twenty-three hours, that would be brilliant,' I said, crossing my fingers and hoping beyond hope that somehow it would all come together.

Hanging up, I glanced again at the clock. 'Honey,' I shouted.

Cordelia's muffled reply came from upstairs.

'Tonight is concert night!' I shouted.

The morning came far too quickly, and with a deep sense of fatigue, I headed downstairs. It had been a great night – despite the fact that if any of my friends ever got wind of which musician I had taken Cords to see, I'd never live it down, we had both really enjoyed ourselves. Not having a visit until the early afternoon, my plan was to recover with a strong cup of coffee and go through the entire monthly invoicing – a horrible, tedious task, but one that was essential to the running of the business. I also wanted to try a few other possible homes for Bracken, in case Holly decided against the idea.

I said goodbye to Cordelia, who, true to her invincible nature, seemed totally recovered and all set for work, then settled down to get on with things. Just as I began to sift through the endless papers, the phone shrieked at me from the counter.

Leuwen whimpered underneath the desk.

'Hello, Luke,' came a voice. 'This is Ian Myrtle, vet from the other side of the forest, Hazel Vet Surgery.'

'Hi,' I replied. 'How can I help you?' I vaguely knew of Ian's practice but had never had any dealings with him.

'I was wondering if you might be able to help us out?' Ian Myrtle had a kindly, whispery voice that put me in mind of a particularly dear grandfather. 'Inspector Henwood from the RSPCA booked me to go on a visit today with them but, unfortunately, one of my vets has had to call in sick and I'm stuck. I was wondering if you might take it on.'

'This morning?' I replied, glancing at my watch. It was seven thirty a.m., there were seven hours to go before my visit and before I was due to phone Tony about Bracken.

'Yes, I know it's incredibly short notice – but I've only just found out I can't do it. I hate to let them down. It's a welfare assessment for a farm about fifteen miles away from you. Fairly low key. I'd call and cancel it but I know they've put so much effort into arranging it for today that it would totally let everyone down – not to mention the animals.'

'What sort of animals?' I asked. 'I'm mainly a farm practice and, to be honest Mr Myrtle, I've never done an RSPCA investigation before.'

'I've heard nothing but good things about you and your practice. Aren't you setting up as mixed soon? You'll be fine, I assure you. They really need a vet like you, someone who can assess everything. The place is in quite a built-up area and it's mainly dogs and cats. There's a horse and a couple of cows out the back – seems a bit of everything lives there!'

I hesitated. I'd never been on a welfare visit before and this suggested a world of confrontation that would thrust my fledgling practice into the local limelight. An RSPCA investigation into a smallholding was not something I really wanted to get involved with.

'Well, to be honest,' I wavered, 'isn't this a bit close to home for me to get involved with?

'It's right on the periphery of your area, that's true, but it's the same for us. It won't cause you any problems. These people just need a lot of help and a stern word. The RSPCA are so close to getting these guys straight, it would be maddening to see it fall through now – it's taken months of planning and co-ordinating for this visit.' Ian paused. 'Luke, you'd be doing us all a huge favour. It's fairly low key, they just need your independent assessment – it'll all be confidential – and the RSPCA will take care of the rest.'

I thought about it. It was, I supposed, ironic that I was so keen to champion animal welfare overseas and yet, here I was, dallying about visiting a farm only half an hour away.

'How long do you think it will take?' I said, glancing again at my watch.

'No more than a couple of hours,' he replied confidently.

A sudden thought entered my head. If a job like this had come along to Mr Spotswode or Giles, neither of them would have flinched from the task just because it was local. People who abused animals needed to be caught and, as a vet, I should be championing welfare no matter where I was, no matter what it did to my business, or what people thought of me.

'OK,' I finally said. 'I can do it this morning. Shall I meet them at the farm?'

'Oh, that's wonderful, Luke, thank you. Best if you go to the police station, I think – everyone's rendezvousing there and you'll all go on together.'

'The police are involved?' I asked, surprised. 'I thought you said it was low key.'

'Oh, it's a co-ordinated effort,' he explained. 'Local police, trading standards and the RSPCA, you know how it is.

Everyone works as a team these days. Don't worry, it'll be really simple. Do you think you can get there in, say, forty minutes?'

'Forty minutes?' I exclaimed.

'That's the briefing time.' Before I could get a word in, he ploughed on, 'Thanks again, Luke. Don't forget, the contact you need is Inspector Henwood. She's a lovely lady. I'll phone her and tell her you'll be coming along in about half an hour or so.'

'Half an hour, I thought it was forty minutes away?' I stuttered, Ian, ignoring me, continued.

'On the plus side, they pay well for this sort of thing. Hope it all goes well, Luke. Best of luck.'

The dialling tone buzzed in my ear.

I scrabbled about to restock my medicine box, unsure of what I might need to take with me. Telling Leuwen I'd have to do this one solo, I reminded myself that I'd need a notepad and pen for the report, so, grabbing one of each, I hopped in the truck and roared off.

The police-station car park was completely full of white vans with a scattering of police cars. Finding a space on a nearby street, I walked into the building and told the officer on duty who I was and what I was there for. With a stern face, he disappeared, only to return moments later with a badge to pin on my shirt. After that, he issued me with hasty directions to go down the corridor, take the second left and proceed to the meeting room at the end.

Wearing my shorts and a short-sleeved brown shirt with my homemade Pilgrims logo emblazoned over the left pocket, I felt somewhat out of place. A stream of uniformed officers surged past me, heading in the same direction. It was with a sinking feeling that I realised they were all going to the same room as I was.

On the tail of the policemen, I found myself in the middle of a sea of about thirty bodies. Tables were placed in the centre of the room with chairs all around them. Every seat was full and, as I pushed myself back against the wall, I scanned the crowd observing a mix of civilians, RSPCA officers and police.

'Ladies and gentlemen,' a distinguished-looking policeman addressed us, 'thank you for coming. Today's briefing will be carried out by Chief Inspector Plimly.'

A thick-set police officer rose from the head of the table and scanned the room. In his late thirties, he looked every inch the commander. All eyes were fixed on him as he spoke.

'Today's operation will commence at oh-nine thirty,' he began. 'Sergeant McGinley will be leading the raiding team. We have some civilians who will be accompanying us. If we can now go round the table, starting on my left, in a clockwise direction, so everyone can introduce themselves with a short explanation of their role, that would be a useful step.' The Inspector nodded and looked to his left.

A thin lady with greying hair smiled and cleared her throat. 'I am Inspector Henwood from the RSPCA,' she announced. 'I am the investigating officer for the charity and represent the prosecuting body for the case and seizure.'

As she finished her short, succinct description, an icy feeling gripped my stomach. This wasn't shaping up to be the low-key visit Ian had talked about.

'Good morning, everyone,' came the second voice. 'I am Janet Funroe from Trading Standards. I have been actively involved in bringing today's action to bear and have visited the site on three previous occasions. My role is to enforce animal-welfare legislation and serve notice, as required, on, primarily, the livestock and horse that are resident at the premises.'

And so the introductions went on: two local dog wardens, another Trading Standards representative, a couple of dog handlers who had been contracted to assist.

Then, finally, all eyes shifted to me.

I stood there, uncomfortable, in my shorts, my hair all over the place, looking every inch the village yokel who had stumbled into the wrong wedding party. 'Hello,' I stumbled. 'My name is Luke – Luke Gamble. I'm a local vet and I'm here to, well, assist the RSPCA in their investigation.'

A few wry smiles appeared among the officers. I looked at Inspector Henwood and raised my eyebrows. She nodded briefly and turned her attention back to Chief Inspector Plimly.

'Our brief today is to serve this warrant for a full premises search and seizure, as required. We are looking for animals the suspects are said to have on the premises, namely a large number of attack dogs. These dogs are being bred illegally. The residents are farming puppies and the suspects have become increasingly aggressive in response to visits from RSPCA and Trading Standards, in relation to allegations against them of cruelty and other breaches of animal-welfare issues. Notice has been served. On the premises there are also noted to be a large number of cattle, ponies and horses that the suspects trade with.'

Janet Funroe cleared her throat. 'According to reports we had from a witness, who wishes to remain unidentified, they have allegedly killed some of the dogs and fed them to the others.'

There was a collective gasp from some of the officers. I

shook my head, not at the news from Janet, but at the predicament I was in.

The chief inspector raised his hand. 'During this raid, it is important that we do not get emotional and remember the task at hand. We are going in large numbers, due to the fact that the suspects have alleged they will release the dogs on us if we enter the premises. To that end, we have been lent the support of a squad team from Bournemouth, who are going to assist the RSPCA in serving notice and the search warrant.' The inspector paused. 'Can I introduce Sergeant McGinley?'

If the chief inspector was an imposing figure, Sergeant McGinley was in a different league. As he was introduced, the sergeant, who was standing in the hall with his team, ducked in through the doorway to introduce himself. About six foot five in every dimension, he was in full body armour, with a shaven head, and glowered at us from under his cap. I reminded myself never to commit a crime in his neighbourhood.

'I'll be leading the forced-entry team as well as overseeing the raid today,' he began. 'Four of us will be in the advance party to assist with the approach to the premises. We will escalate the necessary actions to ensure safe entry for everyone. Our role is to safeguard the welfare and wellbeing of this team throughout the day.'

'Thank you, Sergeant. In conclusion, the initial approach will be made by Sergeant McGinley and his team, and one representative of the RSPCA, who will serve notice and issue the search warrant to the suspects. The rest of us will wait by the gates and secure the entrance and exit points off the farm. Once secured, the search warrant can be actioned.' He paused, making certain everybody had understood. 'I think this concludes the briefing and introductions. If we could make our way to the vehicles, we will go in convoy and rendezvous outside the farm.'

There were general smiles all around. I watched as Sergeant McGinley ducked back out through the doorway, a huge grin on his face and moved towards three other figures all clad in full body armour. A hand plucked at my sleeve. I turned. 'Luke, thank you for coming along at short notice,' Inspector Henwood said, smiling at me kindly. 'We can't seize the animals without your agreement.'

'I'm totally out of my league, Inspector. Ian Myrtle said it was a low-key affair. I think there are crossed wires. I'm not really in a position to . . .' I tailed off as I watched the Inspector's expression widen in disbelief.

'Oh, Ian is *such* a character! He knew this was a huge operation – we've been planning it for two months. Truth is, he probably didn't realise who the people were until yesterday. That's why he asked you to do it.'

'But – he said one of his vets was sick?'

'Ha-ha! Ian's a one-man band!'

My heart sank. I'd been hijacked.

'Anyway, Luke, so good of you to step into the breach. Don't worry about the family. They won't give you any trouble – the police will see to that. Now, where are you parked?'

My mouth worked like a fish for a moment as I digested what that meant – Ian Myrtle had completely set me up.

'Down the road,' I managed.

'Well, we'll be a big convoy of white vans – you won't miss us and we'll be heading out on the main road. Tuck in behind us and we should be there in about twenty-five minutes.' Inspector Henwood handed me a printed form detailing the planned raid. 'This is the address in case you get lost.'

I looked down and absently noted that Ian Myrtle's name

had been crossed out in pen and someone had written 'shorts?' over the top of it, clearly in appreciation of my attire.

'See you there,' she said, and walked off down the corridor.

I felt like banging my head against the wall. Instead, I gave an almighty sigh and headed off to find my truck.

The convoy was impossible to miss – six white Transits and an RSPCA van with the lettering covered up. I watched in disbelief as they all went past me. Then, fighting the temptation to indicate right and drive off in the opposite direction, I dutifully trailed behind them in my huge red truck with Pilgrims all down the side.

The house was just south of the forest boundary, an area I rarely had to visit. A moderately built up area, drab detached houses flanked either side of the paved street. In front of me, the armada of vans had already parked – and a space had been left for me right outside the entrance to the driveway. The gates were sealed and looked as menacing as those of a prison.

Climbing down from the truck, I looked at the police officer closest to me. 'Everyone's vehicles are unmarked,' I said. 'Even the RSPCA have covered up their signs with magnetic white boards . . .'

The policeman, about my age, grinned back at me. 'Yeah, I was thinking that,' he replied. 'You aren't shy, are you? Even got your logo on your shirt! I guess they'll find out who you are soon enough anyway.'

'Seriously, I have no idea who these people are or what I've been roped into. Who is this family that everyone is so nervous of? Am I asking for trouble coming along on this?'

'Bit late now,' he said, pointing at the house.

I turned and looked beyond the wide metal gates at the huge brick building looming behind them. A curtain twitched in an upstairs window.

'They'll have you marked by now,' the strong voice of Sergeant McGinley sounded behind me. 'Just keep your head down and do your job. We're here to watch your back so it'll be fine.'

'What happens when you've gone and they track down Pilgrims Veterinary Practice?' I said.

'Then you call us,' he grinned. 'They'll be focused on blaming the RSPCA for this. They've instigated everything and conducted all the visits to bring events to this point. The likes of you and me are just part of the process.'

I nodded, as the crowd of officers gathered around. A quick head count told me that twenty-one officers were present. I imagined the crime rate in the rest of the forest soaring as we all stood outside the house, plotting the raid of the century.

Inspector Henwood approached the sergeant and they had a discussion. The sergeant glanced in my direction and I felt my ears burn.

Within moments, instructions were being issued through radios, and officers began to filter away to control the road. Some started to head round the back of the houses to guard a narrow footpath that apparently ran parallel to the road. On the other side of the property, yet more officers stationed themselves outside the large metal gates.

'Luke!' Inspector Henwood called from amongst a cluster of people, including Janet from Trading Standards and the huge figure of Sergeant McGinley and his team.

Not knowing what to expect, I nodded and wandered over to what I assumed was a last minute briefing.

'Luke, Janet and I are going to video everything we see and

begin documenting events as soon as we enter the premises,' Inspector Henwood explained. 'If you could go round the premises, identify animals that you think are suffering or are being kept in unacceptable conditions, those are the ones we'll focus on. Janet is going to bring any prosecution notices in relation to the livestock and the horse. I'll be dealing with the companion animals – the dogs and cats. The dog handlers and the council civilians will come in behind us and take away those animals you're concerned about. Is that OK?'

'Yes,' I replied, feeling a surge of nervous energy. 'You want me to basically point out the aspects I'm worried about and make a note of things for a report?'

'We also want to go round fairly quickly and secure the area, because they will be moving animals as we speak. The important thing is to get some cases we can prosecute on. Courts don't pin individuals down on the general state of things. They want identifiable concrete welfare cases.'

I nodded, and Sergeant McGinley looked at me.

'Ready?' he asked.

'No problem,' I replied. 'I'll just go round with the inspector and Janet here, sounds straightforward.'

'No, son,' he said. 'You're coming with *us*. The inspector and Janet are documenting. We need an RSPCA representative with us when we serve the notice. You're working for the RSPCA today. Welcome to the advance raiding party!' He laughed and clapped me on the shoulder. 'Right, lads, are we ready?' he called.

Three figures materialised from the side of one of the Transits. They all wore helmets, were kitted out in full body armour and carrying large plastic shields. Batons and tasers were strapped at their waists.

'I'm feeling a little underdressed for this,' I murmured. In my hand I had a small box containing some medicines, a notepad and pen.

'Have you got some sedatives?' the sergeant asked as we walked towards the gate.

One of the policemen stationed there opened it and we walked through.

'Er, yes,' I said, twisting round as I heard the gate being shut behind us. 'I have some in the box. Why are they shutting the gate?'

'The same reason we're carrying these shields.' I couldn't see through his face guard, but there was no doubt – I could hear the smile in his voice. 'The family have threatened to set dogs on us. Don't want them getting in the road. These shields pass an electric current that will knock them out. Won't keep them out for long, though, so if we have to pin any, we'll need to sedate them. Either that, or we'll use another tactic to immobilise them – up to you.'

'Do you often get dogs set on you?'

'We often have bigger dogs with us in situations like this – they tend to deal with the problem, but, yes, I've had them set on me in the past. Not great.'

I idly wondered what would happen if a pack of attack dogs did descend on our little group. I had no doubt that the sergeant and his squad would keep off one or two, but if there were four or five . . . I tightened my grip on my box, wondering how much horse anaesthetic I'd packed and if I could get a jab into a furious attack dog.

The walk to the front of the house was about a hundred metres, and there was no sign of life coming from inside. Reaching the door, three of the police officers stepped back behind us, leaving the sergeant and me on the step.

'Give it a knock,' the sergeant said.

I reached out and rapped hard. Nothing. We all waited expectantly.

'I've got a key,' said one of the policemen behind me.

I turned and saw he was holding what looked like a small metal battering ram.

I reached up to knock again. Just as I did so, the door opened and a short, stocky man with cropped black hair and a spotty face looked up at us.

To give credit where it was due, the man didn't seem in the least bit fazed by the gigantic figure of Sergeant McGinley standing on his doorstep in full riot gear, a sight that would have put the fear of God into most normal people.

The sergeant removed his helmet and glowered at the man, who met his eyes with a nonchalant air.

'What?' the man asked.

The sergeant held out a somewhat crumpled piece of paper. 'I am hereby issuing you with a search warrant to be actioned immediately,' he began. 'You are not under arrest, but you are required to remain on the premises while we carry out the operation.'

'What for?' the man challenged, his voice rising. 'You pricks can't come in!'

'Read the paper,' the sergeant replied. 'You know how it works.' Without a second word, he pushed forward into the house, jamming his foot in the door to prevent the man from shutting it.

'No animals in here,' the man said. Then, twisting his head slightly to look at me, his whole face screwed up. 'Who in hell do you think you are? You can just get the—'

'Vet,' I interrupted. I tried not to cringe back, even though I'd been showered with dark grey spittle.

'He's with us,' said the sergeant, as two members of the

team filed into the hallway, leaving one outside, with me and the sergeant still in the doorway.

'You'll disturb my ma,' the man complained. 'She's sleeping.'

'That's a shame,' the sergeant replied, without a trace of sincerity. 'She'll just have to go back to bed when we've gone. Who else is here?'

'Dunno,' the man said, and looked up at the sergeant again, shrugging.

'Right, well, best have a look round for the animals, then,' I said and, trying to ignore the man's belligerent stare, I walked into the house. Beside me, the sergeant spoke into his radio. In the distance, I could vaguely hear the gate opening and the rest of the team coming up the drive.

I walked along the corridor, a policeman following me, and pushed open the door to the kitchen. Instantly, a deep growl sounded from a large Rottweiler, which spun round to look at me.

'Dog!' the policeman shouted.

It was an astute observation.

'Thought you said there were no animals in the house,' Sergeant McGinley demanded.

'Forgot,' the man replied, with a sly smile.

'Does he bite?' the other policeman asked, as we hovered outside the door.

'Only when he's pissed off,' the man said.

'Let's hope he's having a good day,' I said, making the decision to step forward into the kitchen. As the dog walked up to me, I held my ground. As he got near, I let my hand drop and reached out to stroke him as casually as I could.

'Nice kitchen,' I said conversationally. 'Looks quite new.'

'One more word out of you,' the man replied, 'and you'll *get* it.'

The dog, becoming less wary as it heard my voice, seemed to settle and I squatted down to rub his head, face and ears. It seemed to relax him. 'Good boy,' I said, ignoring the threat. 'What's his name?'

'Dunno,' the man said.

'That's an original one, I suppose.'

I moved one hand to catch hold of his collar. The dog seemed fit and strong – there was no welfare issue with him that I could see. And although he might have looked the part, he was no savage attack dog either.

'Good boy Dunno,' I said, slipping a lead over the dog's neck and pulling him gently out of the room where he was led away by one of the handlers.

As I progressed through the downstairs rooms, there was a cage of birds, a glimpse of a cat and, whilst the man had been lying about not having any animals there, they looked in pretty good condition. Generally, the house seemed spacious and tidy.

Just when it seemed as if the whole raid was pointless, I spotted a door at the back of the utility room, which led into a darkened hallway beyond.

The man, seeing my observation, walked in front of me. 'Nosy bastard,' he muttered. 'That just goes to the garage. Easier to get to it going round the front, if you have to.'

'We'll go whichever way we want,' said Sergeant McGinley, moving up beside me.

If the man hadn't called me a nosy bastard, I would probably have gone round to the front. It made little odds to me – but, riled, I ignored him and pushed open the door.

Immediately, a dank dirty smell rampaged towards me.

The passageway didn't lead to the garage at all: it led out to a yard and some buildings at the back of the house. It was strangely silent, and I wondered why the stable doors were bolted both top and bottom. I slid one of the bolts back, edged open the door and tried to let my eyes adjust to the impenetrable darkness inside.

'Anything in there?' the sergeant, standing behind me, asked.

I opened the door a little wider and recoiled in horror at what I could see. The floor of the stable was about three inches thick in dog waste. Two scraggy animals cowered in the far corner. There was no water visible, except for a puddle of fetid liquid that had pooled through a leak in the stable roof in one corner.

The dogs were emaciated, their fur matted with filth, and it took me a moment to realise they were supposed to be German Shepherds.

'We aren't going to be attacked by these,' I said quietly, shutting the lower half of the stable door and moving to the next. Every single sealed stable had two or three dogs in it, all in an equally filthy condition.

Moving rapidly across the yard, carefully instructing the dog handlers not to remove any of the animals until the RSPCA and Trading Standards had gathered their evidence, I opened another stable that was partitioned into four pens. Breeding bitches, each with six or seven puppies, lay on shavings in each pen. Effectively, it was a gruesome puppy farm for supposed attack dogs.

'How much are these puppies worth?' the sergeant asked.

'They probably sell them for between six hundred and eight hundred pounds each,' I replied.

'There are thirty pups in that room alone – that's twenty-four thousand pounds!'

'Thinking of taking up a new trade?' I asked.

'Bloody hell,' the big policeman said, amazed at how the business enterprise added up.

'Those dogs in the stables, they'll be the breeding stock – I presume they're churning them out all year round.'

From the other side of the yard, Janet and Inspector Henwood joined us. 'Exactly,' the RSPCA inspector replied. 'They advertise in the local papers. Each family member has a different dog – by splitting them between themselves, they're trying to get round the legislation that you can't have more than three litters a year unless you're a registered breeder.'

The sergeant looked grim as he digested how the business worked.

'We found the horse,' Janet said, changing the subject. 'The calves have all gone, though.'

'How is it?' I asked.

'Very overgrown hoofs,' she replied. 'Matted mane. Needs worming, but seems to be okay otherwise.'

Shaking my head, I approached a horse trailer that was adjacent to the far block of stables. There was something wet underneath it and I walked round one end to peer into the back. It had been boarded up with plywood, and a big padlock prevented me from opening the ramp. Walking back round to the other side, I had a peek through the jockey door.

Sliding the bolts, I slowly eased it open a few inches, not knowing what to expect. The space was about three foot wide, hardly big enough for the animal within to turn around. Standing in what must have been a week's worth of its own faeces was the sorriest looking mastiff I had ever seen. As daylight spilt into the trailer, it started barking angrily.

'She'll rip your face off,' the man called out.

Keeping the door open just a crack, I peered through the gap and looked at the dog, then glanced at the floor of the trailer. There was a gap under the partition about ten inches high. As I did so, I could make out a little nose, poking underneath.

'She's had puppies,' I said, unable to hide my disgust. 'They must be shut in the back bit.'

'Right,' the sergeant said, turning to the owner, who simply stood there, his hands in his pockets. 'She's going to be a handful. How about *you* get her out?'

He sneered. 'She'll have anyone,' he said. 'That's why she's in there. You want to search, search – but it's *your* job.'

I looked in again. The poor dog had worked herself up, and continued to bark. There was terror and rage in that sound. As all the people gathered outside, I saw Inspector Henwood videoing the proceedings.

I turned my attention back to the dog, and as I did so, the mastiff wet herself.

'Careful, Luke,' Sergeant McGinley said.

'She's not aggressive, Sergeant,' I replied, praying I was correct. 'She's just scared witless.'

Gently edging towards her, dog muck smearing on my legs and boots as I did so, I reached forward. Uttering soothing words, I gently crawled into the trailer. The dog backed herself right up against the far wall of her prison. There was nowhere either of us could go. She was jammed in front of me and I was totally blocking the exit. Having been passed a slip lead by one of the dog handlers, I slowly reached up and looped it over her head. Then, in a whisper, I asked the sergeant to swing the door wide open.

As she hopped down, her skeletally thin frame caused

murmurs of disgust from the police who had gathered behind us.

Two policemen rapidly prised off the padlocks at the back of the trailer and the ramp swung down.

In a heartbeat, the puppies spilled out, ten of them. They had, I decided, been hastily cast inside, presumably when we had arrived at the house that morning. Unbelievably there was also a cage in the back, containing a terrified cat and ten kittens. A cooked chicken carcass lay discarded on the floor.

'Wait!' I heard the inspector call, rushing forwards with her video camera.

I stared in disbelief at the horrible state of the animals.

'We haven't checked upstairs,' the sergeant quietly said to me.

I nodded and went back into the house. Just as I had walked through the kitchen a voice screamed, 'Take your bloody shoes off!'

I looked up. Blocking the stairs was a heavily scarred woman with raven black hair. She was tall, almost six feet, and of medium build. Behind her, two boys, in their late teens, stood and stared at us belligerently. 'Jack's away today,' she wheezed, 'but when he hears about this, he'll tell his brothers and they'll rip your head off.'

'Jack is her husband,' Sergeant McGinley said quietly, behind me.

'Thanks for that,' I said.

'Take your bloody shoes off!' the woman screamed again.

Horrified by the state of the animals, the complete lack of care and consideration the woman had shown, I shook my head and made to move forwards. As I did so, she launched herself from the top of the stairs.

As I tumbled backwards, she clawed at my face. An instant later, she seemed to draw back. A bear-like hand had clamped around her and lifted her, scrabbling, to the bottom of the stairs.

Before I could get to my feet, two of the police officers, complete with their electric shields, had appeared in the corridor, only for one of them to trip over my feet. In a chaos of confusion and limbs, they went careering forward into the banister.

There came a sudden sharp buzz, as the electric shield jarred the railing. The two teenage boys jumped back, a wisp of smoke shooting up.

I heaved myself upright, muttering an apology to the policeman, who gave me a smile and shake of his head.

Glancing at the carpet, I could see the woman's point. Thick mud and dog muck was now smeared all over the hall floor and a dark burn mark had stained the pale oak banister.

'Nothing a bit of shampoo and a good scrub won't clear up,' Sergeant McGinley said, as the two teenage boys mutely filed down the stairs and were led outside. 'Bit like your kennels out the back. Right, let's have a look around, shall we?'

It was half past three when we finally left the premises. More than thirty dogs had been seized, the horse and a cat were left at the house, and all the occupants had been charged with animal cruelty. I glanced at my watch. Thankfully, the farmer I'd planned to visit that afternoon had been happy to postpone until tomorrow and I had thirty minutes in which to phone Holly and Mr Pines.

Bidding goodbye to Inspector Henwood, Janet and Sergeant McGinley, I turned to leave.

'Good work today,' Sergeant McGinley said, walking after me down the drive.

'Certainly an experience,' I replied.

'Look, if you get any bother, give me a phone.' He held out a card with his mobile number on it.

I stopped dead in my tracks. 'What are the odds of me getting a reprisal for this?'

The sergeant paused. 'I'm not sure. At the end of the day, the family will know they were in the wrong and they have honour about that sort of thing. You were just doing your job.'

The sergeant offered me a grin as I shook my head ruefully, cursing Ian Myrtle for getting me into this predicament.

'Where are you off to now?' the sergeant asked.

'Home,' I replied, smiling for the first time that day.

14
A Really Great Adventure

'So Holly said yes, the little dog lives – and you have your own surgery in a month?' Sam's voice crackled down the line.

'Absolutely,' I shouted, the wind threatening to drown out my voice.

'Has your house been burnt down yet?' he joked.

'No, I spoke to a farmer who had connections with the family a couple of days after the raid and explained how I'd been roped into it. He told me that he'd heard rumours that I had been involved through the grapevine but I wasn't to worry,' I replied.

'You and your dodgy pals. You're in with the Mafia,' Sam said, with glee. 'Anyway, breaking news this end is that Jane and I are getting a cat – he's called Montgomery,' Sam continued.

'You've finally got worthy competition for her affections, then. It's all going on for both of us!' I laughed.

'I take on competitions I can win with fresh fish. You take on ones that will probably induce some sort of cardiac arrest,' he said. 'You fly out tomorrow for your little Ironman exercise, do you?'

'Plane leaves at three o'clock. I arrive early evening, and the race is two days later.'

'You're an idiot,' I just about heard Sam say.

'Thanks, as always.'

There was no response. I held the phone out and saw that the reception had died on me. Smiling, I admitted to myself that Sam probably had a point, and thrust the phone back into the little bag that was strapped behind my bike saddle.

It had been a momentous couple of months. My despair at leaving the police raid had quickly dissipated when I'd phoned Holly and she'd agreed to take the plunge and come to work with me and Cordelia. In doing so, it meant that Bracken had had a reprieve; before long, the little Jack Russell and Holly would be inseparable, as she could bring her to work. I'd scrambled to a phone and got hold of Tony Pines just five minutes before the twenty-four-hour deadline was up. He'd agreed to let Bracken have the operation and be rehomed. I even detected a hint of relief in his voice as well.

I'd amputated Bracken's leg two nights later and the operation had gone well. Holly had come in to assist, and even Bob kept popping in to see how she was. True to form, Bracken had healed incredibly quickly and was bounding around almost as fast as she used to on four legs.

The court case for the family we had raided was anticipated to take up to six months to get together – and so, in the meantime, the RSPCA had taken away all the dogs and cats from the farm. It had meant that I'd had to examine every single one of them, writing painstaking reports as to their size, health and condition – but it was good work for the fledgling practice. In the last few weeks several of the dogs had put on over a third of their bodyweight and were still looking lean – a sure indication of just how chronically starved they had been. The case for neglect and cruelty was looking good, and the family would be found guilty as charged.

The only slight cloud on the horizon was that the family had put in a complaint about me to the Royal College of Veterinary Surgeons for unprofessional conduct. It was the only one I had ever received in my career and it was galling, to say the least. In my defence, I had a letter signed by Chief Inspector Plimly, commending me for my participation in the raid – and the RSPCA lawyer informed me it was standard procedure for the defence to try to discredit the prosecution's expert witness.

The biggest problem was, with an allegation of professional misconduct hanging over me, I couldn't volunteer overseas with the charity – no matter how unfounded it was. All the same, I'd been assured that the council of the Royal College would look at my case within the next six weeks – and, with all the training for Ironman, and the looming launch of the Pilgrims surgery, my plans for a charity trip weren't imminent. I crossed my fingers and hoped it would all blow over soon.

My sister's husband, Matt, had clicked with Bob when they had been hunting for Moses and had decided to invest in PetAir. As it turned out, good things had come from that whole escapade: Moses's owners had been on morning television, beamed across from the southern hemisphere, and the story had been reported in most national newspapers. Thankfully, they exonerated us of any blame and advertised the fact that we were flying the dog out there again.

What was really great was that, with Bob taking on large

chunks of the work at the emergency service, and Matt now coming on board to help us run PetAir, I had a lot more time to drive on Pilgrims and spend time at home with Cordelia.

The biggest pressure I'd now brought on myself had been to somehow fit in huge amounts of training for the Ironman triathlon. As soon as the pedals had arrived for my bike, I hadn't wasted a second in trying to learn how to ride it. *Trying* was the key word. It had taken about a week before I could even sit on it comfortably. The saddle was shaped like a knife, and there was huge science involved in positioning it correctly, and even in how many pedal revolutions I was supposed to do in order to gain maximum speed with maximum efficiency. I'd joined a local triathlon club for some tips, but all of the members had assumed I was joking when I'd said I needed to train for an Ironman in a few months. In between the bouts of laughter, they were a great bunch of people – and while I hadn't been able to keep up with anyone for the first month, I had steadily improved and picked up an infinite amount of handy tips and techniques.

Looking at the view in front of me, I took a swig from my water bottle. It was a stunning day and I had ten miles to go to get home. I felt exhausted. Theoretically, I should have been gearing up for a quick run after the cycling, but as I'd have to do it properly in three days' time, there didn't seem much point in exhausting myself. My excuse was that I was 'tapering down'. It was a great phrase that lots of the good triathletes I had met used before a race. Unfortunately, I'd done a lot of that over the last month.

Half an hour later, I swung into the drive and went inside

to have a shower. Cordelia looked up as me as I walked into the kitchen. 'Pasta tonight,' she said with glee. 'Loading up begins!'

'I'll turn into pasta,' I replied.

Cordelia squinted her eyes at me, considering whether or not I could be mistaken for a piece of pasta.

'Certainly not spaghetti,' she said.

'I'll settle for bigoli.'

Cordelia paused. 'Do you need to make any calls to Africa?' she innocently asked.

I looked momentarily confused.

'You know – to get any tips?'

I was still looking at her, blankly. Then it dawned on me. 'Funny,' I replied. 'If ever there was an incentive to get under twelve hours, that image of his hairy chest will do it.'

'Yes,' Cordelia said. '*I* remember that as well.'

'Red rag to a bull,' I said quickly.

'Don't kill yourself to beat Gavin's time. It's ridiculous – you've never even done a triathlon and you're doing this to cut your teeth! Just getting round will make me proud of you. You'll be an Ironman!'

'The winners will do this in eight hours,' I said. 'And word has it that the Austrian Ironman is a fairly good entry-level one. I'm on fire for this.'

'An entry-level Ironman?' Cordelia balked, all thoughts of which pasta shape I most resembled quickly forgotten. 'I thought entry-level Ironman competitions were called normal triathlons?'

'This is a normal triathlon,' I replied, scrabbling for the right expression. 'Just a long one.'

'What about the people who come in last? Is there a time limit?'

'The cut-off is seventeen hours,' I said, feeling the first butterflies in my stomach.

'Seventeen hours doesn't seem all that long. What happens if you get a puncture or your chain snaps on your bike?'

'I'll fix it.' I shrugged. 'Besides, I've got a target of under twelve hours, staying focused, thinking of all the orphan puppies that are relying on my sponsorship money.' I was trying to feign confidence, but Cordelia saw straight through me. She always could. A puncture I could handle, but the chain snapping was something I was just hoping wouldn't happen. I had a chain splitter packed in my saddlebag, and I'd seen the guys at the triathlon club dismantle and reassemble their bikes with practised ease, but I dreaded it happening to me. My bike had been serviced last week and I wasn't planning on touching anything between then and the race. After that – the chain could snap all it wanted!

'Just make it through,' Cordelia said, smiling. 'Get the PR and sponsorship for WVS, then come back here and let's launch the new surgery.'

'I know, exciting times ahead! Are you going to be OK here?' I asked.

She was going to do the farm cover for the next couple of days at the practice. As a small-animal vet, the prospect of a calving was probably making her feel the same as I felt about the Ironman.

Cordelia arched an eyebrow. 'We won't have our mothers with us . . . but we'll cope, won't we, Leuwen?'

At her feet, Leuwen beat his tail in response. That dog was definitely beginning to like being with Cordelia more than he liked being with me.

I shook my head, ignoring the gentle mocking. My mum

was coming out just before the race to cheer me on. I didn't care what anybody thought – she was going to be a massive help. Midway through the race, competitors were allowed to receive some food from a supporter or family friend – and it would have been tricky to get this without anyone who knew me being there.

'Ms Conelson may call,' I continued, pretending I was oblivious to the joke. 'She's had a bit of coughing in her chickens the last couple of days.'

'Don't worry,' Cordelia replied. 'I've handled worse than a coughing chicken before now. And, besides, you'll be back in three days, won't you?'

'With a winner's medal, a load of bucks for the charity and a large Ironman tattoo,' I said, with a hollow laugh, and tripped, stubbing my toe, as I went into the hallway.

The sunlight streamed through the window of my tiny room. I woke up to twitch the curtains that wouldn't quite close. It was just after dawn, and I had a day to prepare for tomorrow's big event. I had arrived the previous night, and the Herculean tasks had already begun in earnest. My first real mission had been to get the bike up four flights of stairs, to a box-like room on the top floor of this hotel. The staircase was only just wide enough for me to get up, let alone turn a corner with a bike and a bag – and it had required a fair bit of contortion.

'The lift is broken,' the lady on the desk had said, with a sympathetic smile on her face.

'Have you got a room on the ground floor by any chance?' I asked hopefully.

'No,' she said, benignly. 'We are full for the Ironman race.'

'Right,' I wheezed. 'It's just going to be a bit hard to get the bike up the staircase. It's very narrow.'

'*Ja*,' she replied, still smiling.

'Anywhere safe we can leave the bikes downstairs?'

The lady folded her hands together like a penitent. 'No,' was all she said.

'Going to be tricky getting up there,' I said again, looking first at the staircase and then back at the lady.

'Are you Swedish?' she asked.

'No,' I replied. 'British.'

Her smile grew slightly wider. At first I thought she was just being friendly – but then I realised what that smile meant. It was a smile of sympathy. A little confused, I took my room key and patiently started to dismantle the bike. I figured it was the only way I might get even part of it safely up the stairs.

Under no misapprehensions that the trip was going to get any easier, I began the hike up the staircase, hoping not to meet anyone on the way. Even having taken both wheels off it was a mission: the staircase went on and on, like some optical illusion Escher might have drawn – but, once happily ensconced in my room, I'd collapsed on the bed in a heap and done my best to get a decent night's sleep.

Just getting the bike into my room had exhausted me. How I was going to complete an Ironman triathlon in under forty-eight hours, I had no idea – but I was about to find out.

The dawn brought with it the sun, and I headed over to the pre-race registration area to get my numbers, attend the morning briefing and work out the set-up for the race the next day.

Weaving among lovingly restored Renaissance courtyards teeming with modern boutiques, trendy bars and rustic beer gardens, I could think of worse places to come and sweat to death. Situated in a province bordering Italy and Slovenia, Klagenfurt was the sort of place I should have been taking Cordelia for a romantic getaway, rather than enduring an epic triathlon – even my pre-race instructions hinted at spectacular scenery, informing me that I should head to the edge of Lake Wörthersee, on the outskirts of the town, at the base of a stunning alpine mountain range.

The plan was that the race would start with a swim in the lake, a cycle around its edge at the base of the mountains, then the run would take me back into the town and out again to the lake. According to the legend printed in the travel guide in my hotel room, the town had been established after a group of villagers managed to kill and destroy an evil dragon that lived there. There was a huge monument to the *Lindworm* monster in the middle of the town, an appropriate landmark to try to spot as I limped through the marathon.

The bright summer sun lit up cobbled streets. Deciding that a walk to the race headquarters would be a bit of an effort in the heat – and wanting to conserve my energy – I did the only decent thing and got on a bus. Ten minutes later, I hopped off. There was no mistaking the huge sprawl of tents, lines of bikes and hundreds of people that marked the headquarters of the competition.

Scanning the area for where non-professional competitors were due to meet, and easing myself through a long line of super-fit triathletes, I cast my eye about to find the place where everyone was supposed to register.

'Who are you here supporting?' a voice said beside me.

'Mainly myself,' I said, to the woman who had spoken to me. She was eating a large ice cream.

'Oh, sorry!' She laughed. 'I thought you were like me, here

supporting someone . . . Not that you couldn't be competing,' she added.

'That's fine,' I replied. 'I'm a relaxed Ironman. Who are you supporting?'

'My husband. He's a doctor.' She hesitated, tongue gangling out over the ice cream. 'Oh, there he is!' she exclaimed, pointing towards two muscular men who stood posing in their Speedos for a woman with a camera. I looked at them for a moment, slightly confused. Then a tall lean man nudged his way between them and walked purposefully towards a tent on our left.

'Ah, the guy walking towards the tent?'

'Yes! *Adam!*' she shouted, waving frantically.

Adam turned his head, saw us, smiled and waved back at his wife.

'Is he registering by any chance?' I asked.

'Yes,' she began. 'It took us a while to find out where to go – but that's the place and that's where the briefing is. It's only for athletes, though. That's why I'm out here with an ice cream. I'm Heidi, by the way,' she said, holding out her hand in introduction.

I took her fingers, sticky with chocolate and vanilla.

'Don't worry,' I said. 'Anyone with any sense in that tent would much rather be outside having an ice cream on a day like this.'

I bid a hasty goodbye and made a beeline after Adam.

Easing my way into the tent, I found the stewards. Promptly, they ticked my name off a long list. Collecting my competitor's bag of goodies, I spotted Adam and walked over to say hello. He was chatting to three other men, all of whom looked incredibly fit. They smiled at me welcomingly as I introduced myself.

'Are you Swedish?' a wild-haired German asked me. His eyes were steel grey and his face heavily bearded, with long hair sticking out of the top of his head. If he hadn't been standing in the Ironman tent, I might have mistaken him for a tramp.

'No, British,' I replied, wondering if I had a Swedish flag stuck to me somewhere.

'Ha! British!' he declared. 'I go to Wales every year!'

I didn't know what to make of that.

'Wolfgang here is an avid fan of racing horses,' Adam cut in, by way of explanation.

'Racing horses?'

'*Ja!* I will win next year!'

'Basically,' Adam laughed, 'he runs twenty-two miles against fifty-odd horses and several other human competitors. It's cross-country and if he wins, he'll get all the prize money.' Adam shook his head. 'Got to be easier ways of earning a few thousand pounds.'

'One man only has done this. I will be the second!' Wolfgang proudly declared. 'But first, we must conquer Austria tomorrow.'

'I think that's been done before as well,' I said.

Wolfgang let out a mad cackle. 'Have you done many of these?' he asked, heartily.

'I'm an Ironman virgin,' I replied.

There was a moment of silence.

'Ah, tomorrow we will break you as well.' Wolfgang beamed. 'You will be a virgin no longer! I love to meet the virgins before a race!'

I looked at Adam to see if I was the only one who thought Wolfgang was crazy – but his expression pretty much matched my own.

'What is the longest triathlon you have done?' Wolfgang asked.

'Well, I've run a lot before,' I said. 'And I swam as a kid. I also have a decent bike with pedals, so the plan is to put all that together tomorrow.'

Wolfgang roared with laughter. 'You are the most virginal virgin – you have never even been kissed! You are a crazy man. You have never done a triathlon before – the Ironman will be your first ever one. You are a warrior!' He grasped my wrist fervently. 'Tomorrow you will kill yourself,' he said to me earnestly, before roaring with laughter again.

'Don't worry, Luke,' Adam chipped in. 'I'll be dying alongside you – this is my first Ironman race as well.'

'Let me tell you, you young virgins,' Wolfgang chortled conspiratorially, 'it is all in the mind. You need to attack it and whip it and beat it.'

A loudspeaker announced something in German. Wolfgang's ears pricked up.

'I must go,' he said. 'See you in the race, my virginal friends!'

And, with that, he wandered off.

'Well, I'm guessing – no, I'm *hoping* he isn't a typical competitor,' I said to Adam, watching Wolfgang's rangy figure dart around people on his way to wherever he was going.

'Wolfgang's a pro-athlete, would you believe? Before you joined us, he was telling me that he wants this race to qualify him for Hawaii.'

'Come again?'

'This race is one of the World Championship qualifiers. The winners in the groups here will qualify for the final in Hawaii. The ultimate accolade is to win there.'

'I thought this was entry level!'

'Entry for the World Championship series. We're in a qualifier. Tomorrow we're racing against the best in the business.'

Adam seemed to be enjoying just a little too much what must have been an expression of absolute disbelief on my face. 'Are you all set then, Luke? Have you really never done a triathlon before?'

I was beginning to wish I'd lied.

'No, I haven't,' I admitted. 'But I've been training like a fiend for this – and I *have* done some marathons before. I'm just going to take it steady and see how it goes. I've got my gear, I'll check my bike this afternoon and then I'll have a go!' I paused. 'Any medical tips you can give me? Something, say, to prevent a heart attack, or get me through this in one piece?'

Adam considered my question seriously for a moment before responding. 'Save the caffeine until the marathon,' he said, with a gentle nod of the head. 'You're allowed Coke at the drink stops in the race, but if you take it too early on, it'll cause you issues – your stomach acid production will increase. Only have it at the beginning of the marathon – it'll promote the mobilisation of your fat stores, preserve what glycogen you have left until the end.'

'That was a bit more useful than I thought you might say,' I said, digesting the information.

'My issue is the swim,' Adam said.

'The swim?'

'I'm just such a rubbish swimmer. The run and the cycle don't worry me, but the swim is a stress. I've done loads of triathlons but the swim has always been quite short. I've had a heap of coaching for this but, to be honest, I'm dreading it.

I think Heidi's convinced I'll end up at the bottom of the lake . . .'

'I'm the other way around. I'm least worried about the swim.'

Adam looked at me, dumbfounded.

'Well,' I said, beginning to doubt myself, 'it *looks* like a beautiful lake. It's going to be a warm day and, I mean, we could do that distance breast stroke and still make the cut-off, couldn't we?'

'I never looked at it that way. I guess you're right – there'll be a great view at the front, I suppose. But it's not the actual swimming I'm worried about. I mean, the whole start of the sw—'

Adam tailed off suddenly. The loudspeaker was back – and, this time, in English.

'Come on,' I said. 'They're calling us for the briefing. Let's head over and see what the plan is.'

Half an hour later, Adam and I emerged from the tent, our heads full of the intricacies of what was and wasn't allowed in relation to drafting, stopping, starting and a million other things we should do before the race began. I also discovered the checkpoint where a supporter could give a competitor a snack to fuel them. As Adam and I discussed the cycle route, I glanced at my watch. 'Adam,' I said, 'I'll see you tomorrow, I've got to go. My mother's arriving on the plane. She's going to be at the support station and cheer madly on as I puff round.'

Adam laughed. 'Let's meet before the race,' he said. I was glad he didn't make a mother joke. 'Say, six thirty a.m. at the bike station? It's going to be a long day. Maybe she and Heidi can keep each other company.'

'Great plan,' I said, trying not to feel like this was the first day of school and I'd just made a friend. 'And – if you want – we can nail the swim section together. Drafting's allowed on that bit, I seem to think he said.'

I headed back to the bus and got on with my return ticket. When I got off, I glanced again at my watch. Mum was due to arrive at the hotel by taxi in about five minutes. Delving into my pockets for my wallet to pay the driver, my heart sank. It wasn't there. I must have dropped it somewhere at the registration area.

I groaned. At least I still had my wedding ring.

With a silent curse I went to meet the taxi. I just hoped Mum had brought a credit card. If not, checking out of the hotel was going to be difficult.

My alarm went off at five and I sat up groggily. The dawning realisation of what I was about to do sent a surge of adrenalin through my veins. Urgently, I got dressed, checked that the bag with my cycling and running gear was ready to deposit, slung my wetsuit over my shoulder and went downstairs to grab a pre-race snack.

Mum was already downstairs waiting for me. 'Morning,' she said. 'Bit like sports day at school, this – only twenty years later!'

'Be no trophies today, either Mum,' I replied with a smile. 'My heart's still in it, but the results will be the same . . .'

'Always a winner to me,' she replied with a laugh.

I shook my head in despair. 'Come on, let's eat – we've got to get over there.'

'I thought the race didn't start until seven?'

'That's when the starter gun or whatever goes off,' I said, gobbling down breakfast. 'I need to pump my bike tyres up, get into this wetsuit and generally flap about near the start line.' We got up, still chewing, and made for the exit. Outside, the day was already gloriously sunny. 'I've found a friend for you, Mum. Her name's Heidi – she's the wife of a doctor who's also in the race.'

'Oh, that's great,' Mum said, a thousand times calmer than I was feeling. 'There are lots of nice shops here. It's quite a historic town, isn't it?'

'Mum,' I replied, 'I don't expect you to be hanging about for twelve hours solid, but if there's a chance you could meet me at the supporters' aid station and pass me a few snacks as a sort of lunch, that would be great.'

Mum stopped. 'Have you got some lunch?' she asked, suddenly concerned. I remembered that when I was a boy, she was always worrying about whether I was eating properly or not. It seemed that nothing had changed.

'With the money situation, it's been a little tricky to purchase things,' I said. 'If you could grab me a few energy drinks, chocolate bars, pepperoni sausages, that would be amazing.'

'I can manage that,' she said, cheerfully. 'I used to make you a packed lunch for years.'

That said, we got on the early bus service that would take competitors to where they needed to be. As we drove away, I wondered if Mum knew exactly what I was letting myself – and her, if things went badly – in for.

* * *

If the starting area had been full of people the previous day, that morning it was like a city in its own right. The crush of people was immense. TV cameras were trained on entourages of pro-athletes, many of whom seemingly just wanted to be left alone to focus on the job at hand, keeping their heads down, checking bikes and other equipment intently.

The muscular posers who had flaunted about the place yesterday had largely gone, to be replaced with a thousand focused, disciplined, nervous athletes.

Heading over to the bike area, we miraculously found Adam and Heidi. It was a wonder we didn't miss them in the throng.

After introducing Heidi to Mum – I could tell they were going to enjoy this day a lot more than Adam and I would – and making sure they knew where we were going to meet them on the cycle route, Adam and I said our goodbyes, were wished plenty of luck, then headed through to get our electronic tags and don our swimming gear.

Suddenly I stopped, swearing under my breath.

'What is it?' Adam asked.

'I meant to check my bike tyres,' I muttered. 'I haven't done it since we arrived.'

'That's not good,' Adam said. 'They'll definitely have deflated in yesterday's sun. Best get to it, Luke. I'll meet you here in ten. I want to do some stretches at any rate.'

Nodding, I ran over to the hundreds of rows of bikes. Finding my own among them was a momentous task in its own right. At last alighting upon it, I cast my eye around for a track pump I could borrow to check the tyre pressures. It was one of the key things that the triathletes had told me in the UK: get your tyres right and the bike will do half the job for you.

'Luke! Luke the virgin!' a voice boomed.

I turned to see a hairy Viking bearing down on me.

'Wolfgang, would you lend a virgin your pump?' I asked.

Wolfgang roared with laughter and lifted his pump over the row of bikes in front to pass it to me.

I quickly did the tyres, thanked him and, together, we started to walk back to the race area.

'No,' Wolfgang said. 'You must come this way.' I felt Wolfgang's hand closing round my arm. This mountain of a man positively dwarfed me.

'Adam's waiting for me over there,' I replied, pointing to the area where Adam was supposed to be standing.

My eyes must have been deceiving me. I could see no sign of him, just a herd of about fifty Spaniards, all putting on their swimming caps. Everyone was now in their wetsuits with caps in the same colour. It was virtually impossible to make anyone out.

'Come with me,' Wolfgang boomed, slapping me forwards. 'He has gone through! Hurry up! I show you the way to do this!'

We walked through the barriers towards the start area and a loud beep sounded as they read the electronic tags that were clipped around our ankles. Just as we had gone through, I heard Adam's voice and twisted round. He was standing on the other side of the barriers, looking at me confused. 'What are you doing?' he cried.

'I was looking for you,' I said. 'I ran into Wolfgang – we thought you'd gone through.'

'No!' he exclaimed. 'Not yet! What are you thinking? You're in the worst situation there.'

'No problem,' I replied, unsure what Adam was talking about. 'I'll just come back.'

Adam's face twisted up. 'You can't,' he said. 'Once you go through, you can't come back. The machine's read your tag, hasn't it?'

I nodded. 'What's the big deal?' I asked. 'Come on through.'

'This is what I was trying to tell you yesterday,' he said. 'It isn't the swimming bit of the swim I'm worried about. It's the infamous crush at the start. We don't want to be caught up in it.' Adam threw his head left and right, desperate to see if there was any way I could escape.

A steward walked up to me and ushered me forwards.

'I'll hang back and wait for you!' I shouted.

Too late, the steward's hands were on me, urging me forwards.

'You'll never find me!' Adam cried, as I disappeared. 'Take care, Luke! Good luck!'

I tried to resist, but I was inexorably pushed on.

'Come on, Luke,' Wolfgang said, with a maniacal glint in his eye. 'You're in the way! You cannot stand there! Kiss goodbye to the other virgins. Now is *your* time.'

We were swept on, joining the crowd.

'Why have we come through now?' I asked.

'Because you are a man!' Wolfgang announced. 'You need to be at the front to attack it like a warrior!'

I think I preferred Cords' jokes to this.

We had walked to the water's edge. Here, the competitors gathered. There must have been nearly two hundred of us in the advance, all waiting to get in the water.

'Now,' Wolfgang began, 'I must go. You stay here, little virgin – but I want you to catch me. You will be victorious! Just go and swim hard. Ha ha! You want to be on TV – see?' Wolfgang flung his arms at the TV cameras that had appeared, giving me a mad victory sign with two fingers as he waded into the water.

Wolfgang's entrance to the lake seemed to be the cuc for most of the other competitors standing alongside us. I stood there, watching them, and then it dawned on me: they all wore different-coloured swim caps, marking them out as professional triathletes. They had a twenty-metre head-start in the water, away from the rest of the field, to ensure that they didn't get caught up in the mêlée of the beach start. With horror, I twigged what Adam had been talking about.

While I had a great view of the lake, I was standing at the very front of a field of almost two thousand triathletes, all of whom had to get into the water through a fifty-metre-wide section of beach. Bodies began to push against me and, before I could so much as take a breath, a seething mass of wetsuit-clad triathletes was jostling me closer to the water's edge. Almost in the water myself, I gulped.

Helplessly, I looked left and right to see if there was a way back. This time, however, there was nothing to save me. Not even my mum – wherever she was. It was just as Adam had tried to warn me: I was totally pinned in, right in the middle of the front row. I saw Wolfgang spin round in the water among the other pros and give me a mad wave, just as a television helicopter flew overhead, chopping up the water as it angled closer for the perfect shot.

Then, suddenly, the klaxon sounded and we were off.

I would imagine the incentive to swim fast when being chased by a man-eating shark can't be beaten by much, but being chased into a lake by almost two thousand people, all intent on swimming over or through you, must come a close second.

I hurled myself into the water. As I did so, an arm swooped out besides me and knocked my goggles to the side. I stuck my arm out to shove the man away as I tried to adjust them, but I was already out of my depth in the lake. I felt a hand push down on my shoulder, propelling me under the water.

I sprang up, gasping for air, as the crush of bodies powered round me, flailing arms slapping down on everything and everyone in their way. There were already two people seemingly swimming on my back. I couldn't even lift my legs horizontally and I felt a moment of panic as another hand landed on my shoulder, pushing me under again. I gulped a huge mouthful of lake. Thrusting myself upwards, I spluttered on, wondering if this was how I was going to meet my ignoble end.

Realising that the only way to get out of this was to swim faster, I gritted my teeth, and pulled forward with my arms. I couldn't see anything, my goggles full of water, and felt as if I was in the midst of a raging torrent, rather than having a quick dip in an alpine lake in Austria. My right hand connected with someone's face, but I didn't care: this was handbags at dawn. I kicked someone else hard in the ribs, but there were clearly no prisoners and I gained a fraction more space.

Suddenly I was clearing the maelstrom. Someone was drafting me, swimming right on top of my legs; I kicked up instinctively to stop myself being pushed under again and my heel connected with their chin. No one had told me that triathlons were a full contact sport. Free of clinging bodies, I powered on as hard as I could, not daring to look up or around. All thoughts of waiting for Adam were gone: I was just concentrating on gulping air every third stroke, ruthlessly striking out with my arms and legs, irrespective of whoever was beside or behind me, and powering myself forwards faster than I'd ever done before.

Miraculously, I was in a group of about five swimmers ahead of the main pack. I stuck to their rhythm, totally oblivious to the direction I was supposed to be swimming in other than the fact I had to stay in that group. We diverged round a solitary swimmer in front of us – a glimpse of a fluorescent pink hat told me we had caught up with the back of the group of pros who had started twenty metres in front of us. The knowledge gave me new strength and I tried to push on.

Then, finally, after what seemed like an eternity, we were swimming in a narrow channel. Cheering echoed from the crowds strung along its length. Somehow, my feet found a matted ramp and then I was out of the water, gasping air and wondering how on earth I had survived the most traumatic swim of my life.

Dazed, I trotted with the others into the tents. People scurried forward to try to peel off my wetsuit and help me change, but I pushed their hands away, unable to speak. When they wouldn't take no for an answer, I submitted – and, before I knew it, my bike shoes were being thrust on my feet. A large clock at the transition area showed fifty-eight minutes; somehow I had got myself near the front of the field. For a fleeting moment I was in the top one hundred and fifty triathletes – and it was entirely the result of fearing for my life during the last hour.

Still delirious, I recognised Wolfgang in the distance ahead of me, already powering on. Determined to keep myself going, I clambered onto my bike, wobbled dangerously for a moment, and then ground the gears to get into some sort of rhythm.

Catching a glimpse of my mum waving madly as I left the transition zone, I managed a grimace of recognition in return. Desperately, I tried to collect my breath and keep my bike steady as the first surge of competitors raced past me. At least the swim was over, I thought. The sun was shining and it was a beautiful day. I was determined to enjoy the bike ride – and I was even on track for a decent place.

Or so I thought.

Over a distance of 112 miles or 180 kilometres, having

someone overtake you every two-hundred-and-fifty metres for six hours, is an experience all of its own. The route was three laps, each lap tracing along one side of the lake before circling up and around the foothills of the Alps, and then dropping back down to the lake again. Loudspeakers blared, crowds cheered and the sun kept beating down. Drinking as much water as possible, I heeded Adam's advice and steered clear of the Coke – but there were certain rudimentary functions I just couldn't get the hang of without stopping. No one else seemed to have that problem. How they managed it, I don't know, but it did cross my mind that having the swim at the end of a triathlon might be a better idea all round.

About midway round my second lap, I pulled into the support stop and my ever-reliable mum appeared with a bag of food.

'Are you having a good day?' she asked.

'Brilliant,' I wheezed.

'It's a lovely day, isn't it? Lot of people,' she continued. 'Heidi and I are going into town after this, hopefully see you on the run.'

I nodded, fishing around in the bag and pulling out a sandwich. 'Mum!' I gasped. 'You made me sandwiches!'

'It's lunchtime,' she said. 'These are good for you, high-energy ones – jam and cheese.'

I looked at my mother, dumbfounded. I had been expecting a bag of high-energy bars and pepperoni sausages.

'Mum,' I said, distinctly aware that I sounded like I was still fifteen, 'I need high-energy stuff. This race is a killer! None of the other competitors will be having sandwiches. It's not supposed to be a picnic.'

'I spoke to Cordelia,' Mum said, as if that explained

everything. 'You need a decent amount of carbohydrate in you, but sugar overload is not going to do you any favours. Take a bite – you're not leaving here until you finish your meal.'

Despite my exhaustion, I couldn't help but smile. Taking a bite, I chewed for a moment, wondering if my mouth would manage to produce enough saliva for me to swallow it. 'Mum, these are delicious,' I said, gulping them down.

'Mothers always know best, Luke. Now, can you hurry up? I want to go to the shops and I'll miss them if you don't get a move on.'

I took my last bite. 'Great pep talk.'

'Get on with it!'

I laughed, handed Mum the bag and carried on.

The rest of the cycle went well. I had a steady pace and, despite being overtaken so much, I found myself enjoying it. Adam whizzed by on a long downhill stretch, screaming a hello as he went past.

Four hours later, I was midway through the run. The odd swig of Coke was definitely helping and small children lined the roads holding out wet sponges for people to throw on their faces and cool down. The support from the locals was amazing.

'Luke! How are you doing?' a jolly voice sounded beside me. 'You are almost not a virgin now!' Wolfgang had a sponge tucked under each of the straps of his running vest and grinned at me madly. Slowing himself to keep pace with me, he started to chat about the landmarks around us and the history of the town. As he slightly increased speed, I found myself trying to keep up with him. Then it struck me that he had been ahead of me from the very beginning. Surely a pro-athlete would have gone much faster than me on the bike, especially as I had been overtaken by so many others.

'Wolfgang,' I said, managing to collect my breath to interrupt him, 'did you have an accident? How come you're running with me? I thought you'd be far ahead.'

'Yes, I am,' he declared. 'I am running with you because I like you. You are waddling, like a duck. You need to get your rhythm and now we are almost there. You are moving much better. You need to keep going!'

'But what about you, how come you were behind me?' I wheezed.

'Come on, Luke! Think with your head and run with your legs!'

It dawned on me. Wolfgang wasn't behind me at all. Wolfgang was lapping me. He was over eighteen miles in front of me. He was simply keeping me company and getting my spirits up. He was slowing his finishing time because he wanted to help me nail the run.

He grinned at me as we approached a fork in the road.

'When you get here again in two hours or so,' he said, 'you need to go right. Then you are deflowered! I must race again now – I need to go to Hawaii this year!'

He slapped me on the shoulder and powered off. As he left, I smiled and felt my footsteps grow lighter, marvelling at the camaraderie of the man and the generosity of his spirit.

The final stretch was in sight. The cheering was deafening. People lined the ribbons as I surged towards the banner. I ran forward in a desperate sprint finish – and then I was through. It was done. I was an Ironman. Money raised for

WVS, mission accomplished for the charity. A medal was thrust over my head, and I stood there bewildered and amazed.

True to form, Mum was waiting for me, just as she had been on sports day, all those years ago.

I staggered forward. 'Mum,' I gasped. 'I made it! Did you see my time?'

'I'm so proud!' Mum exclaimed, her expression changing from one of joy to mild concern.

'Mum,' I said, noting her expression. 'Are you okay?'

'No, son,' she replied. 'Are *you* okay?'

At that moment, a voice spoke to me from my shoulder. A man in a white medic's uniform had appeared and was telling me, in no uncertain terms, that I should sit down. I waved to him that I was fine but he persisted and another man came up beside him.

'Speak to him in Swedish,' the new arrival said to the medic.

I started to formulate a response to that in my mind. I was not Swedish, I would say, I was British – and I did not need to sit down.

I was about to open my mouth and rebuke them when suddenly I couldn't see them any longer. A sudden wave of nausea washed over me and I collapsed.

The last thing I saw was Mum's face, floating in and out of my vision. It was no surprise to her. You see, I had collapsed on sports day as well.

'You collapsed?' Rob said.

Cordelia, Rob, Holly and I stood in the soon-to-be-opened waiting room of the first ever Pilgrims Veterinary Practice surgery. I had been back two days and, in that time, Cordelia and I had signed the lease for the surgery building and received the keys that morning. There was plenty of work to be done, but the phone was working, Holly was starting and Rob had come over to check the place out and offer some moral support.

'Yes,' I replied, pausing dramatically. 'I collapsed. In fact, I was even dripped by a team of crazy Austrian medics who thought I was Swedish and spoke to me in nothing but Swedish for about half an hour.'

Holly burst into hysterics and Rob just shook his head.

'Not only that but I lost my wallet just before the race and when I finally got back to my car at the airport I had a flat tyre and had to change it. Tricky when I couldn't lift my arms above my shoulders after the swim from hell the day before.'

'And not only are you married to this man, but you're going into business with him!' Rob said, fixing a look on Cordelia.

She smiled in return. 'Means I get to keep an eye on him this way,' she said. 'Make sure he doesn't clutter up the garden with other people's pets.'

'What time did you do it in?' Holly giggled.

'Eleven hours fifty-three minutes!' I replied proudly, still basking in the fact I had somehow done it in less than twelve hours.

'Oh, my goodness, you actually managed it,' Rob said quietly. 'That's good news for Sam.'

'Good news for Sam?'

'Rob had a bet on with him that you wouldn't beat Gavin's time.'

'Very supportive, pal,' I said.

'I always thought you'd do the race,' Rob protested. 'I just never thought you'd be any good at the cycling.'

'To be honest with you, I was beaten by a man with one

leg,' I replied, with a grin. 'And my finisher's photo has a picture of the competitor in front of me, who looks like she could be a pygmy. I'm not exactly in the élite realms of Ironman – but I do qualify for the tattoo.'

Holly was laughing again, but Rob looked at me in abject horror. 'Surely that would be like defacing a sacred temple.'

'Very funny.'

'Not sure how the crowd at your next Will Young concert will feel about having some tattooed fan in their midst.'

My expression of abject horror said it all. Rob bellowed with laughter and Holly burst into hysterics. I looked at Cordelia accusingly and she shot me back a wicked smile. 'He did ask,' she said.

'You promised,' I hissed.

'Just wait until I chat to Sam. I mean, "Come on, baby, light my fire,"' Rob said, as Holly slumped against the wall almost paralysed with laughter.

'Not a word. Please. You'll never have to locum for me again,' I pleaded.

'You're on your own from here, Luke.' Rob grinned. 'I'm setting up Optivet, now I've got my shiny diploma, so I'm afraid that rules me out as your stand-in. Tough times, opening a new place. If you want to use my amazing services again you'll need to be quick because I'm looking for premises myself. I was half thinking that if Pilgrims doesn't fly I could take it off your hands and make it a referral ophthalmology centre.'

'So, the real motive for your appearance today is to scope the place out in case we fail?' I laughed.

'Only a bit. Incidentally, when do you three kick open the doors?' Rob asked, conspiratorially. 'You have the place, you've got the gear, and I'm guessing you have the loan to go with it all. It's all "Changes", isn't it?'

'We open now!' Holly chipped in, shrieking with laughter. 'Team Pilgrim is "My All Time Love".'

'Seriously,' I said, rubbing my temples with both hands, 'let's leave the Will Young thing, okay?'

'It's "Your Game", Luke. I'd hate to mock, I know all "Your Hopes And Fears" are tied up in this place,' Rob replied, deadpan.

Holly, hardly able to contain herself, clutched Rob's arm. 'Come on, let me show you out the back – you haven't seen the operating theatre or the table Luke picked up from the medical auction.'

It was my turn to shake my head in despair. Holly pulled Rob through to the consulting room and I heard her shriek with even louder laughter as she pointed out all the second-hand gear I had somehow managed to acquire.

'Second-hand endoscope – with no light source . . .' I heard Rob muse, as he poked through the boxes we had out the back. 'Handy! I could take some of this gear for my practice, you know.'

Cordelia turned to look at me and held out her hand to stop me following them for a moment.

'What's up?' I said.

'You know about us going into business together?' she began.

Slightly concerned, I fully turned to look at her and nodded gently.

'Well, I've got some interesting news.'

She was about to go on when, suddenly, the phone started to ring.

'Our first client phoning the surgery!' I said, excitedly, looking around for the phone.

'Luke,' Cordelia said, focusing my attention, 'I'm in

business with you and I'll help you all I can . . . but it will only be for a short time. You're going to need to get someone else.'

I froze. Behind me, the phone continued to ring. It was probably a chicken with flu, or a cow with a potato stuck down its throat – another one of the adventures I was getting famous for.

'You mean an assistant?' I said.

She nodded.

'But why?' I asked. 'I thought we'd do this together . . . It would be our thing. We can make this practice brilliant.'

'For both our sakes,' she said seriously.

'What do you mean? I want to do this with you.'

'You need to keep doing your charity work – I know how much you love it. And I have things to take care of myself.'

'I know I've been away a lot, but I'm focused. I'm not going to leave you in the lurch with the practice.'

'Luke, you need the WVS trips – I know what you're like when you come back. It's what fires you, and I'd never stand in the way of that.'

A letter from the Royal College of Veterinary Surgeons clearing me of any misconduct during the police raid had arrived in the post when I'd got back from the Ironman. It meant I was technically free again to start planning my next overseas mission.

'Well, there is this charity in Peru that needs a hand, involves getting a riverboat up the Amazon and going into some remote communities. I wondered if maybe, after we've got this place off the ground, we might get a locum and go off on a trip together . . .'

Cordelia shook her head. 'That sort of adventure is for you and Sam.'

My protests died. I had no idea why she was saying this, not after all the effort and stress we'd devoted to getting this far.

Cordelia paused and just regarded me. The phone stopped ringing and I heard Holly speaking faintly in the background.

'What's up?' I asked. 'I mean, what's changed your mind about everything?'

In reply, only silence.

'I beat Gavin's time,' I said, in an effort to lighten the mood. 'I beat his time and everything.'

'It's your fault,' Cordelia finally said. 'I can't come with you on a crazy WVS trip and soon I won't be able to be counted on to help you full time with Pilgrims.'

'My fault!' I protested, inadvertently raising my voice.

'Yes,' she said. 'All your fault.'

'Cords, you're not making sense. What have I done?' I demanded. 'What's my fault?'

She looked hard at me. For the first time, I saw the faintest trace of a smile playing around her lips.

'Well, if it's not your fault, then we have a problem,' she began. 'Luke, you need to do another WVS trip sooner rather than later because shortly I will need you around and not for Pilgrims . . .'

I looked at my wife expectantly. I was more confused than ever.

'I'm pregnant,' Cordelia said, her face breaking into a huge smile.

I whooped for joy. It was a loud shrick, cut short only by Holly calling me from the hallway.

'Luke, phone!' she cried. 'Our first client to the new surgery!'

I laughed as I shouted back, 'Good news all round!' I beamed. 'Hardcore healing already – bring it on! Who is it?'

'It's a great case, pal – this is going to pave the way for things to come,' Rob's voice replied.

I was talking to Holly and Rob, but I couldn't stop myself from looking deep into Cordelia's eyes. 'Tell me about it,' I said. 'I'm ready for anything right now. Who have we got?'

'It's Mr Baffer!' Holly shrieked. 'He wants to bring one of his frogs down here first thing tomorrow morning.'

Rob appeared around the door. 'Great how life moves on, isn't it, pal?' he said, with a wink. 'Never saw that one coming. How he found out about Pilgrims I have no idea . . .'

I stopped, put my arm around Cordelia. In the corner, little Bracken lifted her head, regarded each of us curiously, and let out a solitary yap.

'Life does move on, buddy – you know that as well as me. I've got a feeling we're just at the beginning of a really great adventure . . .'

ACKNOWLEDGEMENTS

It has been brilliant to write a second book and I've loved every minute of it. Those minutes have been squeezed into evenings, weekends, and any spare time in the working week and without the huge support and patience of Cords, it wouldn't have been possible.

Thanks again to my super supportive agents – Rob, Elly, Heather and Claire, for all their encouragement and help. I am again indebted to Lisa and Valerie at Two Roads who have once again published me – it's an honour to be on their publishers list and they have been fantastic in every aspect of the process. I do appreciate how lucky I am to have found such a supportive and encouraging team to take me on. Thank you.

As before, whilst I have merged many characters and details together – all the animals and people in these books are inspired by the real life cases and clients I have had the pleasure of working with. Many are my friends and form a key part of events that have defined my career. Those whose names I haven't changed in the book will know who they are, those who don't – may have a sneaking suspicion!

Writing these stories enables me to relive some wonderful

experiences. I think I wrote nearly every page with a smile, thinking about colleagues and animals both past and present and how lucky I have been to have gained so much from meeting all of them.

As I have gone on my travels with WVS, the more extreme the situation, the more altruistic acts of kindness I have witnessed towards animals – often by those with nothing themselves. It isn't true that animal cruelty is much worse in poor places, it is simply that the scale of hardship is different and difficult to appreciate from the outside. In slums, townships and compounds all over the world – I have seen people try to care for the most rangy flea-ridden and diseased animals you can imagine. It is an amazing world and I will always deeply admire and respect those individuals that can somehow act so selflessly for the good of both animals and people, often at their own personal expense. I hope, in some way, I can pay a small tribute to them by including some of them in my stories.

I hope you enjoyed this book; it is the foundation of Pilgrims and of many great adventures yet to come – I look forward to sharing them with you and thank you for your support.

LUKE GAMBLE Photograph courtesy of the author

LUKE GAMBLE graduated from Bristol University in 1999 as a vet and spent a year as Clinical Scholar in large animal medicine and surgery at Cambridge University. Although primarily a mixed practice vet and based in his New Forest surgery, Pilgrims Veterinary Practice, his extracurricular work with the Worldwide Veterinary Service charity (which he founded in 2003) takes him much further afield and was the subject of two TV series on Sky 1. He also runs an emergency service for animals in Dorset and a pet travel company.

Luke is a black belt in karate, has run 152 miles across the Sahara to raise money for his charity (and to impress his wife) and in 2010 was awarded the J A Wight (James Herriot) Award by the British Small Animal Veterinary Association for outstanding contributions to the welfare of companion animals. Luke is married and lives in the New Forest with his wife, three children, Angel the ridgeback and a bossy rescue cat named Charlie.

www.lukegamble.com

www.wvs.org.uk

http://www.tworoadsbooks.com/index.php/books/the-vet/

https://www.facebook.com/LukeGambleVet

Twitter: @LukeGamble